Contents

Acknowledgments

This study could not have been accomplished without the generous assistance of José María Veláquez-Gaztelú, Romualdo Molina, Mario Gómez Martín, Pedro Turbica, Paco Lira (both father and son), Gerhard Steingress, José María and Alfonso Eduardo Pérez Orozco, Adrian Shubert, Stanley Payne, Gerard Flynn, Brook Zern, Tomás de Utrera, Richard Pinnell, The Program for Cultural Cooperation between Spain's Ministry of Culture and United States' Universities, Robert Jones and the UWM Library, Jim Parakilas, Pedro Fernández Giménez, David Monroe, Aldis Strazdins, and, most importantly, Catherine Washabaugh. I hope that my writing does not fail to show them the gratitude and respect which they deserve. Finally, let me acknowledge with gratitude the permissions granted for the publication of Chapter 1, an earlier version of which appeared in the *Journal of Musicological Research*, Chapter 2, which reworks an essay first published in *Theory, Culture and Society* and Chapter 5, a revision of an essay originally offered in *Popular Music*.

Preface

Flamenco music is recognized by people all over the world. From New York to Tokyo, enthusiastic crowds have acknowledged the power of Paco de Lucía's guitar and have responded to the passion of flamenco dance, whether in the self-controlled movements of Antonio Gades or in the vintage style of Carmen Amaya, with her inexhaustible passion and penetrating stare. Familiar too, though less so, are the songs – really the wails – that ground both the instrumentation and the dance. These flamenco songs, woven around Haiku-like verses, form the core of the music. Packaged together, the voice, the dance, and the guitar constitute this highly visible and easily distinguished style of popular music.

In North America, flamenco enthusiasts gather their rough-and-ready knowledge of the flamenco style from a variety of sources. Books of many stripes have helped to shape popular knowledge. Guitarists playing both conservative sounds, like Pedro Bacán, and fusion sounds, like Ottmar Liebert, have helped to make flamenco guitar artistry as recognizable as it is. Films from *Carmen* to *Strictly Ballroom* have played up different features of the flamenco style, and flamenco performance groups in many American cities put time and sweat into educating and edifying the American public.

Despite – or because of – this welter of influences, reactions to the style are sharply contrastive. Americans either love it or they hate it. Few people are lukewarm. Ambivalent reactions are rarer still. Some folks celebrate the flamenco style as if were a gospel, a sacred text and a holy ritual all rolled into one. Other folks regard it as if it were the quintessence of kitsch. They find it noisy, gaudy, frivolous and inane.

These rifted reactions suggest something of the importance of flamenco as a cultural phenomenon. Flamenco performances are cultural moraines. They are gathering places for not-yet-well integrated cultural forces. They present divergent messages, and, inevitably therefore, they generate divergent reactions, producing a welter of different impacts on both the artists who perform and on the audiences who enjoy their performances. It is for these reasons that the flamenco style is apt for anthropological study. Its performances are tell-tale signs of social processes, processes central both to Spanish social life and to modern life wherever it is lived. It is as if all the central and most general contradictions of modernity had been heaped together, boiled down, and condensed into a singer's cry and a listener's response.

Most scholars have reduced the moraine of flamenco to manageable singularities. Flamenco is just this. Flamenco is simply that. Most such efforts, however, limp because they are too general, too abstract and too much driven by a passion for the art. What else can one say about the claim that flamenco song liberates one from the claws of time and history (see Grande 1992a) or that the hands of Paco de Lucía have surpassed the humble condition of the human body and have entered into the realm of immortality (Grande 1986)? Clearly, such generalizations are simplistic, being the result of efforts to stand above the whole tradition and to summarize it from the top-down. Top-down methods, as I will call them, tempt one to define a style in terms of its origin and evolution, as if contemporary performances were reincarnations of past realities. As a result, top-down interpretations look to clarify genres from their origins to their present conditions, describing evolutionary processes and periodizing stages of development, thereby making it possible to isolate the different historical threads that get knotted together in contemporary experiences. The major problem raised by such top-down interpretations is "abstract objectivism." As Mikhail Bakhtin and his colleagues have noted, something is wrong with any interpretive method that reifies genres and objectifies abstractions to the point that events in the present are reduced to reflections of the past. Top-down approaches to music are guilty of such abstract objectivism to the degree that they pursue questions of origin and development while neglecting the significance of contemporary performances.

This then is the challenge faced by this book: to find the forest of flamenco without getting hung up in the trees, yet to do so without losing sight of the fact that flamenco music is continually being made in the present rather that inherited from the past. The appropriate analytic attitude is one that sees flamenco reality to be always realized in performance, and always approached as an ever-emerging reality. Every next performance restructures all that has preceded. Though a melody or a lyric or rhythm may seem to be passed down from past artists, it always undergoes transformation in the course of being performed. It is recreated in and through the novel contexts of its production and audition – a condition that is as true of recorded music as it is of live performance. The new contexts in which we listen to old disks help to recreate musical style. Each moment of music carries on a "tacit dialog which lies embedded in the complex circumstances in which it occurs" (Chanan 1994: 42).

No musical style is ever constructed in the past and simply handed down for our enjoyment in the present. To portray music so would be to cast it in the guise of a museum piece, alive in the past but now dead, stuffed, and mounted. Unfortunately, however, most writings that look for general cultural forces, in the flamenco style, approach it in just this way, as if it were some sort of museum piece, something dug up from the past and driven forward into the present by old cultural energies – indeed Caballero Bonald has advanced this archaeological image in a very explicit way (see Carrillo Alonso 1978: 49). Such an account suggests that flamenco is a style that has been crippled by the age-old class contradictions of modern social life and by the noxious ideologies of nineteenth-century society. As a result, performances of the 1990s are liable to the accusation of inadvertently perpetuating the social contradictions of a hundred years ago.

In contrast to such analyses, these chapters on flamenco music credit the flamenco present with at least as much reality as the flamenco past. Against a tradition that attributes the shape of contemporary music to century-old forces, these essays assume that music is renewed on every next occasion of its performance, and that today's artistry paves the way toward tomorrow's renovations. This book struggles to appreciate the significance of today's music, knowing that tomorrow it might be described as traditional.

Besides emphasizing the significance of the *now* in flamenco, these chapters presuppose the importance of concrete events, the actions of artists, the movements of musicians. Flamenco analysis must be expanded beyond smothering debates about the Andalusian mind, its beliefs, its values and its ideologies. The analysis must begin to consider the impact of Andalusian body, including the gender it bears, the wine it drinks, the stages on which it performs, the microphones, disks, and tapes that it uses, and the books it writes. Accordingly, this work will discuss audio recordings, video recordings – legitimate as well as pirated – dramatic productions (e.g. *Quejío* 1975; see Drillon et al. 1975), popular stage productions (e.g. *Flamenco Puro* 1980), feature films (from *Los Tarantos* 1963 to *Carmen* 1983), documentary films (*Duende y Misterio del Flamenco* 1952, "Rito y Geografía del Cante" 1971–3, "An Andalusian Journey" 1989, *Flamenco* 1995), analytic (Steingress 1993), hagiographic (Pohren 1988) and encyclopedic publications (Blas Vega and Ríos Ruiz 1990).

Flamenco from the Bottom Up

Flamenco performances, together with all the recordings, reviews, and scholarly comments that follow such performances, turn on and play off of two kinds of Andalusian social events. The first and perhaps the most important is the gathering of men to drink and sing poetry. The second and somewhat exceptional event is the carnivalesque fair during which women dare to dance outside the conventions that normally constrain their lives. These two events, the male-centered songfest and the bright and blaring fair, provide the conceptual base and the historical context of Andalusian flamenco. Performers continually mine this base, playing, twisting, revising, recombining, and reinventing flamenco as they go. Outside of Andalucía, of course, flamenco operates differently. Here in the U.S., for example, enthusiasts welcome flamenco, less because it reminds them of rituals of night music in a local bar or of festive holidays at a fair, but instead because it is a muscular music that can jolt anyone out of a somnambulant life. Just such a jolt certainly contributed to my own initial interests in flamenco. The event in point took place in Milwaukee, and the blow was delivered by Manuel de los Santos Pastor, "El Agujeta". Agujetas, as he is sometimes called, was in his late forties, tall, muscular, exuding an air of sullen defiance intensified by his unflagging self-confidence. He was dressed all in black. His billows of curly black hair framed a scarred face that Clint Eastwood would covet – a far cry from the frail figure that appears in Carlos Saura's *Flamenco* (1995). About a dozen people gathered late late at night – late at least by Milwaukee standards – in a local tavern. We all underwent rituals of lubrication in keeping with the tradition of flamenco events. And then Agujetas began to sing, though at the time I would have said that his voice was not singing, so much as ripping and tearing at his soul. Standing about two feet from my face singing fire and paid, Agujetas had *me* transfixed and my *wife* stunned.

One night of Agujetas was enough to usher me down a new path of musical appreciation and scholarly investigation. I began to appreciate the flamenco obsession and the passionate commitment of singers, guitarists, dancers, philosophers, painters and writers to the task of explicating flamenco music. I suddenly understood, for one thing, why so much of the literary and philosophical literature on flamenco lingers over some sort of primal flamenco song rooted in the extraordinarily self-reflexive conviviality of Andalucía. Indeed, one might characterize flamenco writing as a devotional literature that aims to encourage a cultural life as much as it aims to cultivate a musical style. This writing roams lovingly over details of the lives and efforts of great artists and over the specifics of poetry that forms the lyrical content of this musical art.[1]

For heuristic purposes, all this literature can be divided into three parts. First, *flamencología* includes popular press, that is, writings aimed at promoting flamenco music, e.g. Manfredi Cano 1973; Monleón 1967a; Pohren 1980; Quiñones 1994; Serrano and Elgorriaga 1991; Woodall 1992, and many biographical writings – the lives of the saints. Such books often stand alongside analytic writings by these same authors. A second body of flamenco writings advances and defends positions on the history and classification of flamenco forms. These writings have been described as "traditional flamencology" by Steingress (1993: 89) who suggests that they regularly enter into regional and ethnic rivalries, with the result that flamenco debates begin to look like football free-for-alls. Andalusians of different provinces try to advance flamenco aesthetics each in his own way (see García Chicón 1987; Quiñones 1964), all the while being chased by Gitanos (Molina and Mairena 1979), by Levantinos (Gelardo and Belade 1985), and by Madrileños (Escribano 1990). Everyone, it seems, wants a piece of the action.

Finally, and most recently, flamenco writings include the "scientific flamencology" of García Gómez (1993), García Matos (1987), Mitchell (1994), and Steingress (1993). These scientific flamencologists argue that traditional flamencologists have been too close and too committed to the music and the people they write about (see Mitchell 1994: 17). They lack objectivity, neutrality, and impartiality. As a result, traditional flamenco-logists produce accounts that are driven as much by personal favoritism as by historical research, and the field of flamenco studies is reduced to an unresolvable debate over musical taste.

The scientific flamencologists propose that flamencology can be set straight if only scholars would divest themselves of their personal interest in the music. With such detachment comes sobriety, clear sightedness, and, accordingly, the true history of flamenco, which, in the cases of Steingress and García Gómez, turns out to be a history that shows flamenco to be much more deeply immersed in general cultural processes of modernization than traditional flamencologists ever imagined.

This scientific treatment of flamenco, while an advance of sorts over "traditional flamencology," is still hobbled by a desire to discover the real flamenco. Though modern and popular, rather than traditional and authentic, flamenco still has a distinct and definable essence that needs to be explicated. Steingress has described that essence as romanticized bohemian music. Mitchell describes real flamenco as maudlin music that lubricates the wheels of an essentially bipolar society and a culture of victimage. And García Gómez describes real flamenco as an intel-lectualized synthesis of regional traditions.

The problem with such scientific approaches is that they deflect attention away from the fact that flamenco music is con-stantly being remade, and not only by artists and impresarios, but also by scholars who write about the music. The flamenco scholar's backward glance towards past facts diverts attention from the role that present-day activities play in shaping flamenco music as a cultural phenomenon. Indeed, this depreciation of the significance of contemporary events seems to be endemic to the top-down, essentialist style of scientific discourse. As soon as one begins talking scientifically about a genre or a style or a cultural object, one inevitably starts roping it off and setting it aside from all that it is not, thereby paving the way for the "abstract objective" handling of cultural phenomena (see Morson and Emerson 1990: 271ff; Volosinov 1973: 65).

Such is the difficulty with top-down approaches to cultural phenomena. By contrast, a bottom-up approach shows little interest in defining genres and identifying objects, but instead concerns itself with the web of significations in which any aspect of cultural life is entangled. The intent of a bottom-up study is not so much to define, restrict, or contain, but to explore the deepest interconnections and the furthest ramifications of an object, event, or person.[2] This present study will deal with flamenco music from the bottom up, starting with concrete and specific flamenco moments.

Politics and Flamenco

With an eye to the most interesting interconnections and most revealing ramifications, we will devote special attention to flamenco and politics. Such a focus is justified because, for one thing, flamenco music has been roundly criticized, especially in Spain, for its politically conservative bent. Along with its cultural sibling, the bullfight, flamenco has been described as "the emblem of all that is regressive in Spanish culture. . .a falsely seductive representation of Spain purveyed by foreign artists" (D'Lugo 1991: 34, 192). Such harsh judgments may unsettle American enthusiasts, especially given the fact that the content of the music is almost totally devoid of political reference. Where, one might ask, is this regressive politics? Our bottom-up exploration of the flamenco style will answer this question, showing that indeed a seductive but tacit strain of backward-looking politics hides beneath the cloak of flamenco passion. But this study will reveal something more – something that is perhaps both more interesting for the general reader and more significant for the theoretician of popular culture. Besides housing the worm of regressive politics, the core of flamenco also encourages progressive inclinations and, during the late-Franco period, was associated with resistance to Franco's dictatorship, a dictatorship that itself advanced a backward-looking politics that narcotized Spanish social life for a good part of the twentieth century. Curiously and paradoxically, flamenco performances during the late 1960s often promoted as much political foresight as regression, as much liberalization of minds as closure, and as much resistance as compliance. Elucidating this welter latent politics will be accomplished only by unpacking multiple layers of what James Scott has called "hidden transcripts" in flamenco perform-ance. For such an approach, it will be necessary to explore the contradictions in flamenco music, contradictions that the artists themselves are often well aware of. An anecdote will demon-strate the point. In the course of a television interview with the celebrated flamencologist Fernando Quiñones in the mid-1970s, the singer "El Chocolate" told a story about a strange con-frontation he had had with a flamencologist early on in his singing career (see p.50). He described himself as impoverished – back then in the 1940s – and desperate to impress this visiting flamencologist so as to further his own musical fortunes. In a very short order, however, he learned that the flamencologist's aesthetic judgments stood in sharp contrast to his own. Renditions that he considered poor elicited the most appreciative comments from his scholarly admirer, and those he considered excellent were spurned. As his story goes, "El Chocolate" pro-ceeded to suppress his own judgments and to confirm those of the flamencologist, dissembling so as to feather his own bed. Obviously he succeeded. By 1970 he had reached the pinnacle of his art. But what is one to say of this strange story as told to a flamencologist-interviewer on television? Is it a true story, or is it itself a fabrication designed to impress the flamencologist and the viewing audience? Is this story a sincere confession or is it another gambit? And if it is a gambit, what is at stake? What ladder might "El Chocolate" be trying to climb now? In what quarrel might he be taking sides? Answers to these questions will emerge, not from analyses of nineteenth-century ideologies that continue to be sounded in the music and with respect to which musicians are "subjects," but instead from a study of the creative and reflexive activities of individuals who self-consciously use their art to respond to those ideologies and who, in tomorrow's retrospective analyses, will be called "agents" of change.

The chapters in this book aim to study such creative and reflective activities of artists, aficionados and audiences. The first set of essays introduces both flamenco music and a distinct-ively bottom-up approach to interpreting flamenco music. "The Politics of Passion" considers the idea that flamenco perform-ances are ambiguous embodiments of political agendas. "The Histories of Flamenco" rehearses four narratives that deal with the same critical moments of the past. Flamenco historians have interpreted these critical moments differently. "The Pleasures of Flamenco" addresses the politics that operates through the enjoyment experienced by audiences, listeners, viewers, aficionados, collectors, etc. "Gypsies" examines the pro-Gitano (pro-Gypsy) arguments that were initiated in 1881 by Antonio Machado y Alvarez "Demófilo" and then developed and applied in new ways in the 1960s by Antonio Mairena. Contrary to those who portray this pro-Gypsy argument as simply an invention of tradition, I argue that it serves multiple political purposes, some far removed from those embraced by "Demófilo" and Mairena. "The Body" contributes to an understanding of the intensely emotional moments of *cante* by arguing that while emotion may be, in part at least, an aspect of a deep Andalusian spiritualism or even of a latent modern romanticism, it can also be understood as an evocation of the body. As such, embodied song is an alternative to the Platonized and mentalized musical experiences that dominate Western aesthetics. "Women" outlines the traditional roles imposed on women who participated in flamenco events and highlights the critical rethinking of those roles that peeks through the cracks of the documentary series "Rito y Geografía del Cante." "Anglo Perspectives on Flamenco Music" explores some theoretical and political contrasts between Spanish flamencology and some recent anglophone writings. The Reflections in "Music, Resistance, and Popular Culture" take advantage of the insights hammered out in these studies of flamenco to rethink politics of popular culture in general. Chapter Nine provides details about, and criticisms of, the 100-program documentary series that was aired on Spanish television toward the end of the Franco years.

In the course of these discussions, it will become apparent that each moment of presentation and representation of flamenco music has the potential of turning back on itself to reinvent both the music and the social life of modern Spain.

Notes

1. Examples of such writing include biographical writings (Blas Vega 1978; Blas Vega and Ríos Ruiz 1990; Ortiz Nuevo 1975a,b; 1987; Nuñez de Prado 1986; Pohren 1988; Quiñones 1989) and compendia of flamenco poetry (see Fernández Bañuls and Pérez Orozco 1983). The more general literature on flamenco, described above as "top-down" analyses of the objectified style, includes accounts by Antonio Machado y Alvarez "Demófilo" (1881) and by Hugo Schuchardt in 1881, criticisms by Eugenio Noel (1916), essays by García Lorca in (1975) and Falla (1947) and books by Carlos de Luna (1942; 1951). Also significant are the writings that appeared at the time of, or in the wake of, the eponymous *Flamencología* by González Climent (1964, originally 1953) including the tendentious contributions by Alvarez Caballero (1988), Blas Vega (1987), Caballero Bonald (1975), Carrillo Alonso (1978), Escribano (1990), Gómez Pérez (1978), González Climent (1975), Grande (1979; 1985; 1992a,b), Lafuente (1955), Larréa (1974), Lavaur (1976), Mairena (1976), Manfredi Cano (1955), Molina (1985), Molina and Espín (1992), Molina and Mairena (1979, originally 1963), Quiñones (1964; 1971), Ríos Ruiz (1972; 1993), and Rossy (1966). Also included in this "top-down" category are the detached and reflective works of Alvarez Caballero (1981; 1994), Barrios (1989), García Matos (1987), Gelardo and Belade (1985), Herrero (1991), and Mercado (1982) and the sociologically sophisticated writings of García Gómez (1993), Mitchell (1994), and Steingress (1993), as well as the musicological writings of Lomax (1968) and Manuel (1988; 1989).

2. These essays attempt to "understand" flamenco phenomena. It should be noted, however, that the term "understanding" is used here in a Bakhtinian sense. "Any true understanding is dialogic in nature. Understanding is to utterance as one line of a dialog is to the next" (Volosinov 1973: 102). To emphasize the dialogic and responsive nature of understanding, Shusterman has characterized understanding as a response launched from a position outside of the event to be interpreted. In his view, interpretation is "a performed ability to respond to the work. . .not to dig out and describe the objectified meanings already carefully buried in the text by its author, but rather to

develop and transmit a richly meaningful response to the text" (1992: 92). As Bakhtin suggested, outsideness is a powerful factor in understanding insofar as it enables us to raise new questions for a foreign culture, ones it did not raise for itself (Willeman 1995: 31). The point and purpose of constructing an "interpretive response" is to join the interpreter's voice to the voices of those who initially produced a work, thereby forming a "fusion of horizons" (see Jay 1993 for a discussion of this Gadamerian concept). Such a "fusion of horizons" facilitates a discernment of the value of a work.

The process of value discernment is an endless one. No determination of value is ever final, and therefore no response to a work is ever complete. Each response invites more responses, which enhance horizons for further value discernment. It follows therefore, that interpretive responses operate as continuations, not finalizations, of a work. By participating in the unending process of value discernment, interpretations extend and transform a text through time. When portrayed in this way, interpretive responses resemble the discursive practices of Rabbinical scholars (Faur 1986; Handelman 1982) whose objective of interpretation is the ramification and pullulation of responsive words to a (sacred) text in such a way that text is developed and extended through time. The delight of such a process is precisely its indeterminacy and its endlessness. If the process goes according to plan, reading "can have no intrinsic or verifiable end." Reading, instead, becomes a dance that, in Steiner's cynical words, "turns never-endingly on itself" (Steiner 1989: 46, 41).

This present study aims to contribute to just such a dance that turns never-endingly on itself. This goal stands first in the order of priorities, subsuming all lesser objectives including the goals of preserving the Other and of understanding ourselves (cf. Bernstein 1992). If you will, the objective to "extend encounters" is akin to the Socratic mandate to "know thyself" and to the Christian commandment "love thy neighbor". Cosmically speaking, the ethnographic objective of "extending encounters" is a grand unifying objective that joins the Socratic, the Christian and the Judaic imperatives into a singularity. "Extending encounters" implies a knowledge of self, a love of neighbor, and a constructive commitment to the human community.

It may sound strange to say that these essays aim to extend flamenco encounters. After all, commonsense tells us that expressive acts are over and done with once they are spoken, once their intention has been made public. However, I assume, here, that expressive acts are always larger than the intentions that might have initially driven them. As Erving Goffman (1974: 2) argued, "most of the time we don't know what we are saying until we look back and see what we have said". In the same vein, Mark Seltzer (1992: 85) has contended, "what (subjects) do has more meaning than what they know". Calvin Schrag (1986: 36–40) says that "expressive discourse and expressive action draw upon a surplus of meanings that overflow the intentions of the particular speaker and particular actor. . .Expressive action should thus not be restricted to the deliverances of meaning through the conscious motivation". Alessandro Duranti (1993: 233) portrays an utterance as incompletely formed with the action of a speaker: "Speakers may hint at possible truths. . .The audience is often expected to do the rest of the job by either accepting or denouncing the potential description of the world more or less vaguely suggested by the speaker."

It would seem, from these alternative points of view, that an actor's intentions have less than full command over the body that carries out those intentions. That is precisely the argument advanced in some recent neuroscientific writings that question the centrality of consciousness and volition in human action. Geoffrey Samuel (1990) and Merlin Donald (1991) criticize the conventional characterization of intentionality (the "about-ness" of thought) as unified and totalizing. In place of that characterization, they offer pictures of multitiered, multimodal – in a word, fragmented – cerebral operations. Even more ambitiously, Daniel Dennett (1991: 241) contends that volition is not only fragmented but also ineffectual, being "as much an effect of the process as a cause." Gerald Edelman argues that "meaning is interactional. . .The environment itself plays a role in determining what a speaker's words refer to (Edelman 1992: 224). In all of these accounts, the overarching message is that habitual practice, achieved through the repetition of action, is a vastly underrated force in human action (see Calvin 1990: 194). Varela, Thompson, and Rosch (1993: 9) repeat this same message when they argue that cognition itself "is not the representation of a pregiven world by a pregiven mind, but is rather the enactment of a world and a mind on the basis of a history of the variety of actions that a being in the world performs." In other words, the brain's operations are dispersed and heavily reliant upon habitual practice. Words – and other expressive actions – are never "fully fixed, self-sufficient, and inviolable objects." One must forsake the "fetishized unity of closure" (Shusterman 1992: 30).

Any work – whether word, or action or object – is always open to development, and is never closed and completed in its intentionality and volition. See Nick Thomas (1991: 3), who contends that "objects are not what they have been made to be but what they have become." See also Christopher Tilley (1990: 333), who argues that "persons define objects in and through their interaction and discourse," and Arjun Appadurai (1986: 13), who contends that we "approach commodities as things in a certain situation. The situation in which its exchangeability for some other thing is its socially relevant feature." The meaning of any text is constructed in the present out of present and past experiences. Accordingly, these essays should be read as acts of "re-membering" (Myerhoff 1982), that is, as acts that articulate flamenco events with sedimented past experiences, thereby helping to fuse horizons towards a new level of musical appreciation.

Chapter 1

The Politics of Passion: Flamenco, Power, and the Body

The flamenco musical style, like most other popular musical styles, exercises political power despite its appearance of political detachment.[1] Its politics is effective but invisible. Its clout is veiled. Here I will show that while political positioning is rarely mentioned by flamenco artists, it is almost always present in their bodies. Elucidating flamenco politics, therefore, means demonstrating the politics of bodies, rather than of minds, and showing how ideologies are promoted physically even though they might stand outside of thought and consciousness.

Any effort to lift the veil on flamenco politics should start, one would think, with a definition of this flamenco style. Ironically, however, the essence of flamenco is, like its politics, hidden, and muddled, and contested, partly as a result of 125 years of commercialization, which, having played havoc with the memories and commitments of its adepts, throws all descriptions, definitions, and illustrations into doubt. Indeed, most scholars recognize that the description and definition of flamenco are hyperpoliticized even if, as they contend, the music itself is not.

Despite these controversies, flamenco can be described for heuristic purposes as a musical style that remembers, celebrates, and plays with seminal but elusive moments of sociality, one male-centered, the other female-centered. The first moment is male-centered and central – though not necessarily original as Ortiz Nuevo has shown (1990). It involves emotionally rich experiences of public fraternity and male bonding in small semi-public gatherings where rhythm, poetry and passion bind together simple folks in southern Spain. Such precious occasions of public fraternity come about in this way. Late at night, in a tavern or bar in southern Spain, some working-class men gather

together. Their comraderie is celebrated with wine and traditional poetry sung at the top of their lungs. The longer they
persist at drinking and singing, the more intense becomes their
reunion. The air, thick with smoke and a musky scent of wine,
starts to resonate with their passion. Eventually, one or another
of the singers produces a texture of sound that sets teeth on edge,
induces chills, and raises goosebumps. This is the quintessential
moment of flamenco song or *cante*.

The flamenco lyrics (*coplas*) that are sung during these events
are bare expressions of elemental emotion. They are simple in
form, often anonymously authored, and usually based on a rustic
poetic style that operates like a psychic key to open up floodgates
of passion. Often this poetical style consists of little more than an
enunciation of evocative terms such as love, hate, pain, death,
mother, prison.

> Por ti abandoné a mis niñas,
> mi mare de penita murió;
> ahora te vas y me abandonas,
> *no tienes perdón de Dió!*
>
> For you I abandoned my little girls,
> my mother died of sorrow;
> and now you abandon me. . .
> may you be eternally damned! (Pohren 1984: 23).

The guitar, for its part, provides musical spice for the *copla*.
Moreover, between *coplas*, the guitarist plays melodic interludes
(*falsetas*), which develop and extend the emotional atmosphere
created by the poetry (Manuel 1988).

The second critical moment in flamenco music is female-
centered, and it stands a pole apart from the dark and musky
experiences of male-bonding. Bright and blaring and daring, the
carnivalesque fair in Andalucía is a seasonal opportunity for
release from the workaday constraints of social life, especially for
women. For three or four days at a time, men and women
gambol with abandon, singing, dancing, drinking, and parading
about. For men, the highpoint of the *feria* is the bullfight, the
moment in which the matador, standing for all that is disciplined,
cultural, vital and bright – wearing his suit of lights *traje de luces*
– confronts and subdues the bull that stands for the wildness of

nature and the darkness of death. For women, the *feria* is a time for walking on the wild side, stepping out and away from the suffocating privacy of the household, parading to the fairground located on the very edge of town where the cultural world abuts on the wild countryside. At this liminal time and in this marginal space, women dress in the most daring clothes and dance the most provocative dances, thereby presenting themselves as hot and "natural" in contrast to cool "cultural" men. This challenging role reversal is nicely illustrated in *sevillanas*, a musical genre perennially popular at fairs in and around Seville and redolent with the very same nature-culture contrasts that are so evident in the bullfight. The woman, with arms curved over her head as if to imitate the horns of a bull, challenges the composure and self-discipline of the cultured man with her wild and dangerous naturalness (Corbin and Corbin 1987: 94–127).

Flamenco performances are riddled with reminiscences of these two kinds of social experiences, the somber song and flashy dance. As such, flamenco performances seem to operate as sacraments through which to remember and reenact the soul of Andalusian social life, playing out, now this way now that way, the twists and turns of Andalusian cultural history. The extraordinary variety of flamenco performances in the twentieth century results, in part, from artists' creative handling of these elemental experiences. In one moment, flamenco consists the sober and soulful songs of Andalusian ne'er-do-wells (Somerset Maugham 1920: 26). In another, flamenco consists of the flash and splash of a dancer like Joaquín Cortes who can stop one's heart with a single step, and of a guitarist like Rafael Riqueni whose wondrous talents have helped to revise the very concept of "flamenco guitar." This whole package, including the signal moments of fraternity and the sizzling moments of commercialized performance, constitutes the flamenco style. And this whole package is implicated in this study of flamenco politics. It may seem obvious and uncontroversial to claim that the flamenco style or any other style of popular music exercises politics. After all, popular music everywhere plays with power in manifold ways. The songs that we hear on the radio, that we play on disk, and that we see performed on stage or in film reinforce authority, resist oppression, intervene in conflicts, and in a hundred different ways resolve the quarrels of public life. Interestingly, however, the most common political moments in popular music, and perhaps the most effective, are moments that we fail to understand, usually because we overlook them. These are moments when bodies are caught up in the politics of music.[2] Beyond the forces exerted by obvious lyrics and by hidden metaphors in any bit of music, politics is also done by bodies.

Getting this picture of music, the body, and politics clear is no mean feat. However, the flamenco style offers itself as a musical laboratory for testing just such issues. The intriguing and problematic feature to be scrutinized is simply this, that the flamenco style is said to be devoid of political significance. Both the content and the unconscious form of flamenco performance suggest detachment from politics. Yet the ideological interest and political persuasiveness of this music cannot be doubted. Thus, flamenco is a perfect test case for exploring a politic that has everything to do with bodies and little to do with thoughts. Where better to look for embodied politics than in a music that is, conceptually at least, apolitical.

Though said to be apolitical, this style has nevertheless grown up in the midst of some of the most highly politicized and bitterly contested social circumstances in the modern world. Specifically, flamenco music arose in a region, Andalucía, which, on the one hand, has been marked by exaggerated social inequities and horrific poverty, and on the other, has served as a playground for nineteenth-century European intellectuals and as a punching bag for Franco's cultural ministries (García Gómez 1993; Miguel 1975; Steingress 1993).[3] Caught up in this milieu of poverty and oppression, the flamenco style could hardly have avoided the touch of politics. Accordingly, I will argue that flamenco politics is primarily an embodied politics that is unintentional, inadvertent, but no less effective than conceptual politics.

In order to argue this case, I will first comment on the absence of political content in flamenco song. I will reiterate the oft-stated observation that flamenco lyrics, the haiku-like *coplas*, rarely speak of political matters, and I will show that the form of flamenco performances suggests, if anything, a flight from politics. At this point, I will turn away from discussing political *ideas*, whether overt or covert, and towards politicized *practice*. I will use the term *metonymy*, unusual in analyses of music and politics, to show how muscles, not minds, accomplish politics in flamenco performance.[4] It is the bodily activity of flamenco artists and *aficionados* that makes politics happen. Flamenco bodies, moving within the long-lived political force fields of Andalusian social life, inadvertently comply with or resist specific political agendas. Finally, I will offer four examples of flamenco political practice.

Politics in Popular Music

A great many musical moments spanning the time from Richard Wagner to Bob Dylan remind us that music mediates politics and that popular music, in particular, has regularly been used to spin political wheels. However, debate persists about how, when, and toward what end any musical style is tied in with a political agenda.[5] The answers to these questions may come easily where lyrics are obviously intended to incite political movements, e.g. songs for labor rallies or national anthems. But after one sets aside these easy cases, the arguments about the politics of popular music rapidly become dense and protracted. My support, in these arguments, inclines toward those who contend that the visible politics of popular music is minimally effective, and that the real potency of the music lies below the waterline, where power is managed through covert strategies and hidden tactics.

The politics that operates in and through flamenco music is most certainly covert. For one thing, flamenco lyrics and performances are rarely, if ever, overtly political. Bernal Rodríguez (1982: 311) has summarized the politics of flamenco in this way: "It is widely understood that political problems and social conflicts traditionally find no explicit treatment in *cante flamenco*, to the point that when such treatments do appear in a song, one doubts its authenticity." Even more peremptory generalizations are offered by Germán Herrero, who contends that the flamenco style has been completely insulated from political life:[6] "A flamenco singer. . .makes no effort to influence the public" (1991: 74); "Scarcely anywhere can we see signs of those who spoke with a tone of rebellion, which may be so because *cante* served to absorb suffering and almost never to invite others to combat it" (1991: 79). This lack of a resistant spirit and of a rebellious attitude in the flamenco style are allegedly due to systematic mystifications. Musicians, it is said, have been benighted by a pervasive Andalusian ideology (see Mitchell 1994: 21). Their consciousness has not been raised to a point at which they might focus on the sources of their suffering. In the words of Gelardo and Belade, the class from which flamenco song springs "feels itself powerless to initiate any kind of struggle and is dominated by fatalism, by tragic fate: hence, their passive attitude" (Gelardo and Belade 1985: 146; see also García Chicón 1987: 186).

Evidently flamenco song overflows with personal sentiment, but runs dry when it comes to political commitment. However, might it not be the case that these flamencologists are placing too much emphasis on words and are relying too heavily on analyses of flamenco lyrics for their discernment of politics in flamenco music? To echo a judgment offered by Ray Pratt, "efforts to establish meaning through apparent substantive lyrical content" constitute "a fallacious but common practice among critics" (Pratt 1990: 8). Better to search for meaning outside the words of a song, as Simon Frith (1987) suggests.

In line with Frith's recommendation, one might search for political significance in the form, rather than in the content. Musical form can, it seems, serve as a metaphor for musical content, including political content. Just so, Lévi-Strauss (1969: 27) found that the forms of modern symphonic performances convey, metaphorically, a struggle with ideological conundrums. Similarly, Charles Keil and Steven Feld found that "metaphorical processes" mediate "special ways of experiencing, knowing, and feeling value, identity, and coherence" (1994: 91). In the light of these precedents, one might expect that the forms of flamenco performance should communicate something of the emotional struggle associated with life in Andalucía. Curiously, however, when one explores the forms of flamenco performance, one finds metaphors that suggest more the absence than the activation of political interest. A revealing example is to be found in the high-profile films of Carlos Saura that feature the dancer Antonio Gades: *Carmen, Blood Wedding* and *Amor Brujo*. These films by Carlos Saura all involve specular frame-within-a-frame imagery (see Molina 1994 for Saura's own considerations of these mirrored images). In *Carmen*, for example, flamenco dance is mediated by mirrors and fractured into moments of rehearsal, and is, by these devices, detached from everyday life. Moreover, performers becomes spectators as they watch themselves in the mirrors, not merely taking in the movement, but interrogating it with the sort of critical eye that ought to, but rarely does, operate in everyday life.[7]

In the light of these foregoing observations, one might well conclude that politics in flamenco music ranges from absent to avoided. The form of flamenco performances makes the absence of politics seem intentional. Unfortunately, such a conclusion does not allow for the sort of politics that is accomplished by bodies, where political significance is not necessarily something that is contained in someone's mind. Political ideology, as Terry Eagleton has argued, "is not primarily a matter of 'ideas': it is a structure which imposes itself upon us without necessarily having to pass through consciousness at all" (Eagleton 1991: 148; see also Duranti 1993: 41). If we take this warning seriously, then we should look outside of lyrics and metaphors for flamenco politics. More to the point, we should attend to musical metonyms.

Generally speaking, metonymy is the use of a part to signify the whole. For our purposes, a musical metonym is musical behavior that is part of politics. Musical metonyms are behaviors that rehearse politics, operating wherever music walks people through a course of action that has the potential of channelling interests and resolving quarrels. Via metonymical action, bodies inadvertently do politics while enjoying music. Unlike metaphors, which operate always from a distance, metonyms practice politics by proximity and contact, and, crucially, the contact is muscular not mental, bodily not conceptual.

Such muscular politics of musical metonymy is nicely illustrated by the chanted dialogs described by Greg Urban (1991: 123ff.). In moments from the ethnographic film *The Feast*, Urban explores some political metonyms embodied by the Yanomamo of southern Venezuela. Two headmen, erstwhile enemies, sit on their haunches, shoulder to shoulder, struggling toward alliance. They do so by chanting a ceremonial dialog. The words of their dialog are relatively insignificant, and its form is unrevealing when analyzed for metaphorical significance. What is remarkable about this chanted dialog is that the co-action of the headmen, specifically their synchronized behavior, models for them the behavior of alliance. Even though their minds might be far afield, their bodies adopt postures of alliance. Their eyes and hands move collaboratively rather than antagonistically, all of which leads Urban to conclude that "social relations are not just, or even primarily a matter of consciousness. They are first and foremost felt or sensed relations. . .To effect coherence it is necessary to suggest it, to make it an aspect of the overall interpretation or feel for the meaningfulness of the event, without simultaneously exposing it to the full light of consciousness" (1991: 145). Political alliance is adumbrated in the momentary behaviors of the headmen. Their chantings exercise the very same muscles that they will be using, hopefully, as they go about establishing and maintaining a long-term alliance. Their chanting action is metonymic in a muscular way. It involves them in a physical preparation for a larger political agenda. It trains their bodies for a political objective, and in the process, it establishes a precedent in social memory for that political objective. Their successful completion of the ceremonial dialog counts as a first phase in their alliance (see Paul Connerton 1989 for more on social memory). The lesson to be learned from this ceremonial dialog is that human politics can be invisibly advanced by muscular metonyms, that is, by momentary bodily movements that are consonant with larger long-lived political agendas.

By focusing on muscular metonymy, one avoids the danger of supposing that politics operates primarily through content and form, both of which involve mental processing. Instead, metonymic analysis presupposes a social life, including a political life, that is a function of the body. As such, this metonymic analysis is altogether apt for the study of politics in music cross-culturally. Such a mode of analysis is apt for advancing the view that Charles Keil seemed to favor when he wrote that "common sense and day-to-day observation of children learning by doing as much as by thinking. . .have demonstrated quite convincingly that our muscles are perceptive. Somehow muscles remember. . .Could it be that in many cultures children learn to listen when they learn to dance?" (Keil and Feld 1994: 56). Keil, for one, recommends a "body-based aesthetic" that looks for politics, not in words or metaphorical juxtapositions, but in the "conversation between dancers and musicians or that between player and instrument?" Here I will search out some such conversations that serve as embodied metonyms for politics in flamenco music.

Political Metonymy in Context

Before detailing flamenco's metonymic politics, it is necessary to map the relevant agendas, ideologies, and political forces that operate, however covertly, in moments of flamenco performance. It should be emphasized that these flamenco forces are most often unintentional. This is so because the metonymic politics of popular music does not express anyone's political consciousness. People are not aware that or how their activities with respect to music are linked to politics. Musicians and listeners cannot be held responsible for agendas that are consonant with their entrainment in musical moments. Similarly, filmmakers produce films which are usually political after-the-fact. Carlos Saura seems to have understood this when he commented on his own work – including *Carmen* – saying:

> There was never any political conditioning that prompted me to make a film. Nonetheless my films evidently were political, first, because I was opposed to Franco, and second, because others made them political (Besas 1985: 237).

In like manner, the political impact of recorded music is registered retrospectively, as listeners accommodate themselves to the music they hear. Such retrospective clout is illustrated by Susan Ossman's observations about reggae in Morocco:

> Some Moroccan youths might see reggae as a secular-liberal attack on Islam, but others explain that they like Bob Marley because his "mellowness" can be harmonized with feelings of piety. In addition, reggae is part of a highly lucrative business for music company executives in the United States. But even promoters dealing in "ethnic music" often see their product as a counter to mainstream, "top forty" music (Ossman 1994: 190).

In Ossman's view, one moment of Marley's music simultaneously favors pro-Islamic, anti-Islamic, pro-capitalist, and anti-capitalist interests. Listeners hear these contrasting interests *in* the recording, as if placed there by the musicians. However, as Ossman argues, it would be more appropriate to say that these influences operate *after* the recording as listeners relate the reggae to their memories of social experiences.

What fixes and channels the political energy of such popular music is not the music itself so much as the listener's articulation of the music with some discursive community, with some shared contextual frame (see Hutcheon 1995: 123). The political punch of music is a function of its potential to be intercalated into ongoing ideological discourses and inserted into pre-existing political narratives. When such intercalation occurs, the music effectively, even if inadvertently, reiterates, clarifies, reinforces and or objectifies features of those discourses and narratives (see Ossman 1994: 191). In consequence of being inadvertently linked to such a discursive context, the sound of the music is registered, defined, objectified, and transformed from an individual's momentary tactic of listening into a more widely shared strategy of social action.[8]

One need not dig very deep into the history of Spain to discover welter of diverging political contexts: "In the last hundred years or so Spain has twice been a republic (1973–5, 1931–9), twice a constitutional monarchy (1875–1923, 1976 onwards), and twice a military dictatorship (1923–30, 1939–76). . . . The attendant ideological conflict has been equally diverse. Numerous explicit "isms" – monarchism and republicanism; regionalism, liberalism and socialism; fascism, marxism and anarchism – have advanced their claims and sought adherents" (Corbin and Corbin 1987: 128).

Here, seven such ideological claims will be discussed as contexts in which flamenco bodies work out their politics metonymically. These seven narratives of Andalusian and Spanish social life are driven by distinctive political, economic, and intellectual interests. All are widespread and buoyant. For heuristic purposes, I will refer to them as *nacionalismo, romanticismo, fatalismo, modernismo, franquismo, andalucismo* and *gitanismo*.

Nacionalismo

In the period following the Napoleonic wars, the burgeoning middle class of Andalucía, with ideas borrowed from German nationalists, sought legitimacy in the face of their political nemeses by locating or inventing traditions of folksong and dance (see Brandes 1990; Burke 1992: 295f.). Local academies promoted and sponsored traditional performances in order to distinguish Andalusian life from the dominant courtly and ecclesiastical life of the times (Steingress 1988). Popular literature in the *costumbrista* style depicted the practices of the common folk, portraying such customs as reflections of past Andalusian authenticity (see the comments on literature and *casticismo* by Steingress 1994: 13). Thus, for example, *Escenas Andaluzas*, written by Serafín Estébanez Calderón in 1847, is filled with reflections on the historical contributions of Gitanos and Moriscos to the contemporary musical – and therefore cultural – life of Sevilla. Such writing encouraged artists and writers in the second half of the nineteenth century to pursue the musical style called flamenco so as to highlight Andalusian roots and legitimate a distinctive identity.

Romanticismo

During this same post-Napoleonic period, European intellectuals turned their attentions and their longings in the direction of Andalucía. Specifically, and despite the rampant poverty and tenurial injustice of this region, French and English romantics joined their voices with Spanish expatriate intellectuals to celebrate the vitality of the Andalusian people, portraying this vitality as a precocious form of poetic spontaneity and liberal individualism. Commonly enough, Andalusian balladry was both the object and the medium for these Romanticist celebrations of Andalusian vitality (Steingress 1993; Zavala and Diez Borque 1974). Songs that celebrated the Andalusian spirit were themselves much sought after for their own spirit. Thus, by 1850, the "Spanish art" was extended throughout Europe, so much so that the most prestigious ballerinas of the theater were converted into "Gitanas" or artificial "Andalusians," as is illustrated by the cases of the Viennese Fanny Elssler and Marie Gestiginer, Taglioni, Guy-Stephen and Eliza Gilbert – alias "Lola Montes" (Steingress 1994: 12).

Fatalismo

The Andalusian community of the late-eighteenth century was a two-class system, with only a very small percentage of the population owning land and controlling resources. In the nineteenth, the privatizations of public and ecclesiastical properties (1827, 1829, 1836, and 1855) only reinforced the contrast between Andalusian haves and have-nots (Gilmore 1980: 24). This bipolar social system was maintained by equal parts of guilt-catharsis and fatalism. The elites, emulating the character of the saintly Miguel Mañara – a seventeenth-century figure whose life evidently served as a replica of the character of Don Juan (Mitchell 1990: 53ff.) – expiated guilt by participating in over-wrought displays of penitential emotion. The poor, for their part, employed similar displays as vehicles for expressing their consummate frustration with poverty and oppression. The maudlin sentimentality that characterized both religious practice and flamenco song thus served as a double-edged sword to free both the rich and the poor from their emotional burdens (Mitchell 1988; 1994).

Modernismo

In the late nineteenth and early twentieth century, and especially after the military debacle of the Spanish–American war in 1898, intellectuals sought to reinvigorate the humiliated global image of Spain. Fractious politics, backward economics, and alleged moral bankruptcy as revealed in lascivious music called flamenco prompted intellectuals simultaneously to explore the causes of Spain's political spinelessness and to advance programs of cultural reinvigoration by availing themselves of the modernist quest to go behind appearances and discover universals in forms that underlie experience (see Huyssen 1986: 53). Amongst the most celebrated of these modernist intellectuals were García Lorca and Manuel de Falla who attempted to redeem flamenco music by calling it *cante jondo* and by portraying it less as a national or regional or Gitano art than as a crack in the cosmic egg of culture (see García Gómez 1993: 119), an aperture through which streamed the universal power of *duende*, a transcendental passion sufficiently powerful to free humans from the claw of history and from time itself (Grande 1992a,b). García Lorca (1975) and de Falla (1947) understood nationality to be rooted in just such a deep and universal dimension of experience, which they illustrated by referring to

Gitanos who experience life as a "no one" – Gitanos having been marginalized by everyone – and therefore as a unique "someone" whose vitality consists of a noble suffering core that is exposed only when all superficiality has been stripped away (see Grande 1992b: 88; Monleón 1974: 38).[9]

Franquismo

Between 1939 and 1975, the Franco regime ransacked the past in search of symbols upon which to rebuild a new and unified Spanish identity, an identity that might be attractive enough to lure tourists and centralized enough to be tweaked as needed for promoting the national interest. Following the Spanish Civil War (1936–9), Francisco Franco began to refashion the Spanish state, shrewdly but ruthlessly. His policies were more strongly influenced by fascist ideology in the early 1940s than in later periods of the regime. Characteristic of the early period was the suspension of individual rights, censorship of the press, mass imprisonment, and execution by edict. Economic and foreign policy was xenophobic and isolationist. Internally, the ministries of the *franquista* regime promoted centralization of administration with a focus on Madrid – hence the antipathy toward Madrid amongst *antifranquistas* (Burgos 1980). With regard to cultural politics, *franquistas* sought to fashion a single national identity, not so much by imposing one culture on the diverse regions of Spain, but by portraying Spain as a mystically unified ensemble of cultural varieties. The mystical body of Spain was, for Franco, perfectly analogous to the Mystical Body of the Church (Payne 1987: 58). Regional and ethnic variation was tolerated and even celebrated, but never as a competitive or contestatory or oppositional force. The cultural climate during the Franco regime was characteristically polite and silent, especially regarding all matters political. One can appreciate the suffocating cultural atmosphere that dominated the Franco years by reading Diaz-Plaja's satirical parody of one of the self-serving television serials that was promoted by the Franco regime:

– I see that there is a program on National Television called "Chronicle of a Town," which faithfully reflects the happenings in a small village. You know, of course, that National

Television always reflects faithfully the events that occur in our country.
- Is that right? I wouldn't know. I've lived here (in Germany as an expatriate) for many years and haven't visited Spain.
- Well, then, let me tell you about it. The documentary series deals with aspects of workaday life in a rustic town. It's really just a collection of small houses, with a small population, but, in this town, everything is always harmonious.
- Everything?
- Everything. Once in a while there is some small incident, almost always provoked by the arrival of a foreigner who makes mischief or at least tries to. But he leaves quickly and then the waters resume their normal flow.
- So, there is water then?
- Oh sure. There is never a shortage. The fountain gushes continually in the plaza. But really, the important story lies in the human element. The mayor, for example, is super. He is always preoccupied with the interests of the citizens, restoring order in the streets, settling debates. . .
- Oh, so there are debates?
- Yes, but nothing of importance, just talk that passes the time (Diaz-Plaja 1974: 61–8).

In this stifling cultural climate, folkloric performances were cosmetically retouched to obscure any indications of provincial loyalties. Traditional flamenco venues, such as bars and taverns, were shut down because they spawned dissent and subversion (see Gilmore 1985). Other venues that were less threatening to the regime flourished, e.g. *festivales*, *tablaos* and *peñas* (see Carrillo Alonso 1978: 180, 197). The *franquista* political cooptation of flamenco music in this period, especially on stages in Madrid, earned it the demeaning sobriquet *nacional-flamenquismo* (Almazán 1972; Alvarez Caballero 1992; Moreno Navarro 1982: 360).

Andalucismo

Variants of early-nineteenth-century regionalism and nationalism have persisted in southern Spain and have broken out into the open about every thirty years during the past two centuries

(Acosta Sánchez 1978; Moreno Navarro 1993: 106–23). Blas Infante, murdered in 1936, was this century's great martyr to the cause of Andalusian independence. He set the agenda for twentieth-century *andalucismo* by portraying the Andalusian community as a polyethnicity, contending that, prior to 1492 when Madrid imposed its centralizing authority on southern Spain, Andalucía was a paradise of Christian, Jewish, Moorish, and Gitano diversity. The conviviality of this period is remembered primarily through its remnants and vestiges, especially its popular culture including its music, preserved most faithfully by contemporary Gitano Andalusians (Acosta Sánchez 1979: 41; Moreno Navarro 1982: 362). It may well be that this regionalist fervor in southern Spain began as a reactionary movement amongst elites against industrialization and land reform – parallel in some respects to the nostalgic and conservative regionalism of southern United States – but over the years this Andalusian regionalism has shifted gears and undergone revisions. Whatever the root and source of the movement, the 1970s saw the quest for Andalusian autonomy emerge as a formidable force, albeit scattered, and never so well organized as the regionalist politics of the northern Basque and Catalan provinces (Corbin and Corbin 1987: 159).

Gitanismo

In the late nineteenth and early twentieth centuries, Antonio Machado y Alvarez "Demófilo" (see Steingress 1993: 103ff.) and Federico García Lorca (García Gomez 1993: 119ff.) advanced, each in his own way, a strong pro-Gitano argument about flamenco music. Both contended, for example, that Gitanos (Gypsies) made genre-defining contributions to the flamenco style. These arguments, along with numerous others that celebrated the contributions of marginalized minorities to flamenco, resonated with the *andalucismo* and the *modernismo* described above (Blas Infante 1980, originally 1930; Cansinos Assens 1985, originally 1933; Nöel 1977). However during the Franco regime, there emerged a new pro-Gitano ideology which was increasingly independent of the older political agendas. One source of this new ideology was the selective favoring of Gitanos in Franco's Spain.[10] Specifically, the future brightened and the stars rose for Gitanos with weak or weakened ties to Andalucía, e.g. for Carmen Amaya from Barcelona, and for the Manolo Caracol and Pastora Imperio, both from Seville but residents of Madrid during their glory years. Over the long haul, this favoritism encouraged a new sort of *gitanismo* that promoted the appreciation and betterment of a distinctly Gitano ethnic group. Just as the Black Power movement in North America was promoted through the celebration of a distinctive Black aesthetic in the 1950s and 1960s, so too the "Gitano Power" movement of Spain in the 1950s and 1960s was promoted through an analogous Gitano aesthetic, primarily rooted in flamenco music. Antonio Mairena stands out as the driving force behind this new *gitanismo* (Molina and Mairena 1979; Mairena 1976). The BBC documentary film "An Andalusian Journey" (1989) illustrates this new *gitanista* discourse, with its overtly political treatment of flamenco music.

Metonymic Aspects of the Flamenco Style

Flamenco music almost always trains muscles and steers social memories towards these agendas. Performers and audiences, though lacking explicit political intention, reinforce agendas by just practicing behaviors. Though these behaviors may be ambiguous in isolation, they become defined in the specific moments in which they are played out, defined in part by the sedimented political memories of the bodies that perform them and in part by the contexts in which they are performed and witnessed. Thus, the bodies of artists and listeners invisibly accomplish politics, often undermining the visible politics with "interpellations" that are directed by their sedimented social memories – here, using the Althusserian term "interpellation" in an expanded sense (see Silverman and Torode 1980). With regard to the flamenco style, I will illustrate some divergent inter-pellations with respect to some specific musical characteristics, notably "orientalization," "synchronization," "dys-appearance," and "recording."

Orientalization[11]

The term "orientalization" refers to practices that assimilate flamenco music to a Moorish model by using traditional rhythms of North Africa, by playing North African variants of musical modes, by using Moorish instruments such as the *'ud*, by emphasizing quarter tones and melismas, or, most remarkably, by singing *coplas* in the Arabic language. Orientalizations, under the specific conditions and according to the specific dispositions of listeners, operate in service to a number of the different ideologies described above. For example, Lole Montoya's rendition of *tangos* in Arabic ("Rito y Geografía del Cante", 1973) promoted in practice, though not in word, the *andalucismo* that was being rekindled in the late 1960s. Her orientalized rendition emphasized the links between contemporary Andalusians and their Islamic forebears (as discussed in Acosta Sánchez 1978 and Noakes 1994). Paradoxically, this very same orientalization was interpellated by *franquistas* as permissible, if not desirable, because of its power to attract foreign tourists. For *franquistas*, whatever undertones of *antifranquista andalucismo* may have been touched off by Lole's Arabic lyrics, her subversiveness – like the subversive behaviors of other Gitanos (Pohren 1994: 1714) – was tolerable because her behavior on the whole could be nicely articulated with the *franquista* project.

This one moment of performance also exercised *gitanismo*, which was new in the 1960s insofar as it celebrated Gitano ethnicity as something independent of Andalusian ethnicity. (Subsequent performances which advanced this agenda of *gitanismo* include Juan El Lebrijano's recording *Dame La Libertad*, 1985.) Montoya's orientalized song also served the interests of both *modernismo* and *romanticismo* insofar as it emphasized exotic "oriental" passions which bespeak a mystical universality (see also the recent disk *Flamenco Mystico* by Gino D'Auri, 1992).

Synchronization

"Synchronization" refers to the coordination of behaviors of improvising artists. Just as conversationalists synchronize their spates of talk, their emotional displays, and their gestures (see Kendon 1981), so flamenco singers, dancers, and guitarists coordinate their movements in the course of performing. The challenge of coordination is heightened by some distinctively flamenco features of song, dance, and guitar accompaniment. First, since singers select the *coplas* that they sing on the spot, in the moment of performance, guitarists are challenged to select appropriate chords for accompanying the singer's melodically distinctive *coplas*. In the face of this challenge, guitarists tap a variety of musical competencies. They fall back on deep reservoirs of melody-knowledge and *copla*-memory. Good accompanists, it is said, possess an encyclopedic knowledge of song and are often themselves accomplished singers – an allegation that is born out by the performances of Pedro Peña in the "Rito y Geografía del Cante" film series. In addition, guitarists may either lag behind or forge ahead in their playing, on the one hand, following the lead of the singer towards a critical note, or on the other, pointing the way towards that note with an anticipatory chord. Such guitaristic techniques require great sensitivity to the singer's style.

Second, dance in flamenco performance presents its own coordination challenges to both singers and guitarists. For one thing, dancers regularly locate a performance groove as a result of a momentary combination of musical elements. For another, the different flamenco forms contain different segments that dancers handle with distinctive movements. For example, *alegría* consists of sections called *castellana, escobilla,* and *silencio,* each with choreographically and guitaristically distinctive movements and with distinctive signals, such as *llamadas, remates,* and *desplantes*. Dancers initiate all these sections, providing signals that accompanists and singers must discern in the course of an improvisational performance.

Finally, the rhythmic structure of certain flamenco forms presents a unique challenge to artistic coordination. Forms such as *alegrías, bulerías, soleares,* and *seguiriyas* all involve a 12/4 Andalusian rhythmic phrase (*compás*), with stress on the 3-6-8-10-12 (see Vittucci 1990: 271–6; Woodall 1992: 102f.). This phrase, constantly repeated throughout the performance, presents singers, guitarists, and dancers with a unique challenge. As they improvise their music and dance, and coordinate their improvisations with each other, they must always and above all, attend to their place in the twelve-beat phrase. Their handling of beats 5 and 6, for example, will differ from their handling of beats

11 and 12 in all these modes of performance.

Given these many dimensions of coordination and synchronization in flamenco performance, it will not be surprising to learn that some scholars have focused special attention on synchronization. Notably, Anita Volland analyzed one particular spate of *bulería* performance (recorded in the "Rito y Geografía del Cante" documentary series, 1972) involving Diego del Gastor, La Fernanda de Utrera and three flamenco dancers (Volland 1985). She noted that flamenco "performance requires not only a knowledge of one's own role, but a great sensitivity to and awareness of the roles of other performers" (1985: 161). She attributed this sensitivity to Gitano culture, thereby interpreting the *bulería* synchronization as a metonymic reinforcement of *gitanismo*: "I am suggesting that the pattern of Gitano social interaction may, like the formal structure of the *bulería*, be one highly adapted to creative, even 'playful', manipulation by individuals and sub-groups. At the level of values the penchant for manipulation of people and events lies at the very core of Gitano culture" (1985: 162).

Despite Volland's argument for synchronization as a Gitano trait, synchronization is common to many varieties of flamenco performance besides Gitano. Minimally, some such synchronization is required for any successful collaboration between *cantaor* and *guitarrista*, and, when absent, can be the pivot around which some very heated words will turn. Given the ubiquity of synchronization in flamenco performance, it is plausible to argue that its political force is retrospectively defined in the light of a variety of community-oriented agendas such as *andalucismo* and *nacionalismo*, as well as *gitanismo*. Such an argument will be illustrated below with a specific discussion of events that took place during the festival at Montellano in 1994.

Dys-appearance

"Dys-appearance" is the term used by Drew Leder (1990) to refer to the behavior of bodies-in-pain, specifically to their withdrawal from outgoing practice as they turn reflexively inward. Such behaviors characterize the musical performances of many highly-regarded flamenco singers. Grande, following García Lorca, contends that, at his best, "the flamenco (singer) is explicitly concentrated in himself, self-absorbed" (1992a: 82). The acclaimed singer José Menese describes something akin to "dys-appearance" when he says that when he is singing, "unexpected things come out of his mouth," as if his conscious self had been totally overridden as a result of his inward turn (Alvarez Caballero 1981: 172). Afterwards he is "wracked, destroyed, literally broken" by the experience of song (1981: 48).

Mitchell has portrayed the self-absorbed lamentational quality of flamenco as an indication of the prevalence of the agenda of *fatalismo*, but Grande interprets such behavior in terms of García Lorca's *modernismo* (Grande 1992b). On yet another tack, one can note that "dys-appearance" prepares one for an experience of "flow," that is, for a complete loss of self in one's activity, an experience associated with communitas, the non-conscious delivery of one's self into the hands of others (Turner 1969). Understood in this way as an embodiment of communitas, flamenco "dys-appearance" becomes a musical reification of communality consonant with *gitanismo* or *andalucismo* or *nacionalismo*. However, paradoxically, "dys-appearance" is also an embodiment of resistance to communal power, specifically, a resistance to oppressive social constraints. It is in this way that Leder himself celebrates the experience of "dys-appearance", that is as a form of resistance to the oppressive dualism of Western life (Leder 1990: 121ff.). With respect to resistant "dys-appearance" in music, Ray Pratt (1990: 29ff.) argues that American popular music has the capability of cutting one off in time and of establishing a dimension of the "present" that is independent of a past so heavily burdened with its baggage of memories. Living thus "in a moment with no memory or anxiety about what has come before," persons can be reconstructed and if necessary recreated, "an important matter, if only for its functional necessity to revolt." Such revolt through "dys-appearance" is precisely what surfaces in José Menese's musings about his own labors as a singer. He says, for example, that when he is completely self-absorbed in song, he should sing in such a way as to "pinch" his listeners and "turn them around" (Alvarez Caballero 1981: 172).

Recording

Here our attentions are directed to the medium of music. Recording practices frame the music, and carry it from place to place and from time to time. Though recording is a matter of "medium," still it enters into the retrospective politicization of flamenco events. Sometimes recordings comply with "corporate manipulations," and at other times they serve as "grassroots expressions" in opposition to hegemony. Peter Manuel contends that recordings negotiate these and "other dialectics, such as traditional/modern, young/old, male/female, city/countryside, regional/pan-regional" (1993: 10). The weight thrown one way or the other by any recording is not so much a function of who controls the media as of how the recordings are integrated into the ongoing political lives of participants in a musical event, especially listeners. Applied to flamenco music, this understanding helps to account for the manifold ways in which flamenco recordings advance political agendas.

Any one recording can be negotiated in contrasting directions by different listeners. Consider, for example, the film series "Rito y Geografía del Cante" (1971–3). Currently, these film recordings of flamenco performances form part of the videocassette library at the "Centro Andaluz" in Jerez de la Frontera, where they, along with audio-recordings, books, essays, and photographs form one of the world's premier museums of flamenco artistry. In Jerez, ensconced in video carrels, eager young students – as many from beyond Spain as from within – access the world of the "flamenco past" even as the floor-pounding sounds from across the patio attest to the vitality of the "flamenco present." In such an atmosphere, it is hard *not* to read these films as "nostalgia films" (Jameson 1983). They serve, in Jameson's words, the interests of those who would recover the "feel" of the past without recovering its historical meaning. These films are, in a sense, required viewing for those who would cultivate flamenco sensibilities. Evidently, one must see Diego del Gastor, Juan Talega, Pepe Marchena, Manolo Caracol, young Paco de Lucía, and young Camarón de la Isla as they were then, in order to feel flamenco now. To approach flamenco artistry without seeing these figures would be like traveling to Granada without seeing the Alhambra. As such, the politics of this series tends to be a politics of *romanticismo*, a politics which coopts historical representation to authenticate contemporary practice.

However, when these films were originally aired on Spanish National Television, they were frequently viewed by quite a different set of *aficionados* and were interpellated in altogether different ways. One clue to this divergent interpellation is the fact that the films were broadcast on Channel Two, a television channel which was grudgingly tolerated in Franco's Spain – grudgingly because it occasionally aired subversive material.[12] Channel Two viewers were therefore already predisposed to see the films of the "Rito y Geografía del Cante" series as a realistic historical challenge to Franco's loose play with history. When viewed with this disposition, these films became the very antithesis of "nostalgia films." In content, the films of the "Rito y Geografía del Cante" series contrasted the warmth and candor of Andalusian song to the brashness and contrivance of Madrileño performances. They favored non-professionals over professionals, family-life over club-life, and Gitanos over non-Gitanos. By favoring these topics, the "Rito" films advanced a modest and covert resistance to Franco's *nacionalflamenquismo*. Like similar ambiguous and deniable acts of resistance that were occurring elsewhere in Spain (Johnston 1991: 182), these films were subversive only in their uptake. They were perceived as oppositional efforts by viewers predisposed to find *antifranquista* resonance in what others would interpret as politically neutral material. Viewers had to exercise a fairly sophisticated interpretative competence in order to find political opposition in topics and treatments of this film series, though in Franco's Spain in the late 1960s and early 1970s such competence was not in short supply (D'Lugo 1994: 338; Maravall 1978). Consider for example the reviews by Aguirre (1972) and Almazán (1971a) that appeared in two of the most prominent left-leaning, and therefore notorious, periodicals of the day. The clarity and depth that they applaud in the "Rito" series is a veiled criticism of the media cosmetics in the documentary projects produced under Franco:

> After a number of ill-fated attempts, with expectations inevitably rising that television would focus on flamenco, this excellent series has finally jelled. "Rito y Geografía del Cante" is the best of the materials that has been offered on the small screen until now, whether reckoned in terms of quality and sampling of artists, or

with respect to well documented information expressed in a convenient, succinct, and clear manner (F. Almazán, *Triunfo*, 1971a).

For the first time, popular music is depicted within the network of cultural and human presuppositions in which such music is rooted (Angel Aguirre, *Cuadernos Para el Diálogo*, 1972).

It can be argued that those who produced this series were guilty themselves of inventing the past. José Blas Vega, whom I interviewed during the summer of 1994, argued just this point, that the series inflated the historical importance of Andalucía, of Gitanos, and of family life. Without denying this charge, one can also recognize that the filmmakers, whatever the basis of their historical representations, were primarily interested in debunking the histories offered by Franco's purveyors of nostalgia. Curiously, then – and paradoxically – this one series of documentary films is consonant with contemporary politics of nostalgia and also with the contrary politics of those bent on overthrowing Franco's politics of nostalgia.

On the Politics of Interpretation

Participants in a musical event need not interpret metonymy for it to be effective. Their bodies do politics regardless of their conceptual activity. However, flamenco enthusiasts regularly do interpret their acts of enjoyment, often with an intensity that rivals flamenco performance itself. They offer responses to momentary musical experiences in such a way as to work some features of those momentary experiences into the context of prior and plausible experiences (see Keil and Feld 1994: 86; see also Shusterman 1992: 92). In other words, interpretations make explicit the implicit politics of metonymy. They render conceptual what has been, until then, muscular. In the course of this explication and conceptualization, the ambiguity of muscular politics is resolved into forms that are clear but fixed, if not frozen, cartoons of the complex force fields within which bodies move. These cartoon-like depictions of embodied politics inevitably get inserted back into the fields of social energy within which all subsequent performance occurs.

The connections between metonymic body politics and interpretive discourse were placed in high relief, for me at least, during August of 1994 when I attended the flamenco festival in Montellano about sixty kilometers from Sevilla. I accompanied José María Pérez Orozco, his brother Eduardo, and Paco Lira. We arrived at Montellano around eleven in the evening, well before the beginning of the concert, and so we used our time to enjoy some wine with a street-side snack while visiting with friends. The featured artists in this festival were Diego "El Cabrillero" and Mayte Martín (see García et al. 1991). As is customary, they were preceded on stage – outdoors, set with conventional symbols of rusticity including an oxcart and clothesline of drying clothes – by a *cuadro* and by some less well-known singers. Guitar accompaniment for the singers was provided by a technically advanced young Catalan and by a very young Sevillano whose skills had not yet matured, but whose promise was great. Diego El Cabrillero, whose powerful songs sung in the style of Utrera had attracted us here, was accompanied by the Catalan. Martín was accompanied by the Sevillano. I sat amidst José María, Eduardo, and Paco as we listened to the performers, and I drank in their comments knowing, even before they were introduced by the master of ceremonies as visiting dignitaries, that these were men who knew *cante*. However, I was not prepared for the suddenness of their judgment regarding the Catalan who accompanied El Cabrillero. No more than two minutes into their performance, José María was shaking his head, and Paco was already calling it a mess (*fracaso*). The guitarist, they said, did not know how to play.

This comment struck me as odd because I had just then formulated my own opinion that this guitarist was truly a marvel, capable of uncommon speed and intensity. But my comrades explained that it was not that the guitarist didn't know how to play the guitar itself. Rather, he did not know how to accompany a singer. He had no sensitivity to the song and was overplaying at all the wrong moments, destroying the very emotion that El Cabrillero had worked hard to establish. The evening went from bad to worse – though my enthusiastic consumption of manzanilla served to brighten my own personal view of just about everything I saw and heard. By the end of the festival, my colleagues were calling it a disaster. After the artists received their final applause, and after the bulk of the crowd had dissipated, a smaller group of obviously exercised *aficionados* remained behind. They gathered round the festival organizer and

complained loud and long about his ill-considered allocation of
guitarists to singers. It would have made more sense, they
contended, to pair the Catalan guitarist with Mayte Martín,
herself a young Catalan. On the perimeter of this contest, I saw
Diego El Cabrillero approach the young Sevillano. He gave him
encouragement, along with a word of lament that they had not
worked together. It was at this point, while the battle of words
was still raging behind me, that Paco introduced me to Diego. He
greeted me warmly and apologized for the evening. As if to make
up for its failures, he sang a *copla*, unaccompanied, to me.

The evening in Montellano saw the movements of artists'
bodies subjected to a variety of interpretive discourses. Regional
interests generated a great deal of talk, most of which turned on
either El Cabrillero's emphasis on the song style of Baja
Andalucía in contrast to Mayte Martín's favoring of the style of
the Levant, or on the differing guitaristic styles of the
accompanists. Superimposed on this confrontation of regionalist
agendas were the interpretations of musical coordination and
synchronization, or lack thereof: the Catalan guitarist and the
Andalusian singer were said to be out of synch. Interestingly,
these layers of physical activity were then translated into elegant
and well-measured interpretive words by José, Eduardo, Paco
and other members of the audience. They transformed the
implicit contents of regional variation and musical coordination
into an explicit musical aesthetics. The Catalan, it was said, did
not know how to play. Not to say that judgments about musical
beauty are inexorably and inevitably driven by political interests.
Rather, what happened in Montellano is what happens in so
many other venues of popular musical performance: the
boundary between aesthetics and politics gets blurred in such a
way as to facilitate the politicization of aesthetics.

Conclusion

Spinning a record backwards may reveal its devilish agenda, but
the experience of politics in popular music is far more workaday
than this weird gyration suggests. Unfortunately, we have all
been led to suppose that politics consists solely of ideas, whether
in lyrical contents or in metaphorical forms, and that these ideas,

having been embedded in musical acrostics, beg for cabalistic analysis. Here I have shown, however, that the politics of popular music lies as much in its doing as in its thinking. To participate in music is to engage in behaviors that are consonant with political agendas and that, after the fact and under the influence of sedimented force fields, become complicit with those agendas.

Aspects of flamenco music have been presented here to confirm this claim and to illustrate this argument. The words of flamenco songs are virtually devoid of political significance, and the forms of some recent flamenco artistry do little more than suggest political agendas, but the workaday behavior of those who participate in flamenco music embodies the music's deepest and most potent political forces. The politics of flamenco is advanced by muscular means rather than by mentation. Specifically, as artists intimate the Arabic past, as they synchronize behaviors in performance, as they turn attention utterly inward, and as they make use of recordings, they are accomplishing politics. Their bodies accomplish politics when they inadvertently resonate with and reinforce political energies consonant with existing political agendas. Such political actions of bodies making music are both more potent and more enduring than the political messages of songs, whether played forward or in reverse.

Notes

1. The term "political" refers to "sub-politics" which Ulrich Beck (Beck, Giddens, and Lash 1994: 21) describes as "contradictory multiple engagement which mixes and combines the classical poles of politics so that, if we think things through to their logical conclusion, everyone thinks and acts as a right-winger and left-winger, radically and conservatively democratically and undemocratically, ecologically and anti-ecologically, politically and unpolitically, all at the same time. The current clarities of politics – right and left, conservative and socialistic, retreat and participation – are no longer correct or effective."

2. Of course, minds have their role to play, thinking politically and deciding on courses of action that will sort out and resolve conflicts. It is obvious, for example, that lyrics do politics in a conceptual way. Conceptual, too, are the workings of the alleged unconscious musical faculty. This faculty discerns political metaphors hidden in musical structure, and, in its manner of operation, attests to the unity of the listener, a unity which is itself a significant principle of political ideology (see Chanan 1994: 103 for illustrations of the working of this faculty, and see Eagleton 1991: 35ff. and Barry 1987 for discussions of the ideology of the unified subject). However, whether conscious or unconscious, conceptual politics is just one aspect of musical politics, and not necessarily the most powerful or the most interesting.

3. The rancor of Andalusians who spoke out against Franco was not at all diminished by the fact that Franco's creative reinvention of Spanish national identity drew heavily on Andalusian cultural practices such as bullfights and popular religious practices. The writings of Burgos (1971; 1980) and Moreno Navarro (1977), for example, look beneath the artifices of Franco's andalucization of Spain to find loathsome processes of cultural homogenization and social central-ization. Franco's cultural politics, even though heavily weighted with Andalusian themes, was never absolved of its sin of centralism in the eyes of the Andalusians who suffered during the Civil War and the years that followed.

4. Scott Lash has counterposed "mimetic art" to "conceptual art" in a manner similar to my contrast between *metonymy* and metaphor (Beck, Giddens, and Lash 1994: 135ff.). The term "metonymy," however, is preferable to "mimesis," insofar as it avoids reliance on the notoriously ambiguous notion of "iconicity" (see Eco 1976), and insofar as it has nothing to do with the potentially confusing notion of resemblance (see Rosen 1995: 54).

5. For example, "noisy" music in modern Western social life has been portrayed frequently as a Dionysian threat to an Apollonian order (Attali 1985: 21-4; Chanan 1994: 34; Leppert 1988). Simon Reynolds doubts the neatness of such portrayals (Reynolds 1990: 59), and Evan Eisenberg suggests that noisy music plays a role in micro-level face-to-face relations as well as in macro-level politics (Eisenberg 1987: 44). Obviously, the

final word on the politics of "noisy" music is still a long way off.

6. Ortiz Nuevo (1985: 13) claims that systematic forces have erased political content of flamenco from both performance and memory. Cruces Roldán (1993) and Gelardo and Belade (1985: 133) suggest that the process of commercialization is primarily responsible for this erasure; lyrics were softened and the performance style sweetened so as to assure a successful marketing of flamenco performances to the widest possible audience. However, it should be noted that, according to a few intellectuals, flamenco song, especially when presented in private gatherings, *does* give voice to social frustration, if not to explicitly political intentions. Notably, Grande portrays *cante* as a silent accusation and a secret rebellion (Grande 1992b: 91). Carrillo Alonso claimed that some varieties of *cante* harbor an underlying political agenda: "Where it is an expression of marginalized and frustrated lives, *cante flamenco* is converted into a clear denunciation of the unjust social situation, being – essentially – the sole medium of liberation for some human groups who live isolated and forgotten lives" (1978: 12). Vélez, brandishing Marxian argumentation, argued that flamenco "is a cultural revolution of the whole community. . .We affirm the existence of classes and of the struggle between them. We affirm that this struggle is antagonistic and to the death. We affirm that, given this class struggle, nothing escapes its influence and that in art – while classes exist – there will be ideological defences of the one or the other. We affirm that the interpretation of flamenco by certain *flamencólogos* is such an ideological defence – in the final analysis – of the interests of one of the classes" (Vélez 1976: 27).

7. This filmic structure, so characteristic of Saura's films of the 1980s, developed out his attempts to deal with the heavy-handed censorship of the early 1960s under Franco. Saura began collaborating with the producer Querejeta who, "still opposing the regime, was looking for a way to 'negotiate' a film through the bureaucratic machinery so that it might actually receive the necessary support of the government while, in effect, critiquing from within the very system that supported it" (D'Lugo 1994: 340). Paradoxically, the success of this Saura–Querejeta tactic of negotiation runs contrary to one

of the major messages of these films, namely, that Spaniards, whether workaday citizens or flamenco performers, are "locked in the trap of. . .the social and historical constraints of Spanish culture" (ibid.) Obviously, the trap can be sprung by creative forms of resistance. Such paradox, however, is to be expected in the Manichean world dictated by Franco's cultural politics where statements of intent had to be expressed with consummate caution. How else to interpret Saura's claim that "there was never any political conditioning that prompted me to make a film" (Besas 1985: 237) in the face of his equally emphatic statement that "I believed that when Franco was still alive, I had a moral obligation to do everything that was possible within my form of work to help change the political system as quickly as possible" (Kinder 1983: 57)?

8. The process of constituting social action retrospectively is one in which actors find themselves "floundering through mere happenings and then concocting accounts of how they hang together" (Geertz 1995: 3, 166; see Goodwin and Duranti 1994 for another take on this same process, and see John Doe 1988: 201f. for an extraordinarily enlightening Bakhtinian account of the role of retrospective narrative in social practice; finally, see Keil and Feld 1994: 85 for a discussion of "musical–extramusical dialectics").

9. Both García Lorca and Falla attributed the flamenco style to Gitanos (Falla 1947: 122; García Lorca 1975: 24). These attributions were not intended as direct promotions of contemporary Gitano social life, but rather as idealizations of *cante*. García Lorca commented on his *Romancero Gitano*, for example, saying that "though it is called Gitano, it is really the poem of Andalucía; and I call it Gitano because the Gitano is the most elemental, the most profound, the most aristocratic in the land, the most representative of this style and guardian of the flame, the blood, and the letter of the universal Andalusian truth" (quoted in Grande 1992b: 88). Such comments make it clear that Lorca was using "Gitano" to symbolize the distinctive and exotic roots that, he said, ground and support Andalusian social life. Interestingly, this idealization, as a rhetorical tactic, devalues the concrete and workaday experiences of Andalusian life, whether Gitano or not, as García Lorca's critics have eagerly pointed out. "The world of song according

to Federico García Lorca is nothing more than a concatenation of personal aesthetic allusions which afterwards was mounted on the foundation of *duendes* and dressed up with trifles" (Burgos 1971: 164; see Monleón 1974: 38). A kindred observation, though made with a cup-half-full perspective, has it that "Federico dispensed with superficialities – for example, the facts – and approached the universe of laws" (Grande 1992b: 85).

No less ironically, Manuel de Falla, though having argued with Lorca for a Gitano origin of flamenco song, nevertheless found it necessary to expel some noisy Gitanos from the *Concurso del Cante Jondo* in 1922 because they persisted in clapping time – irreverently in Falla's estimation – to a *soleá* (Rossy 1966: 60).

10. The favoring of Gitanos must be understood in the context of *franquismo* where to be permitted was tantamount to being promoted. Though the regime may not have actively promoted or celebrated Gitano ethnicity, it did permit such promotions as a sop to intellectuals who claimed that resistance was always muzzled in Franco's Spain. Such permissions constituted no great concession by the regime since Gitanos were, though often critical of Franco, politically unorganized and therefore unable to transform their sporadic criticisms into strategic political action.

11. "Orientalization" here refers to a European romanticization of Arabs and Islam "which for almost a thousand years together stood for the Orient" (Said 1979: 17).

12. See Chapter 9 for a discussion of the history of Channel Two and of the "Rito y Geografía del Cante" series.

Chapter 2

The Histories of Flamenco

Existing discussions would have one believe that all beauty, truth, and meaning lies in flamenco's moments of intimacy and that commercialized flamenco, by contrast, is the site of mystification, superficiality, and artificiality. The banalities of commercialized flamenco are so insulting to the authentic tradition that, as Yogi Berra would say, they aren't even worth ignoring. Indeed, many of the flamenco historians who seem willing, if not eager, to disagree at every turn, nevertheless share this same Adornian disparagement of commercialized artistry (see, for example, Molina 1981; 1985 and Mitchell 1994). This chapter addresses one small feature of this broadside of criticism heaped on commercialized flamenco spectacles now and throughout flamenco's history, namely their political meaning or lack thereof. In contrast to those who would argue that the non-commercial flamenco of private gatherings is politically – as well as aesthetically – rich in meaning, and that commercialization erases or hides such meaning, I will argue here that every flamenco performance, commercial or non-commercial, is a multidimensional, multiaccentual experience that almost always includes crosscurrents of political signification. Commercialized flamenco spectacles are not political voids, banalities to be ignored, but are instead enriched cultural experiences. Flamenco spectacles are knotted and snarled performances of complex meaning that deserve careful interpretation.[1]

This chapter will begin by examining the flamenco commentaries that dwell on the taproot of flamenco intimacy, and that treat public spectacles as if they were silly deviations from the trunk of the tradition. In particular, I will focus on histories that, like Cruces Roldán's (1993), treat the political vitality of flamenco as if it were to be found always and only in non-commercialized venues. Having outlined four such approaches to flamenco politics, I will re-examine some major public moments in flamenco history – namely the *café cantante*, the *ópera flamenca*, the *Concurso del cante jondo* and "Rito y Geografía del Cante" – and will demonstrate the multidimensional political significance of each moment.

Traditional Histories of Flamenco

Restricting themselves for the most part to non-commercialized flamenco, historians have constructed stories that celebrate the meaning and value, including political, of the flamenco tradition. These stories vary insofar as they are built around distinct ideological principles. Here, four such stories are labelled "Andalusian", "Gitano", "populist", and "sociological." Each is long-lived and widespread, and each claims itself to be the proper and true history of flamenco. And indeed, each *is* a proper and true history, depending on who is narrating it. Common to all four is the claim that commercialization has clouded or erased the true meaning of flamenco music.

One line of flamencological argumentation emphasizes the Andalusian character of flamenco music. Anselmo González Climent promoted such a view in his *Flamencología* (1953) which is considered a genre-defining opus. He described flamenco as a mysterious song, an "intuitive metaphysics" (González Climent 1964: 166), an embodiment of the fundamentals of human experience (1964: 168), a musical realization of what Unamuno described as "the tragic sense of life" (González Climent 1964: 170; Ríos Ruiz 1988: 242; 1993: 33). This musical metaphysics is portrayed as a swelling river produced by the confluence of different cultural streams. The epic song traditions of the late Middle Ages were shaped by contact with Islamic, Jewish, Christian (liturgical), and Gitano (Gypsy) influences. Over many centuries, these influences were completely amalgamated (Ríos Ruiz 1972: 32; Rossy 1966) so that by the end of the eighteenth century one can speak of a fully-formed and deeply-rooted Andalusian cultural song style. Gitanos, on this account, ranked amongst the finest performers of this Andalusian tradition (Manfredi Cano 1955: 43–4).

The Andalusian argument goes on to say that in the nineteenth century, this Andalusian song style was popularized in the taverns and the *cafés cantantes* of southern Spain. Through this popularization, flamenco emerged as a crystalline human expression – both transparent and dense – which, though distinctively Andalusian, had the power to speak to all humans: "In the tragic profundity of song, the Andalusian succeeds in concretizing the experience that is fundamental to himself and to the world" (González Climent 1964: 168).

The last half of the nineteenth century, with its flourishing *cafés cantantes*, is often described, in this account, as the golden age of flamenco (Riós Ruiz 1993: 11). Those who advance this Andalusian argument contend that this golden age was a period during which artists refined Andalusian song, strengthening its already strong metaphysics (García Chicón 1985: 44). Artists from the different provinces of Andalucía contributed to this enhancement by elaborating their regionally distinctive substyles.[2]

In the second half of the nineteenth century, Europeans turned their admiring attentions to Andalucía, and tourists began flocking to flamenco performances (Steingress 1993: 323). According to the Andalusian argument, the tourist fanfare weakened the pure stock of flamenco. Then in the early twentieth century, garish flamenco spectacles orchestrated under the high-flown label of *ópera flamenca* attracted even larger audiences. These baroque spectacles are said to have obscured the rock-solid Andalusian core of the music. When coupled with the Gitano style of flamenco, such spectacles soon earned this music an ugly reputation in the popular press (Ríos Ruiz 1993: 37ff.) By 1950, the true Andalusian character of flamenco is said to have been thoroughly obscured in the crush of journalistic assaults on popular spectacles: "Among the Andalusian, the flamenco and the Gitano, the Andalusian is categorical; flamenco and Gitano effects came afterwards" (Manfredi Cano 1955: 29).

In 1922, Manuel de Falla, Federico García Lorca, and other notables from Granada sought to revitalize Andalusian flamenco by promoting the *Concurso del Cante Jondo*, a two-day contest of song held in the Alhambra of Granada (Falla 1947; García Lorca 1975; Stanton 1978). They rejected the name "flamenco" in hopes of circumventing the criticisms that that term had attracted. Instead, they embraced the term *"cante jondo"* ("deep song") to emphasize a style of song that, they contended, ran a silent course below the surface of popular culture. *"Lo jondo* was not imported into Andalucía from the outside, but was one, and perhaps the only, survival of the oldest aspects of Andalusian culture itself" (García Chicón 1987: 28). *Lo jondo,* it is said, was never appreciated by the masses, but was always cultivated by those in touch with the soul of Andalucía (1987: 25).

According to the Andalusian argument, flamenco song after the *Concurso* was torn between the glitzy delights of ersatz flamenco and the heroic spirit of true and pure Andalusian flamenco. The ersatz flamenco generally prevailed until the 1960s when artists and scholars began recovering the "authentic" Andalusian style. This recovery was advanced and illustrated in the Spanish National Television documentary series, "Rito y Geografía del Cante" (Blas Vega and Ríos Ruiz 1990: 741), in which terms like "authenticity" and "purity" became flamenco watchwords.

In contrast to this account that emphasizes the Andalusian character of flamenco, a second account contends that flamenco is the ethnic music of Gitanos. Antonio Mairena spearheaded this Gitano account in the late 1960s with his claim that flamenco is, at its heart, a Gitano invention (Mairena 1976; Molina and Mairena 1979). Mairena claimed, in effect, that "the first sounds of flamenco were Gitano" (see Woodall 1992: 94).

Gitanos, it is said, were sequestered and persecuted during the 300 years between 1492 and 1783 (Alvarez Caballero 1988: 54; Caballero Bonald 1975: 20; Grande 1979). In the face of this persecution, they shut themselves off from their threatening surroundings, and, during what Caballero Bonald described as "a long phase of hidden and impenetrable invention," they developed the core forms of *cante gitano,* i.e. *tonás, soleares, seguiriyas, alegrías, bulerías.* These are the songs with which "the Gitano Andalusian community gave voice to its bitterness and powerlessness for four hundred years" (Drillon et al. 1975: 10). Mairena contends that these were songs that Andalusian Gitanos "developed and preserved in a subterranean form," that is, in the privacy of Gitano weddings and baptisms (Mairena 1976: 20). Alvarez Caballero argues that Gitanos *created* these flamenco songs. More than just students who learn a local song tradition, and more than merely performers who sing and play with a distinctive flair, Gitanos, for Alvarez Caballero, were nothing short of the prime movers of flamenco (1988: 70).

This pro-Gitano history of flamenco contends that the Gitano creation of flamenco was obscured when the music became popular and professionalized in the late nineteenth century. The gritty Gitano songs of old were softened and sweetened during this era by non-Gitano singers and promoters, notably Silverio Franconetti – though Steingress (1993: 357) offers an alternative interpretation of Franconetti's art. Antonio Machado y Alvarez "Demófilo," the great nineteenth-century folklorist, contended that this sweetening dealt a deathblow to flamenco (Alvarez Caballero 1981: 81); "Authentic and genuine *cante*," he said, "ought not to have departed from its obscure surroundings" (Molina and Mairena 1979: 20).

In the *cafés cantantes*, Gitanos, it is claimed, were reduced to the level of prostituted performers who were trotted out onto stages and into private parties (*juergas*) to delight wealthy gawkers attracted more by the romance of the Gypsy than by the value of *cante Gitano* (Grande 1979: 343). To these injuries, the era of theatrical flamenco only added more insults. New forms of flamenco derived from Andalusian (e.g. *fandangos, fandanguillos, malagueñas, granainas*) and Latin American folk traditions (e.g. *rumbas, colombianas, guajiras*) hid the true Gitano art "under a huge black cloak," displacing and obscuring the heart and soul of flamenco-Gitano (Mairena 1976: 29).

The Gitano account contends that flamenco lost its way and forgot its roots during the period between the mid-nineteenth century and the mid-twentieth century. The sound of Gitano flamenco would have been lost altogether were it not for the efforts of artists like Manuel Torre and Pastora Pavón, who, in the Gitano argument, are portrayed as stalwart defenders of the Gitano heritage. Pavón, according to García Lorca (1975: 46), was forceful enough to "kill all the scaffolding of the song and leave way for a furious, enslaving *duende*, friend of sand winds, who made the listeners rip their clothes." Their ineffable *duende* – "muse, angel, demon" (García Lorca 1975: 43), "worm" (Bergamin 1957: 1), "hypnotic energy" (Vitucci 1990: 74) – is said to be part of the biological heritage of Gitanos (Mairena 1976: 79f.; Molina 1985: 62; Serrano and Elgorriaga 1990: 35).

The organizers of the *Concurso del Cante Jondo* tried to encourage rare artists like Torre and Pavón, but the times were not favorable, and, it is assumed, the *Concurso* had little lasting impact on the art. However, in the early 1970s, the documentary film series "Rito y Geografía del Cante" struggled to reinvigorate the Gitano aesthetic, appealing in a special way to anglophone aficionados among whom gitanismo has become an especially popular dimension of flamenco (see "Rito" programs nos 68, 85 and 96; Volland 1985; Woodall 1992, and the 1989 BBC television documentary "An Andalusian Journey").

In contrast to the emphasis on ethnic origins, whether Andalusian or Gitano, a third account portrays flamenco as a voice of opposition. According to this "populist" view, flamenco is a "weapon of cultural resistance" (Whitney 1974: 25), which, like other such weapons wielded by the marginalized people of Andalucía (Scott 1990: 27), cries out for "salvation from the conditions of poverty and abandonment, from the pain of prejudice and social oblivion" (Woodall 1992: 115). The conditions that prompted the appearance of flamenco, according to this account, have less to do with ethnicity, whether Andalusian or Gitano, than with the structural conditions of oppression in which people find themselves, i.e. landless, jobless, and bullied by the corrupt elite. The argument for flamenco as a voice of resistance claims that marginalized artists were the ones who created and performed flamenco music (see Cruces Roldán 1993; Vélez 1976).

Herrero (1991: 42) advances this claim by likening the history of flamenco to the history of jazz: "Both are rooted in the lower classes, the poor and the oppressed. . ... These two communities considered, and continue to consider, as theirs the single form of expression that they have within their reach: music." Twenty years earlier, Brook Zern had made a similar comparison between Black Americans and Gypsies who:

> found themselves in the south end of a new and strange country. . .and thus began for them an era of persecution and misery. . .. As a result of this traumatic experience, they forged a dense and pessimistic musical style. This music, which never left the house, served to give voice to the enormous racial tragedy that they had suffered, and also to document that tragedy for their children and for history. It was a living testament of their anguish (Zern 1973).

This populist account suggests that the flamenco style persisted in Andalucía for nearly 500 years. However, during the nineteenth century that resistant song of the lower classes began to lose its bite: "With the professionalization of song in the *cafés cantantes* and above all with the commercial developments of the late nineteenth century, the singer becomes an individual paid, generally speaking, by the wealthy classes who integrated him into their *fiestas*, into their *juergas*, or their *cafés*. The content of the flamenco, the verses or *coplas*, were softened little by little to please the middle class that pays its way into the *cafés*, and with this softening *cante* lost the tragic force that it originally possessed" (Gelardo and Belade 1985: 133).

For populists, the writings of both García Lorca in the 1920s and Mairena in the 1960s, although oriented towards Andalusian and Gitano interests, respectively, nevertheless emphasized the role of resistance and opposition in the flamenco song style. In the populist's lexicon, *duende* is a faculty that generates liberation for, and cohesion among, the oppressed (Grande 1992a; Zern 1975), and flamenco aesthetics is rooted in an appreciation of "prolonged poverty and oppression" and in the recognition "that Andalucía is exploited and neglected and that its culture is being debilitated" (Manuel 1989: 63). Flamenco as a weapon of the weak was, it is said, a major theme in the television documentary series "Rito y Geografía del Cante" (see Zern 1987) and in the musical production *Flamenco Puro* that opened in 1980 and which, like its sister-productions *Black and Blue* and *Tango Argentino*, was intended as a celebration of what one critic called "the art of the excluded."

Finally, the sociological history of flamenco is a demystifying modernist account of the power of economics and politics to blur the vision and numb the mind of people in everyday life. Hugo Schuchardt outlined such a view in 1881 as a rejoinder to the gitanismo of "Demófilo." García Gómez (1993), Mitchell (1994), and Steingress (1993) have contributed theoretical sophistication and historical detail to this scientific sociological view, thereby countering the Andalusian, Gitano, and populist accounts. Flamenco, according to this sociological view, is a spectacle through which oppressed people voice their misery in such a way as to evoke expressions of guilt-driven pity from wealthy listeners. The song, on this account, performs a double catharsis, exposing and relieving both the pain of the poor and the guilt of the wealthy. The upshot of the song is this: both the poor and the wealthy, having been relieved of their psychological burdens, walk away content with the world as it is. Hence, flamenco song is fundamentally a homeostatic device that knits together the elements of the bipolar society.

The sociological account emphasizes a few critical features of flamenco social history. First, in the eighteenth century the defiant backward-looking style *majismo* emerged in opposition to the francophiliac elite of the day. Second, early nineteenth-century romanticists exploited *majismo* in pursuit of their romanticist interests.[3] Third, the nationalist intellectual labors of Johann Herder and the German Romantics encouraged Andalusians to search for folk traditions that might provide them with a distinctive identity. Fourth, with rise of the urban middle class, romanticisms and nationalisms were repackaged as commodities for trade and profit in *cafés cantantes* and, later, in *óperas flamencas*. Fifth, Andalusian intellectuals emphasized the importance of critical self-reflection after the Spanish–American War in 1898. Amongst such self-reflective efforts was the *Concurso del Cante Jondo* promoted by Lorca and De Falla in 1922. Finally, the sociologists emphasize the dark night of mystifying *franquista* ideology that encouraged flamenco song to hide the oppressions and contradictions of Franco's cultural politics. A tell-tale indication of the power of this *franquista* ideology is evident in the television documentary series "Rito y Geografía del Cante," a series that Jameson (1983) might describe as "nostalgia film" filled with appreciations of the "feel" of the past yet devoid of efforts to recover the economic and political realities that generated this "feel."

Ironies in the History of Flamenco

Flamenco writers over the past 40 years have spent their time honing their criticisms of professionalized flamenco, demonstrating that commercialized spectacles have diluted the Andalusian soul of this music, or cloaked its Gitano heart, or blunted its oppositional edge, or intensified its power to delude the masses. In all these efforts commentators have operated as if the historical evidence should support one or another account, but not all four. In contrast, I contend that the critical moments in the history of flamenco music are those that involve multiple, countervailing, parallel forces. They are moments in which flamenco is simultaneously Andalusian and non-Andalusian,

Gitano and non-Gitano, resistant and compliant. Embodying as it does these simultaneous opposites, flamenco should be described as an ironic musical style, and one should expect to discover that irony pervades public spectacles as well as in private gatherings.

I will develop this account in two ways: first, by demonstrating the prevalence of ironic social processes in Spain from the sixteenth to the nineteenth centuries – that is during the period of time that precedes the popularization of flamenco music – and second, by demonstrating that the flamenco landmarks of the nineteenth and twentieth centuries, i.e. the nineteenth-century *café cantante*, the early twentieth-century *ópera flamenca*, the *Concurso del Cante Jondo* of 1922, and the film series "Rito y Geografía del Cante" of 1971–3, must be understood as heteroglossic and multi-voiced events (Bakhtin 1981).

Spain, from 1492 to 1850, was the site of intensely ironic social practices. On the political front, strong resistances to oppression often took the form of conservative and accommodating practices. On the personal front, people played with identities to the point of losing track of their own artifices. By the time flamenco became popular in the nineteenth century, the people of Spain were already 300 years into the practice of irony.

The stimulant for this spate of ironic practices was the conquest of Granada in 1492, followed by the imposition of religious, cultural, linguistic, and political homogeneity on the newly united Spain. The Inquisition imposed both religious and cultural homogeneity on the Jewish and Muslim peoples who were especially numerous in southern Spain (Root 1988; Shell 1991). Antonio de Nebrija's grammar of Spanish, the first grammar of any European vernacular, explicitly promoted linguistic and political homogeneity (Illich and Sanders 1989).

Popular responses to these impositions of homogeneity were covert and varied. Some Jews and Muslims feigned compliance to the authorities. Others feigned compliance to their compatriots. For many, life became one huge protracted artifice. Sometimes people lost the ability to distinguish their real selves from their feigned selves. For example, many of the Spanish Jews who escaped the Inquisition by fleeing to Amsterdam found that they had forgotten how to be Jews; others found themselves longing for the Christianity that they had so long been feigning (Yovel 1989: 41ff.). Elsewhere, Muslims pretended to be Gypsies, and Gypsies, who usually eschewed agricultural labor, adopted the rural life style of Muslims (Barrios 1992: 47). Little wonder that ethnic identities were vaguely and inconsistently defined during these centuries.[4]

Many persons resisted the monarchical efforts to centralize Spanish politics and to homogenize the Spanish nation during this period, though usually their acts of resistance were invisible, like the "hidden transcripts" of opposition described by James Scott (1990). The proto-novel *La Celestina* (Yovel 1989: 96), the hyper-Catholicism of the Spanish mystics (Certeau 1986: 88–100; Yovel 1989: 25), and the independence of the holy women, *beatas* (Perry 1990: 97f.), all exemplify such invisible resistance.

The seventeenth century, with its economic and political crises, witnessed a redoubling of political oppression. Throughout this tumultuous century, the oppressions as well as the resistances turned on artifice and irony. José Maravall portrays the politics of this century as a smoke-and-mirrors affair (Maravall 1986: 236, 253), the epitome of a "seductive use of spectacle" in "a cynical festering of mass culture" (Jay 1993: 46).

In the eighteenth century, the poor – and especially the Andalusian poor – embraced a resistant conservatism that, ironically, resembled the oppressive and coercive conservatism of the previous century. With the Bourbon accession to the throne and with the attentions of the Spanish aristocracy turned towards Paris (Mitchell 1991: 58), the poor resisted by vaunting all things old and common thereby "inventing tradition" (in the sense described by Hobsbawm and Ranger 1983). They refashioned themselves as *majos*, a *majo* being "a bold self-assured malapert" who more-or-less consciously rejected "the alien and overrefined fashions and behaviors of the upper classes of the early eighteenth century" (Mitchell 1988: 176) *Majos* resisted by defiantly opposing everything associated with the francophiliac Spanish aristocracy (see Steingress 1993: 316).

Majismo as a cultural style might not have flourished as it did had it not been for the ironies of the early nineteenth century. First, the *majo*'s rude defiance acquired a positive value when it was juxtaposed with the morally decadent refinements of the French court (Berlin 1991: 246). Second, the European literati heroized Andalusian *majismo*, especially after the War of Independence (1808–14) during which a ragtag Spanish army, aided by gun-toting monks and scissor-wielding women, successfully opposed the French Republic's soldiers (Mitchell 1991: 62), while embattled patriots in Cádiz promulgated a stunningly liberal constitution (Steingress 1993: 284ff.). Thereafter, according to Michael Jacobs, "The attention of Europe was turned increasingly towards Spain, and in particular Andalusia." "In no other part of the country," wrote George Dennis in 1839, "is the liberal part stronger than in Andalusia" (Jacobs 1990: 174). As the British saw it, the military ineptitude of the *majos* of Andalucía was more than adequately offset by their defiantly liberal spirit.

The attentions paid to Andalucía by the British were not lost on the many Spanish intellectuals who had sought refuge outside of Spain during the war. When those Spanish intellectuals returned to their homeland in the 1830s, they took up the theme of celebrating Andalucía, singing *coplas* (verses) celebrating the courage of the peasants during the War (Ortiz Nuevo 1985: 75). In short, the new crop of Spanish intellectuals found themselves revaluing their homeland, its customs, and its expressions, including its music. "The first overtures of peninsular romanticism were from amongst the exiled. . .Not only did they accept a principle of nationalism that was incompatible with neoclassical universalism, but they allowed themselves an enthusiastic turn towards primitivity and spontaneity, represented above all in popular song" (Zavala and Diez Borque 1974: 17). José Caballero Bonald contends that the War of Independence prompted a "revaluation of some unappreciated popular traditions" and "enthusiasm for renewing long forgotten traditions" (as quoted in Alvarez Caballero 1981: 36).

Ironically, this celebration of *majo* resistance was initiated in Britain at the very moment when the British were limbering up their own imperialist practices. The British "often criticized the place for the same reasons that they found it so exciting" (Jacobs 1990: 181). For example, British "orientalist" writing (that is, its imperialist rhetoric) persistently infantilized the same Andalucía that the British honored, as evidenced in Havelock Ellis's portrayal of the Spanish as "primitive" (1908: 36), W. Somerset Maugham's characterization of Andalusians as simple and natural (1920: 27), Collin's claim that the Spanish are child-like (1931: 26), and V.S. Pritchett's description of Spaniards as pre-modern (1955: 180).

In retrospect, it is apparent that multiple traditions of ironical

practice were solidly established in and around southern Spain
well before the popularization of flamenco. The precedent for
irony includes the slippery resistances by sixteenth-century Jews
and Muslims to inquisitorial oppression, the use of artifice in
seventeenth-century politics, the reinvention of cultural style
by eighteenth-century *majos*, and finally the celebration of
Andalusian resistance by the very people whose abiding interest
in Andalucía was imperial control. Mindful of these multiple
traditions of irony, we should revisit four landmarks of
commercial flamenco – the *café cantante, ópera flamenca*, the
Concurso del Cante Jondo, and "Rito y Geografía del Cante" – in
order to see, in them, ironies similar to those described above.

The period of the *café cantante* is one that seems to celebrate the
voices of quotidian life in Andalucía by putting flamenco song on
stage. In the *cafés*, patrons could sit down to hear the sounds that
they would otherwise hear only in the streets and courtyards of
the city. For example, *café* patrons could hear the voices of street
vendors whose songs (*pregones*) were commonly used to
notify residents that vegetables were en route. In short, the
cafés acknowledged the importance of Gitano traditions, of
Andalusian traditions, and, more generally, of the social life of
the poor of southern Spain.

However, appearances can be deceiving. The staged sounds of
flamenco song were detached from the street sounds of flamenco.
Singer's voices were refined. Raw lyrics were smoothed over,
and, as a result, the voices of the *cafés* ended up hiding, as much
as celebrating, the voices of the street. The *pregones* of the street
vendor only seemed to appear on stage. In reality, patrons heard
a retouched facsimile of the street vendor's song.

A struggle to appreciate the voice-of-the-street in the voice-of-
the-stage is evident in scholarly commentaries on the cáfe. Ortiz
Nuevo (1985) and Alvarez Caballero (1981) argued that, in the
early nineteenth century, every individual in a flamenco musical
event was an active participant. There were no passive and
detached audiences. Everyone, in pre-*café* flamenco events,
contributed something. In contrast, the flamenco in the *café
cantantes* was sung to paying audiences, with the effect of
reducing the vitality of the song, but increasing its popularity.
The *café*'s staging of street music was stimulated by "the great
increase of enthusiasm for *cante* that had then occurred. The
increase of fervent admirers, which had appeared in all social

classes, was a powerful stimulus that motivated some shrewd *café* proprietors to organize, in their halls, spectacles of the art of flamenco (song and dance), assured that habitual clientele and tourists would support the endeavor" (García Matos, quoted in Molina and Mairena 1979: 47).

Ironically, the invented songs of the *cafés* were reconstructed as authentic songs. Authenticity was achieved by preserving their linkage to Andalusian street life. But, also, in order to survive, the flamenco songs of *cafés* had to be promoted to the middle classes, whose expectation was that if flamenco songs were culturally valuable (i.e. "real"), they would not bear marks of authorship or signs of their development from street life (for more on "realist" assumptions, see Abercrombie, Lash, and Longhurst 1992: 131ff.; for more on the construction of "the real" through the management of social relations, see Grossberg 1992: 48). In effect, this ironic reconstruction of flamenco in the *cafés cantantes* required that flamenco song be both found and "*not* found in any context of daily life" (Poster 1990: 63; see also Corbett 1990). As a result, the musical presentations in *cafés* involved both the celebration and suppression of the linkage of music to the street. The celebration of the street was consistent with Romanticist impulses, but the suppression of the street was necessary if this music was to seem well-defined, was to appeal to diverse audiences, and was, thereby, to earn its stripes in popular perception as real music. Grande seemed to appreciate this paradoxical situation when he wrote that "the majority would not warrant performances of the pre-*cafés* variety as real" (Grande 1979: 355).

Following the era of the *café*, the music of the Andalusian streets was muted and overshadowed by the professional sound of flamenco. The *ópera flamenca* advanced this process, but added an ironic twist. The *ópera* in *ópera flamenca* is a reminder of influence exercised over Andalusian song styles by the Italian operatic tradition (García Gómez 1993: 32f.; Lavaur 1976: 38), itself a multidimensional tradition (Chanan 1994: 46f.; Taruskin 1993: 37). However, in its twentieth-century Spanish realization, an *ópera flamenca* was extravagantly staged flamenco spectacle that sometimes involved elaborate ensembles of performers accompanied by orchestral instruments and occasionally interspersed by performances of juggling or prestidigitation.

According to Escribano, the *ópera*-style was launched in 1893 in Madrid's Barbieri theater with performances of "show songs" (*cuplés*) by the German singer Augusta Berges, and, later, by the Madrileña Pilar Cohen (Escribano 1990: 59f.). Thereafter, Amalia Molina and Pastora Monje Imperio married this style with flamenco song and dance, paving the way for Antonio Chacón's promotion of theatrical spectacles. Once launched, theatrical flamenco became wildly popular. Staged events drew people in great numbers, and not merely as passive spectators. Everyone contributed to the commotion, creating a carnivalesque atmosphere and transforming the musical moment into a boisterous affair reminiscent of Parisian concerts in the mideighteenth century and American Shakespearean plays in the mid-nineteenth. The Spanish term *bululús* for such moments seems an appropriate descriptor even in English. Today, one can still appreciate the noisy tenor of these *óperas* by experiencing contemporary flamenco festivals, born just as the *ópera* was dying out in the 1950s. In festivals now, as in earlier *óperas*, audiences bubble with activity as people pass glasses of sherry up to performers, exchange food amongst themselves, chatter across rows, and linger at the *ambigú* (the refreshment bar) – some folks even attend to the music. Such activity is, and was, the target for purists' barbs on the assumption that audience commotion indicated their ignorance and their failure to appreciate the music and its roots (see program no. 31 in the "Rito" series). Ironically, however, such criticisms miss an important dimension of the *bululú*: the noisy tumultuousness of *óperas* signaled an acceptance of audience activity and an affirmation of their contemporary sociality.[5] By contrast, purists' criticisms signal a willingness to subordinate the present to the past, and to sacrifice today's interactions on the altar of yesterday's art. The critics may have been on target when they claimed that the music (*cuplés*, show songs) and the audience behavior of theatrical spectacles ignored the past voices of everyday life. But by seeking to tame the audiences, the critics were, in effect, discounting the importance of contemporary social relations. In Spain as in America of the same era, critics of boisterous artistic events became "active agents in teaching their audiences to adjust to new social imperatives in urging them to separate public from private feelings and in training them to keep a strict reign over their emotional and physical processes" (Levine 1988:

199). In the process of trying to enrich the social sense of self by recommending a serious attention to the music of the past, critics promoted a consummately modern and repressive "segment-ation of the self."

The fact that these theatrical flamenco performances were often schlock presents us with a second dimension of operatic irony. The shows were often put-ons and fakes that transformed "real" flamenco for the sake of box office appeal. Even the title *ópera* was a ploy of cynical promoters who registered this name in an effort to slip their extravaganza under the tax-exempt umbrella of "legitimate" opera (Yerga Lancharro 1991). This fakery of the *ópera* is a reminder that it, and all similarly counterfeit spectacles, were instruments of commercial exploit-ation. However, like other forms of kitsch that found a comfortable and profitable niche in the first half of the twentieth century (Calinescu 1987), an *ópera* was flamenco-with-a-wink, a performance event that reminded audiences of its own fraud-ulence, inviting audiences to look behind appearances and to question all displays, including displays of political authority.

In the midst of the early twentieth-century era of theatrical flamenco, the *Concurso* of 1922 made its momentary appearance. Spearheaded by intellectuals and non-professional artists, the *Concurso* was intended to be a pure cultural event mounted in opposition to the decadence of the *ópera*. The idea behind the *Concurso* was a public celebration of the authentic traditions that the *ópera flamenca* was obfuscating. Given its anti-*ópera* orientation, it is certainly ironic to see the *Concurso* of Granada now described as the real moment of lift-off for the *ópera flamenca* (Cobo 1994: 77). Its effects have, evidently, headed off in a direction diametrically opposed to its objectives.

The efforts of Manuel de Falla, Federico García Lorca, Andrés Segovia, and other organizers of the *Concurso* were motivated by questions about where Spain was heading in the years to come. The organizers sought answers to their questions about Spain's future by considering Spain's past. To know where Spain was heading, one had to know where Spain had been, and especially, where Spain had been musically. They rejected the tawdry and superficial flamenco of the *ópera*, and focused their attention instead on *cante jondo* ("deep song"), the Andalusian song that preceded the modernization of flamenco. *Cante Jondo*, they argued, is not only the root of Andalusian flamenco, but it is also the root of Spanish identity, a rich and distinctive identity shaped by the experience of living life in the face of death. But despite the best intentions of the organizers, the *Concurso* became an ironic, janus-faced event. While the *Concurso* may have cut through oppressive commercialism,[6] it was also an occasion for advancing the oppressiveness of folk culture.

It has been argued that folk cultures were invented in the nineteenth century (Anderson 1983; Burke 1992; Hobsbawm, and Ranger 1983). As such, folk culture served, initially and especially in Germany, as a resistance to the oppressiveness of the French regime. However, folk cultures themselves soon became oppressive in the sense that people were pressured into conforming to a folk culture's codification of authentic practices (Chambers 1994: 38, 82). Ironically, this promotion of "the folk" served the interests of elites more so than the interests of the common folk: "The invention of the folk concept serves to protect the ruling class from the threat and suffering of proletariats by first exoticizing them and then absorbing their cultures into their own" (Keil, paraphrased in Middleton 1989: 134).

The *Concurso*'s promotion of Andalusian and Gitano folk culture paved the way for the cultural oppressions of the Franco regime. Its expression of cultural authenticity which, in 1922, was intended as an act of resistance, was used as a club under Franco after 1939, at which point flamenco became "a political tool" (Hooper 1986: 163) used against its very creators, the people of Andalucía (Isidoro Moreno, in Mitchell 1990: 87). "Franco's Spain, isolated and blocked internationally, needed a prideful national symbol of its worth to show the world and to reduce, finally, its internal diversity to a firm, clear and manageable unity" (Francisco Almazán quoted in Alvarez Caballero 1992: 110).

Folk culture, in the twentieth century, has cut two ways. On the one hand, it has provided a platform for resistance by marginalized people. On the other hand, it has been used to press marginalized people into compliance with dictatorial authority. Thus, despite the benefits gained through the *Concurso*'s revitalization of folk culture as a weapon of the weak, the *Concurso* nurtured a concept that in Franco's hands became a weapon of oppression.

A fourth landmark in all four histories of flamenco music is the televised film series "Rito y Geografía del Cante." One of the great ironies of this film series lies in the fact that the "Rito" films both support and undermine Gitano ethnicity. The "Rito" films play a role in supporting Gitano ethnicity, certainly by referring to the historical role of Gitanos in the formation of flamenco, but also, by portraying flamenco song as a mainstay activity of Gitano families. These films portray flamenco as a significant familial activity in nineteenth- and twentieth-century Gitano families – such a portrayal is clear in programs that feature prominent flamenco families (nos 19–21, and especially in the program on Christmas activities, no. 10).

It is important to note that the "Rito" portrayal of flamenco as a familial activity is coupled with an almost complete silence about the role of decidedly non-familial activities of the *juerga* in the shaping and developing of the flamenco style (see Howson 1959; Pohren 1980). The impact of the disassociation of flamenco from the *juerga*, in the "Rito" films, and of the reassociation of flamenco with family ought not be underestimated. Similar manipulations have elsewhere provided pivots for the recon- structions and reinventions of ethnicities. For example, Ferraro (1989) argues that the film *The Godfather* concocted a bond between commercial and familial activities of Italian-Americans, thus providing a basis for a reconstruction of Italian-American identity. In exactly the same way, the "Rito" characterization of flamenco as a Gitano familial activity forges a new foundation for Gitano ethnicity.

Ironically, and at the same time that the "Rito" programs support the reconstruction of Gitano ethnicity, these programs also undermine that ethnicity. They do so by handling flamenco song and Gitano ethnicity as if they were objects in a musical museum. Just as American Blues has been "museumized" in retrospective codifications and recordings (Middleton 1989: 143), so flamenco song has been "museumized" by the "Rito" films (see Preziosi 1988: 79 for a discussion of the link between "museum" and "film"). Like any modern natural history museum (Ziolkowski 1990: 355), these films present broad- ranging and balanced displays, that draw evenly from different historical periods and geographical regions. The balance of these exhibits is a sign that the documentarians did not let themselves be personally biased by any single period or community. This balance and panoramic breadth in the "Rito" documentaries suggests that the musical curators behind these programs were eager to show sympathy for all and partiality toward none. They divested themselves of involvement with the people of any particular time and place, and became guardians of the whole. For example, in the "Rito" programs, *fandangueros, malagueñeros* and *sevillaneros* are on an equal footing. Programs on Manolo Caracol and Pepe Marchena, whose stocks had risen during the *época teatral*, stand right alongside programs devoted to their critics, e.g. Antonio Mairena. This balance contrasts with the acerbity of many of the scholarly works that deal with these artists (see Alvarez Caballero 1981; Gómez Pérez 1978; González Climent 1975). Evidently, the curators of the "Rito" programs were willing to buck strong currents of Andalusian factionalism in order to maintain their balance.

Such balance is not, however, and has never been characteristic of flamenco circles, nor of social life in southern Spain (Alvarez Caballero 1993; Mitchell 1990). More often than not, flamenco adepts were versed in three or four (out fifty or so) flamenco forms, and clung to those with a passion, spurning all others as relatively worthless. But the "Rito" documentarians have hidden any such provincial allegiances, and have instead emphasized the value of all flamenco varieties. True, the tensions of provincial life in southern Spain peek through "Rito" discussions of the musical styles of Gitanos versus non-Gitanos, of elderly artists versus young artists, of *gaditanos, sevillanos,* etc. However, these moments that acknowledge diversity and difference are nullified by the synoptic and encyclopedic form of the "Rito" series, a form that encourages viewers to conclude that flamenco is ultimately one single and integral phenomenon. Moreover, the breadth and balance of the films serves to redirect the attentions of viewers back onto themselves, promoting as much self-appreciation and music-appreciation. Viewers are implicitly encouraged to see themselves controlling the music, choosing it, and using it at will (Corbett 1990: 99), and, as a result, they inadvertently become the masters of all the music they survey (Kirshenblatt-Gimblett 1991: 413; see also Preziosi 1988: 68). Ultimately, the films enhance the viewers' self-worth at the cost of reducing the value of the very artistry that the programs had wished to celebrate. In the end, the Gitano ethnicity advanced by the content of the series is undercut by its viewer-enhancing form. Being antiquities collected in a filmic museum, *cante Gitano* in these documentaries loses whatever power it had to revitalize Gitano ethnicity.

"El Chocolate"

The four major flamenco landmarks discussed here are ironic moments in the histories of flamenco. Each is a moment of countervailing practices, a moment in which flamencos create what they destroy and accommodate what they resist (see Marcus 1992: 313). I am not contending that flamenco music or its histories are flawed or rendered less valuable because of their ironic complexity. On the contrary, flamenco is probably no more complex, in this respect, than any other social style or cultural development. Irony is everywhere. However, despite the ubiquity of irony, historians and ethnographers, have persistently hidden complexity behind narratives that emphasize simple structures and consistent processes.

This flamenco account moves against this grain by emphasizing the complexity of flamenco music rather than its simplicity, and by exposing the ironies of flamenco history rather by hiding them. It is particularly important to note that public spectacles of commercialized flamenco are no less ironic in their political significance than are private flamenco happenings. During the period of the *café cantante*, musicians on stage cultivated an appearance of authenticity by emphasizing their linkages to Andalusian street life, but they cultivated a semblance of reality by systematically detaching themselves from that same street life. The real and authentic flamenco of the *café* period is achieved, ironically, by simultaneously embracing and rejecting Andalusian street life. During the period of the *ópera flamenca*, flamenco was staged with elaborate contrivances that exaggerated the separation of staged music from everyday life. But the elaborate contrivances of the *ópera* also served to highlight its own fictitiousness, its own manufactured nature. Like other forms of kitsch, the *ópera* exposed what it pretended to hide. The *Concurso* sought to distance itself from the oppressive contrivances of both the *cafés* and the *ópera*, but in doing so, the *Concurso* unwittingly armed folk culture for later service as a device for homogenizing Spain (for more on the *Concurso* and nationalistic movements of the day see García Gómez 1993: 122). What was intended as a tool of resistance became a tool of oppression. Finally, the "Rito" film series helped to advance the cause of Gitano ethnicity by realigning flamenco song with

Gitano family. Yet, at the same time, the synoptic form used in the "Rito" series served to weaken the ability of flamenco song to serve as a feature of Gitano ethnicity.

Ethnographers of all sorts, including historians, poets, essayists, and cinematographers, have generally misread the history of flamenco music. They have interpreted that history as if it were singularly Andalusian, or wholly Gitano, or purely a matter of resistance.[7] However, this present account of ironies in the history of flamenco should indicate that flamenco events are almost always double-voiced, heteroglossic events (Bakhtin 1981) that are not susceptible to singular interpretation or totalizing description.

The flamenco artists who perform the music sometimes display a better understanding of flamenco heteroglossia than do the scholars whose job it is to make sense of the music. We can see an example of such understanding in an autobiographical anecdote told by the great singer Antonio Nuñez "El Chocolate"

> An occasion when I was 12 years old, and I grew up in the Alameda (a section of Sevilla). There were a lot of drunks in the Alameda, and I dedicated myself to the drunks, that is why I go. . . there are two epochs I lived in. . . and I found a man that bragged that he was a flamencólogo, and I was very grateful to him because he gave me two or three hundred pesetas, and I could eat for a month for that – this is twenty five years ago. Well, whenever I sang for this man I was always tired, because I would sleep in a chair in Alameda in my clothes. One day I found him in a bar when I was well rested, and my voice was clear and fresh. I was so happy that he was going to give me another three hundred pesetas, and I could eat for two months. I said to myself, now I can finally repay him for all the money he gave me because I am in good (*limpia*) voice. And here's what happened. He said, "Sing an old song for me," and I started singing. But in the moment I started singing he got real serious and said "Your voice is horrible today." And I didn't know what to say, and I said, "Well, I don't know." This man was accustomed to hearing me sing with a rough voice (*voz ronca*) rather than a clear voice (*clara*). It gave me a great pain when he said that my voice was horrible, but I had to go with the *favoritismo*, and I said to him, "It's just that today I haven't rested, I haven't slept, I'm just bad."

This story – told, ironically enough, to a flamencologist – presents the case of "El Chocolate's" self-denial. Knowing full well that he was in good voice, this great singer confessed to the flamencologist that he was singing badly. He did this, he says, because he had to "go with the *favoritismo*."

By going with the *favoritismo*, "El Chocolate" may have helped to confirm the scholar's singular definition of flamenco as a song sung by the weary. But, as his story makes clear, his confirmation is fraudulent. Flamenco is not a song sung by the weary, but a song sung by weary singers pretending to be strong, and by strong singers pretending to be weary, and, sometimes, by singers who are neither, pretending to be both. Flamenco is an ironic practice.

Notes

1. To interpret is to respond (see Gardiner 1992: 87; Holquist 1990: 48). In anthropology, however, the activity of responding has generally been subordinated in importance to that of sense-making. Regularly, anthropologists have produced neat ethnographies that adduce "simple structures" to account for complex experiences (Comaroff and Comaroff 1992: 18–31). Such ethnographies often fare well as sense-making discourses, but they induce a contentment and complacency that stands in the way of constructive responses to those experiences. In order to counterbalance this tendency, ethnographers would do well to offer complicating representations as well as traditionally simplifying analyses. Such complications will encourage readers to respond creatively to the experiences that confront them (see Chambers 1994: 10f.).

2. The value of these distinctive contributions is continually debated along partisan lines. For example, García Chicón has nominated Málaga as the site of the late-nineteenth-century perfection of flamenco song: "The *malagueña*, already formed and in the splendor of its beauty, cannot compete in any way in deep rootedness and antiquity with primitive deep songs;

nevertheless given the order of the classification that we offer, we suppose that it can be considered as the most modern and evolved form of deep song" (García Chicón 1987: 44).
3. Flamenco is one of a number of ironic musical styles that emerged out of late nineteenth-century romanticism. As such, its sentimentality of expression became one of its characteristic selling points (Featherstone 1991: 65ff.; Steingress 1993: 361).
4. Scholars from Salillas (1898) to Steingress (1993) and Mitchell (1994) have contended that Gitanos do not form a clearly defined ethnic group. Without rejecting these arguments, one might also contend that Gitano ethnicity is a construct that "cultivates its own marginality...not (as) a buried master narrative, but rather as a conscious cultural politics that survives by 'floating and hovering,' never quite existing and never quite vanishing, the ultimate camouflage for the difficult but necessary work of building a historical block" (Lipsitz 1990: 159).
5. Equally rich in crosscutting politics are the reflections of Manolo Caracol on the *ópera* (see nos 53 and 54 in "Rito" series). An advocate of the style of the *ópera*, Caracol contended that it broadened the appeal of flamenco artistry by couching flamenco song in innovative dramatizations that were meant to attract female audiences on the assumption that women lacked the aesthetic mettle necessary for appreciating the traditionally plain rendering of *coplas*. His observations about the broader appeal of *óperas* may be accurate, but his observations about the aesthetic sensibilities of women may not.
6. The *Concurso*'s efforts to side-step commercialism were inconsistently implemented and ultimately counterproductive. First, the organizers of the *Concurso*, the *Centro Artístico y Literario*, restricted participation in the *Concurso* to professionals under twenty-one years of age, their intent being to open the way for commercially untainted adepts of older and purer forms of *cante jondo*. However, they found it necessary to fall back on professional artists to shore up the scanty talent that showed up, and they ended up presenting first prize in the *Concurso* to Diego Bermúdez "El Tenazas" who had been a professional singer as a young man (Ríos Ruiz 1993: 29).

7. Hayden White has argued that historians create simple and internally consistent narratives because of "a desire to have real events display the coherence, integrity, fullness, and closure of an image of life that is and can only be imaginary" (White 1987: 24).

Chapter 3

The Pleasures of Music

The production of flamenco music gets the press, but its consumption is largely responsible for its character. Accordingly, in order to balance our responses to flamenco experiences, we should attend as much to the spectator's pleasure in witnessing flamenco as to the performer's passion in producing it. That is precisely what this present chapter aims to accomplish by considering questions such as: What pleasure does one derive from hearing a brawny man wail in public? Why does one's spine tingle in direct proportion to the speed of a guitarist's fingers? What drives one to search the shops for the latest flamenco disk?

To begin, two proposals about the pleasures of witnessing flamenco dominate the current literature. A traditional view has it that the anguished song style of, say, Manuel Agujeta acts like Proust's madeleine to jar the mind into resurrecting memories that, upon release, liberate the listener. On this account, *cante* is an instant that "literally takes us out of ourselves, separates us from our history, gives us a push towards reintegrating ourselves with our lost innocence, a push that raises us up to recover our own wonder....This self-reflection enables us to know the pure and absolute air of liberation" (Grande 1992a: 83). So goes the traditional flamencological argument.

The second view, a scientific view, assumes that the listeners who are attracted to Agujetas are less repressed than benighted. They are subject to a false consciousness, and are attracted to the anguished song of flamenco only because of its meretricious appeals to tradition and community. Mitchell (1994) and Steingress (1993), for example, both contend that the late nineteenth-century fascination with flamenco was driven by the interests of the rising middle classes in Andalusian cities. Their interests in flamenco music helped to legitimize their individualistic economic and political practices. Wealthy

Andalusian *señoritos* celebrated this traditionalist song style that provided them with a distinctive identity while simultaneously expressing their sympathy for the downtrodden. The *señoritos* emerged from such flamenco performances, with a clear sense of their identity relative to the masses of impoverished Spaniards, and with a sense of justification – having undergone a ritual of absolution via *cante*. The poor, for their part, embraced the "romantic" song style of flamenco because it expressed their anguish, and because it referred them backward in time, rendering their miserable pasts rosier in hindsight, and holding out a hope, however faint, that the sincerity of their song would qualify them as bonafide cultural heroes in the future.

A major problem with the former view, traditional flamencology, is that it is provincial and freighted with ideology (see Vélez 1976: 27). Mitchell (1994: 17) argues that it is developed with an insufficiency of critical reflection by scholars who care too much about a narrow range of Andalusian and Gitano interests. However, the latter view, scientific flamencology, has its own distinctive drawbacks, some of which will be familiar to those who have traveled the path of critical social theory (see Honneth 1991). The scientific view wants to treat the flamenco-lover's romantic consciousness as an historical dead end or an epiphenomenal effect. *Cante*'s passion, it assumes, does nothing more than mask reality. Such an assumption, however steeped in the writings of Marx, is naive insofar as it portrays consciousness – false or true – as a mere by-product of social life. An alternative to this scientific view – as well as to the traditional argument – begins with a recognition that utterances and expressions – including songs and dances – can be productive forces in human history (Fiske 1993: 3-34; Gardiner 1992: 59-80). As Simon Reynolds says, music "can be sufficient intoxication to induce a different state of being other than the one in which you exist" (1990: 46). Artists' bodies do more than reflect social relations, they "mold social space" (Franko 1995: xiii). An alternative to both traditional and scientific flamencology treats social life, not so much like a billiard table on which the economic/political cue ball shakes up and restructures experience, but like a jungle, where new life forms emerge to create new realities, and where the rules of the game are constantly being revised (see Terdiman 1993: 23f.).

Both the traditional and the scientific accounts of flamenco are static and one-dimensional (see Lipsitz 1990: 99ff.). In contrast, the alternative view presented here will acknowledge the evolution of multiple flamenco pleasures. It will contend, for example, that "romantic" flamenco was a productive force in Andalusian history, and therefore partly responsible for the way everyone in the twentieth century enjoys flamenco song. Pleasures of the past are not lost to the present, but are transformed into radically different aesthetics by the manifold forces that operate through time (as suggested by Vélez 1976: 25).

The forces that have given, and continue to give, shape to flamenco pleasures are manifold. However accurate may be the historical analyses of García Gómez (1993) and Steingress (1993), their work falters insofar as it encourages readers to think that flamenco aesthetics is simply a function of the intellectualizations in which the music is couched, as if any experience of pleasure is built upon some prior intellection of pleasure. This analysis will show that the source of flamenco delights is as often technological as intellectual and material as well as mental.

The Romance of Flamenco

This account of the attractiveness of flamenco is a generational account in the sense that each generation of flamenco enthusiasts, starting in the early nineteenth century, builds new pleasures on top of old, and adds fresh memories to existing recollections (see Featherstone 1991: 32). As we chart this generational construction with its sedimentation of memories upon memories, we will have occasion to discuss the emergence of an urban middle class in early nineteenth-century Andalucía, the influence of German and French Romanticisms on members of that middle class in the nineteenth century, and, in the twentieth, the development of new technologies, specifically, audio, cinematic, and video recording for witnessing flamenco.

The year 1789 marks a social memory disruption of seismic proportions (Terdiman 1993: 5). The official institutions of memory in the Old Regime – the court and the church – were neutralized. In consequence of that neutralization, people were no longer sure what past they should be attending to. Of this period the Mexican poet and critic Octavio Paz says that modernity is "cut off from the past and continually hurtling forward at such a dizzy pace that it cannot take root, that it merely survives from one day to the next: it is unable to return to its beginnings and thus recover its powers of renewal" (quoted in Berman 1982: 35).

In Andalucía, the reaction to the turmoil induced by 1789 was strongly colored by the immediately forthcoming events: the War of Independence (1808–14), moments of hope for liberal reform in 1812, and the reassertions of dictatorial conservatism in 1814, 1823, and 1833. The population, swelled by immigration, flooded into southern cities. The ranks of the liberal urban middle classes grew. Nationalistic movements emerged and gained strength,[1] and Andalusians found themselves dancing the old dances and singing the old songs, thereby advancing a defiant message of group identification. Like people of other regions of Europe, they used music to help construct a culture for themselves (García Gómez 1993: 27–48; Martin Moreno 1985: 297; see also Burke 1992: 295; Scott 1990).

The songs and dances, it should be emphasized, were the old songs and dances. In particular, the *romances*, the epic ballads that date back to the time of struggle between Christians and Muslims, were revitalized after centuries of being ignored (Bryant 1973; Escribano 1990: 41; Steingress 1993: 280), and were augmented with lyrical tributes to those who fought in the War of Independence (Alvarez Caballero 1981: 36). Moreover, the preferred style of musical performance was the defiantly traditionalistic style of *majos*, a style that itself had arisen as part of the popular opposition to the French-leaning aristocracy of the eighteenth century (Mitchell 1990: 176). Thus, in content as well as style, songs and dances of the late eighteenth century in Andalucía were sticking places for memories that had come unglued in 1789.

Ironically, it was the quintessentially old songs and dances that were called upon to shore up the foundations of the consummately modern society of Andalucía (Steingress 1993: 225). The old was reinvented to serve new functions. The music, in particular, can be said to have been reinvented, "not because the songs were faked – although this happened from time to time – but because they were attributed to particular people, despite the fact that many ballads did not respect political or even linguistic frontiers" (Burke 1992: 297).

At the same time that the old songs and dances were reconstructed to serve new social identificational functions, they were also being deconstructed. The "institution" of memory, as Terdiman says (1993: 23), always involves some amount of "destitution" of memory. New moments of remembering come paired with new moments of repression. In the particular case of Andalucía, new musical styles presented urban middle class Andalusians with the challenge of embracing characteristics that might signify independence from the Old Regime while suppressing features that might smack of lawlessness and libertinage. In response to this challenge, Andalusians cultivated the political defiance of the bohemian style, while repressing its "uncontrolledness" (García Gómez 1993: 49; Zavala and Diez Borque 1974: 24; see also Stratton 1989). One indication of their repression of uncontrolledness is the cultivation of *escuelas boleras* and *academias de bailes* in the early years of nineteenth century (Steingress 1993: 349ff.). These gentile institutions were dedicated to the restoration, preservation, teaching, and renovation of "decent" dances. As happened elsewhere in Europe – and especially in Germany (García Gómez 1993: 77) – "the middle class succeeded in replacing the working-class expressive dancing with a new set of rationally based dances in which the importance lay in correct performance rather than in the opportunity which dancing provided for a loss of reflexivity" (Stratton 1989: 41).[2] The flamenco dances of Andalucía emerged from the theaters[3] that sprang out of the *academias* and *salones* in which defiant but edifying folkloric songs and dances were enjoyed. In this way, the rise of flamenco music traced a circular path of development, going "from the popular to the intellectual and to the professional, and, from there, it gradually came to be imitated in popular circles" (García Gómez 1993: 45; see Chanan 1994: 139f.).

In the last half of the nineteenth century, the decline of the public sphere in Europe ushered in a new era of flamenco pleasurability (see Steingress 1993: 280). The decline of the public sphere meant – from Habermas's perspective – that:

> Civil society was changed by the establishment of a world of work as a sphere of its own right between the public and the private realms. Large organizations, both public and private, played the central role in separating work from the purely private sphere of the

household. The private sphere in turn was reduced to the family. An "externalization of what is declared to be the inner life" occurred (Calhoun 1992: 22).

This externalization of the inner life promoted a general sentimentality toward persons (Calhoun 1992: 24; see Wouters 1986). Inner life, with all of its irrational and uncontrolled desires, now became less a source of repulsion and titillation than an object of focused gaze, a new site for the workings of memory, a new site for recovering what had earlier been forgotten, and the new place for pleasure (Huyssen 1986: 50; Kittler 1990: 124; Pratt 1992: 76), at once consummately secular, yet still strangely religious, as Franko suggests in his characterization of sentimentality in the dance of Isadora Duncan:

> The expressive idea informing Duncan's concept of the activity of *dancing* was iconostatic (religious allegory) inasmuch as her body was a means to an elsewhere rather than an autonomously independent material. "Do you not feel an inner self awakening deep within you – that it is by its strength that your head is lifted, that your arms are raised." Expressivity, then, is inseparable from an idealist perspective in which the body acts as a "medium" giving the spectator access to an extracorporeal self of which the body's movement furnishes traces (Franko 1995: 1).

The enjoyment of flamenco as an expression of an awakened inner self was strongly influenced by French, rather than by German, Romanticism. "This other romanticism, less educational, spiritual and essential than the German, impregnated the artistic manifestations of sensuality, exciting mystery, eroticism and ardent passion, of blood and of sand" (García Gómez 1993: 79). Romanticized flamenco pushed listeners to confront inner demons and repressed desires, carnivalesque reversals, symbolic disorderliness (for a discussion of the controlled decontrol of emotion see Featherstone 1991: 81). During this time, people took pleasure in flamenco because it facilitated their release from external disciplines and their development along paths illuminated by inner lights. This romantic flamenco became an instrument for remembering one's detached identity, for "rescuing the self from the claw of Time and History, and for revisiting a transcendental intimacy, a paradise of innocence" (Grande 1992a: 85).

At the same time that late nineteenth-century flamenco romantics were swooning over images of Carmen, *antiflamenquistas* were flooding the newspapers and *revistas* with unrelenting criticisms of the inauthenticities and moral debasements of flamenco performances. Ironically, this broadside of criticism *against* popularized flamenco was nurtured by the same romantic principle that prompted that popularization in the first place, namely by the principle that culture is an externalization of an interior life (Ríos Ruiz 1993: 38). The *antiflamenquistas*, however, contended that interior life must be sifted and winnowed so that only the most highly perfected of internal experiences is given public expression. For Eugenio Noel (1916), appropriate flamenco should consist of only those private experiences that time has elevated to the level of national art (García Gómez 1993: 109). In this view, a worthy public expression of interior life should be one that finds a common denominator in the refined and unifying sentiments that *should* arise within individuals, rather than encouraging raw and diversifying feelings that *do* arise. For these *antiflamenquistas*, as for the American critics of the popular arts at the turn of the century, audiences should "separate public behavior from private feeling. . .and keep a strict rein over their emotion and physical processes" (Levine 1988: 199). The watershed of opinion that separated the flamencophobes from the flamencophiles of this period was, not so much a disagreement over the importance of expressing interior life, as a disagreement over when, where and how interior life might be fit and apt for public presentation. The flamencophobes railed against the swells of untutored popular experience that the flamencophiles encouraged, and in this way these two romantically driven approaches to flamenco showed themselves to be at once elitist and conservative but also populist and progressive (see Ríos Ruiz 1993: 44f.).

Manuel Machado and García Lorca celebrated the spontaneous musical irrationality of their day with as much vigor as the traditionalists and *antiflamenquistas* who criticized it (García Gómez 1993: 109, 126). However, their celebration of culture included mystifications and inventions. García Lorca, for one, was only distantly familiar with the actual performance styles of the *cante jondo* he touted, and was poorly apprised of the literature surrounding those styles. He misspelled the name of

Manuel Torre – rendering it "Torres," an error that then gets repeated (see Bergamin 1957: 1) – whom he heralded as the avatar of the spirit he preached, and he was unaware of the work of Antonio Machado y Alvarez whose writings of the 1880s virtually launched the genre of flamencology (see Grande 1992b: 25). Moreover, he portrayed *cante jondo* as a popular development whose roots extend backwards to "time immemorial" while simultaneously deprecating its professionalization. Grande summarized Lorca's position, rightly I think, by arguing that the qualities in *cante jondo* that Lorca admired were the very qualities that had come about through a process of professionalization during the period of the *café cantante* (Grande 1992b: 28). In the same vein, García Gómez finds the work of Lorca, along with other pro-Gitano scholars of this period, enmeshed in a paradox: "They refused to acknowledge the contemporary professionalization (of *cante jondo*) at the same time that they were making its reality clear" (García Gómez 1993: 154; see also Vélez 1976: 47 for a defense of flamenco's commercial popularity). Scholars such as Lorca appreciated the candor and spontaneity of flamenco performance partly because that spontaneity, though a product of professionalization, seemed antithetical to the artifices of the professional stage. The appeal of polished-but-spontaneous performances is of a piece with the contemporary passion for commodities manufactured to seem unmanufactured, like cloth mechanically produced with thread-pulls that simulate the hand-made (Orvell 1989), like CD disks dubbed with scratches to suggest the authenticity of phonographic recording (Corbett 1990), like staged blues performances that play up the moldy fig image of the old, unlettered, but heroic singer. Like so much else in consumer culture, flamenco promised "at least the illusion of connection with the past" (Lipsitz 1990: 11). Flamenco presented itself as "the exotic elsewhere, the untouched different, the world of the 'natural' and the 'native'. . .an authenticity to be held against the corruption of modernity" (Chambers 1994: 12).

Music at the turn of the century had become a detached commodity that appealed to the detached identities of listeners. The appeal of music lay in its power to express inner realities and reveal personal authenticities. Turn-of-the-century romantics in Spain embraced with specific vigor the backward glancing music of flamenco and used its historical orientation to sound a new theme of self-construction in place of the earlier theme of group-construction. This shift of themes coincided with a change from theatrical and folkloristic flamenco to the *cafés* and *juergas*, a change that is part of the massive reshaping of social memory that was occurring at the time.[4] In consequence of these cultural shifts, the Andalusian working classes, the Spanish middle classes, and the European touring classes found the sentimental song of flamenco singers newly attractive (García Gómez 1993: 313ff.).

Technology and Pleasure

The preceding paragraphs have underscored the speed and depth of changes in musical pleasure as they evolved under the influence of romanticist thought from the folkloric theater in the early nineteenth century to the *juerga* and the *café cantante* in the late nineteenth century. Below, it will be argued that other developments, inaugurated by the appearance of recording technology, had a similarly rapid and dramatic impact in the twentieth century on how music was enjoyed (see Chanan 1994: 251).[5]

Flamenco records appeared at the turn of the century, earlier than one might have expected. A large number of flamenco artists recorded cylinders at the end of the nineteenth century and in the first five years of the twentieth. The first flamenco disks were recorded between 1901 and 1902 featuring El Canario Chico, El Mochuelo, La Rubia Niño de Cabra, Niño de la Hera, and Sabastian Scotta (Blas Vega and Ríos Ruiz 1990: 252f.). From 1903 to 1912, the International Zonophone Company, with home offices in America, dominated the flamenco recording scene. Thereafter, the French company Du Gramophone La Voz de su Amo, dominated flamenco recording. The fact that these flamenco recordings were produced so soon after the invention of recording devices – the first jazz record did not appear until 1917 – and the fact that the recording companies were American and French, should help to dispel the popular literary image of flamenco music as a backwater song comparable to early blues, a view popularized by writers such as Irving Brown (1929), John Dos Passos (1926), Waldo Frank (1926), Somerset Maugham (1920). It is rather the case that flamenco was, even at the turn of the century, a shrewdly marketed urban song style that was promoted successfully to both tourists and the indigenous middle classes.

Blas Vega seems convinced that the most profound consequence of the very early recording of flamenco is anthological. Extant records, he contends, give us access to more than a hundred years of song, 80 percent of the total range of historical styles and variations of flamenco song. The recording industry, he says, "introduced us through records to the forms and manners closest to the origins of flamenco" (Blas Vega and Ríos Ruiz 1990: 253). However, the impact of records has been far greater than merely tapping origins or popularizing artists who were then beginning to perform in large theaters, *plazas de toros,* and *concursos*. The larger impact is that flamenco records established a new site for memory and pleasure.

First, records helped to transform flamenco music from a commodified folk music to a commodified art music (see Arrebola 1991: 57). As a folk music, flamenco had been improvized and passed along by word of mouth rather than by musical notation. However, in the phonographic era the flamenco tradition suddenly acquired exemplars, canons, and prescriptions for how the art of flamenco should be performed. Once recorded, the songs were scrutinized and analyzed. Their aesthetic rankings were assigned, the assignments were reconsidered, and the whole business of flamenco appreciation began moving out of the bars and theaters and into the offices and studies of flamencologists. In this way, a flamenco canon was formed and erected as the single most important counterforce to the stinging barbs of the *antiflamenquista* journalists. Records conferred legitimacy on flamenco, as they did on other styles of popular music (Eisenberg 1987: 125, 150).

Records also affected the acquisition of musical skills. As they became more prevalent and more affordable, apprentices began acquiring their art from disks as well as from flamenco masters, studying the acoustic notations on disks in lieu of visual notations on paper. Still, however, the tradition of studying flamenco artistry in face-to-face encounters between masters and apprentices persisted into the present.[6]

Besides altering the process of learning and appreciating the music, recording technology also changed the music itself. Specifically, the microphone and audio amplifier facilitated the coordination of guitar and voice in flamenco performance. Prior to the mike, the guitarist and the *cantaor* formed a mismatched pair. The guitar was a quiet introspective instrument, generally incapable of projecting anything but vague percussive sounds over long distances.[7] The *cantaor*'s voice, however, was formed in early-nineteenth-century Andalucía under the influence of Italian operatic styles (Lavaur 1976: 35ff.; Martin Moreno 1985: 284; Steingress 1993: 224), and was a powerful projective instrument. Like a horn, the flamenco voice carried force and volume to the distant corners of any hall. In 1925, with the development of the microphone and the audio amplifier, the guitar came into its own. Amplification released it from its acoustic constraints, and the guiding hand of musical geniuses such as Ramón Montoya led it to new heights, so that today flamenco guitarists approach – and sometimes even challenge (see Chapter 1) – the prestige of *cantaores* in flamenco performances.

Besides expanding the potential of the guitar in flamenco performance, the microphone also expanded the possibilities for the voice. Suddenly, a *cantaor* had at his disposal not only the capability of projecting a powerful voice even further, but also the capability of deploying gentler and subtler voices. Antonio Chacón's falsetto voice and the murmured dreamy vocals of Pepe Marchena were suddenly available to large crowds. Henceforth, the singers became solipsists. Though they were seated on a stage before an audience of thousands, they could moan and whisper as if they were entirely alone. . .if they had a microphone.[8]

Not only did the increased use of microphones, phonographic recording equipment, and, in the 1930s, radio transmission, favor a new and softer song style, these technical developments also undercut the popularity of other, previously popular, flamenco sounds. For one thing, the limitations of fidelity, especially in radio transmission, discouraged the high-volume shrieks that had characterized some traditional artistry. For another, the space limitations on phonograph records imposed new constraints on the length of songs. Such selective discouragements, along with the equally selective promotions of certain sounds by the new technologies, resulted in a transformation of artistry. They inaugurated a new wave of flamenco. In the 1930s, this wave was capped by the *fandango* form that enjoyed dizzying heights of popularity for a number of decades (Molina 1995: 7).

On another front that might be described as more symbolic than technical, the recording industry altered flamenco music by creating a closer link between musician and machine. Specifically, music heard on disk invited the listener to blur the boundary between the artist that plays and the machine that plays. The machine that plays, plays perfectly and consistently, over any number of repetitions. An artist in the world of records was expected to display similar abilities.[9] This expectation encouraged the development of a musical "machine culture" (Seltzer 1992: 79). The speed and consistency that characterizes machinery became desiderata of artists. The effects of this shift were especially apparent in the development of the art of the flamenco guitar. Ramon Montoya, Niño Ricardo, and Paco de Lucía honed superhuman skills and thrilled audiences with their machine-like abilities. Flamenco guitar, like American bluegrass of the same period, "does not mime the movement of the body it mimes the movements of the machine that reproduces it" (Stewart 1993: 12). Ironically, however, this newly emergent fascination with speed and consistency in flamenco guitar was interpreted in terms of generationally prior principles. Félix Grande, for example, comments on Paco de Lucía, portraying the machine-like power of his hands as a romantically liberating force:

> Paco de Lucía has delved into flamenco music and come up dripping wreckage and memory; but he emerges also distributing disobedience, power and liberty; burning like a firebrand. The hands of Paco de Lucía respect the profound laws of Andalusian music, but they disobey the lawmakers. In the world of guitar, the hands of Paco de Lucía are a new law. . .Paco with the musical labor of his hands, transforms us from mortals into resurrected spirits (Grande 1986).

Setting aside such anachronistic aesthetics, we are now in a position to see that flamenco music in the last half of the twentieth century has moved into hyperreality as a result of technological innovations. Disks and tapes gradually coopted the semiotic place of flamenco performances. Recordings became "signifieds" and performances became "signifiers." Listeners began attending performances as copies of recordings, reversing the original intention of records to represent performances (Attali

1985: 84). On one occasion, the guitarist "El Ingles" confessed to me that he would rather listen to Rafael Riqueni on disk because a well-engineered disk makes it possible to hear subtleties that are lost in a live presentation. He argued that the recorded disk sounds, to use Evan Eisenberg's words, "bigger than life" (see Eisenberg 1987: 153). In this newly rearranged world of musical signs, the live performance has become an occasion for imitating and verifying the recording. Its new function is to bear witness to the singular and authentic source of the recording (see Stratton 1989: 45). One attends a concert, not so much to hear the music – which can be more comfortably and more clearly heard on disk – but to bask in the presence of the performers.[10]

In the wake of this audio revolution, the interests of listeners are refocused onto disks. The disks themselves – the physical objects – become pleasurable (see Corbett 1990 on the art of the disk jacket). The disks are new sites for memory, new places for pleasure. Some appreciation of the dimensions of this new pleasurability can be gained by exploring the popular passion for collecting recordings (see Eisenberg 1987: 1ff.). Flamenco anthologies appeared, beginning in 1954 with the *Antología del Cante Flamenco*, a retrospective collection under the direction of Perico El del Lunar (Hispavox). Since that date, an uncountable number of similar anthologies have appeared. On a related front, the anthological "Rito y Geografía del Cante" provoked a thirst for filmic and video anthologies in the early 1970s. This new pleasure of collecting and this new passion for anthologizing led aficionados to recalculate their statuses in terms of their personal collections of recordings – pirated cassettes, CD remakes, and the unauthorized distribution of video recordings have been playing havoc with these status-definitions.

The pleasure of collecting recordings is built upon a foundation that springs from, but which has grown larger than, recording technology (see Stewart 1993: 151f.). It is part of the modern pleasure associated with the privatization of properties and the acquisition of goods, and, as such, is associated with a modern redefinition of what it is to be a human being. "The individual, as both producer and consumer, is decomposed and a new unity is created consisting of a unique package of saleable parts. Desirable social relations tend to appear mediated by purchased objects" (Goldman 1992: 23). A person is assayed in terms of the objects that he or she has purchased and collected.

"For the individual who has 'only one life to live' there is a vast array of interpretations of cultural goods, experiences and lifestyles all of which point to the capacity for self and lifestyle transformation" (Featherstone 1992: 115).

This new pleasure is supported by a revised rhetoric of authenticity. The authenticity of the collection is no longer lodged in the music or even in the dark and dangerous interiority of the listener, but now in the listener's choice. Record collectors operate authentically when they *decide* to participate in this or that aspect of the artistic manifold that surrounds them. Flamenco enthusiasts in the second half of the twentieth century derive joy from *choosing* to explore and sample the diversity of the music. Flamenco aficionados in this age of the recording indulge passions similar to those of World Music fans. They are "a new incarnation of the economically driven explorer, the sort of rough and rugged type who is able to make the difficult journey to distant lands and return with new treasures for sale in the home markets. . .all to indulge Western fantasies of exotic 'native' peoples in touch with the primal rhythms of the earth, (and) provide consumers with musical trophies of their enlightenment" (Mattelart 1992: 109).[11]

At the center of this pleasure is the aficionado-as-explorer, the self who wades through diversity, picking and culling for a noble cause. These new musical explorers enjoy flamenco with a curious blend of guilt for past cultural arrogance towards marginalized people and elation at the prospect of redeeming both ourselves and those marginalized Others by valorizing their life ways in the present. The avid anthologizer revels in the delight of redeeming both self and Other by gathering objects (disks and videos), and occasionally even listening to them.

Such an explorer is driven, in part, by a quintessentially modern contradiction between a commitment to root values roots and an interest in opening self to all possibilities. He displays "a desire for clear and solid values to live by," but also "a desire to embrace the limitless possibilities of modern life and experience that obliterate all values" (Berman 1982: 35). The explorer resolves this dilemma by ranging over all the musical possibilities, and then, in a moment of choice, by selecting one facet of that range for complete and total commitment – at least until something new comes along. "Cultural practices become merely the occasion for a temporary and intense affective investment, for a constant movement between emotional highs and lows. It is as if it were only necessary to feel something more intensely than is available to us. While it is necessary to feel something – anything – that strongly, it is irrelevant what one feels because no particular feeling matters in itself. What matters is affective excess" (Grossberg 1988: 45).

Conclusion

The historical manifold of flamenco pleasureability is present in each moment of performance, so that enjoyment can be simultaneously traditionalist and progressive, romanticist and nationalist, egocentric and sociocentric, compliant and oppositional. One can experience disdain for the banalities and insipidities of a commercial performance, and, at the same time, one can celebrate its spontaneity and authenticity. Everything is present in any performance. Musical pleasure, in other words, is like a television broadcast signal. It is manifold, ubiquitous, and integral. But the breadth of its pleasures is essentially unavailable because those pleasures are diffused, scattered in the musical atmosphere, useless without a receiver. In the consumption phase, listeners tune into this or that pleasure, exercising the agency necessary to decode its delights, but thereby diminishing the fullness of the broadcast by their focused enjoyment. In this way, the consumption molds the social space of ensuing social relations.

Notes

1. These "ethnic nationalisms," it can be argued, were spawned by historically "civic nationalisms" of popular opposition prior to monarchical rule (see Greenfeld 1992; Olivia Smith 1986).
2. British scholars of the 1830s argued that the involvement of the masses in music was controlled in its uncontrolledness by

reason of the operation the "invisible hand" of custom. Such a British interpretation of music may well, as Zavala suggests (1974: 17), have shaped the romantic folkloric interests of the Andalusian intelligentsia of the time. For more on this British interpretation of music and culture, see the comments on the writings of Adam Smith by Kevin Barry (1987: 106) and Christopher Herbert (1991: 79f.).

3. The theater was a favored place for gathering, and conversing (see Eisenberg 1987: 74; Johnson 1995: 9–34), and remembering. It was one of a number of different genres of new memory institutions on the scene in the nineteenth century, including newspapers (Terdiman 1985), salons (Burke 1993: 87ff.), and coffee houses (Schievelbusch 1992: 49ff.; Stallybrass and White 1986: 94ff.).

4. "Cuando llegó la muerte y el tiempo se hizo de silencio, volvió de nuevo el cante disminuido a los teatros y comenzó la larga agonía de la juerga. . .Las relaciones de producción que allí también, aunque de forma a veces encubierta y a veces no, se mantenían entre señoritos y cantaores, y que, a su modo, evidenciaban explotación y dominio flagrantes, no aconsejan, desde luego, un regreso a lo que fue." With these comments, Ortiz Nuevo (1985: 11f.) describes the oppressiveness of the epoch of the *juerga*. Similar to this description is Chambers's account of the oppressiveness of the contemporary musical marketplace:

> Subordinate subjects have invariably been ordained to the stereotyped immobilism of an essential "authenticity," in which they are expected to play out roles, designated for them by others. . .for ever. For many, the blues and R&B, or Rastafarian "locks," are considered more "authentic," somehow closer to a "black" essence – while the glitzy styles of Tamla Motown, the artifice of disco, the electronic plagiarism of house music, straightened or permed hair, represents obvious forms of betrayal, a denial of roots. The corollary that seals this logic and finally condemns the subordinate to the eternal role of "authenticity" is that success is suspect: it automatically suggests a sell-out (Chambers 1994: 38).

5. Phonography began in 1877 with Edison invention of the foil-cylinder "talking machine." In 1887 Emile Berliner patented the gramophone, a phonograph that used disks instead of

cylinders. Soon thereafter Berliner devised the technique of pressing records from a master – prior to 1890 each disk had to be individually recorded – and in 1892 "After the Ball was Over" became the first million-seller. At the turn of the century, phonographs and disks were inexpensive and within reach of the working class as well as the wealthy (though see Eisenberg 1987: 16 for an alternative account). In 1925 recording was first done by microphone, as opposed to acoustic recording through a pick-up horn. In the late 1940s the recording process was further developed. Instead of recording from mike to disk, engineers began recording onto a master tape where splicing and mixing could then be used to enhance the recorded sound.

6. What Phillips (1987) calls the "natural" method of dance acquisition is matched by a similarly face-to-face and rote method of guitar apprenticeship. For example, Eduardo El de la Malena, in 1987, was reluctant to allow me to use a tape recorder to facilitate my learning of guitar *falsetas*. Such reluctance was part of the climate of artistic paranoia associated with the age of recorded music. Just as Freddie Keppard passed up the opportunity to be the first musician to record jazz in 1917 because he was afraid that others would steal his music (Eisenberg 1987: 143), and just as Manolo El de Huelva became an artistic recluse in Sevilla in the 1950s, refusing to record for fear that others would copy his style (Blas Vega and Ríos Ruiz 1990: 367), so Eduardo El de la Malena was reluctant to allow a tape recorder into a guitar session.

7. Guitar was the original instrumental accompaniment to Argentine Tango, but when the tango moved out of small bars into large halls at the turn of the century, the guitar's role in that style was replaced by the bandoneon, violin, and piano. That replacement gave rise to the popular expression "Awkward as a guitar in a tango!" *Guarango como guitarra en tango* (Pinnell 1993: 25).

8. For festival performances, *cantaoares* have adopted the curiously vestigial practice of taking a few moments to stand aside from the microphone so as to demonstrate the raw power of their voices.

9. Recently, I chatted with Jack Grassel as he relaxed between sets. A local jazz guitarist with prodigious talent, Jack

explained that he and the others in the group had come together for this one-night gig so as to rehearse for a CD that they were to record the next day. To my question about whether it was possible to record a whole CD in one day, Jack responded in this way: "Oh, you mean the problems of errors and the need for retakes? Well, we just won't make any errors. Hey, we haven't made any tonight." His retort suggests that music should be made with, and appreciated for, its machine-like automaticity, break-neck speed notwithstanding. Such an ideal depreciates the monumental importance of failure in human practices, and the inestimable value of learning to pick up the pieces in the aftermath.

The contemporary flamenco guitar artistry of Paco de Lucía, Vicente Amigo, and Gerardo Nuñez is cultivated with an eye to a similar ideal of automaticity, but other artists march to a different drummer. In my studies with both Eduardo El de la Malena and Juan del Gastor, I found that speed and accuracy were always subordinated to tonality. The artist, according to these latter guitarists, should cultivate rich, and often unsettling, sound textures to complement a singer's expression, sometimes even exploiting noisy "dirty" sounds. As in baseball where players strike out at least as often as they hit home runs, guitarists should expect to fall short of producing satisfying accompaniments with perfect consistency, but should instead look forward to those rare occasions when the setting is apt and when the coordination amongst artists is at its peak.

10. Program no. 31, Festivales del Cante (29, May, 1972) of the documentary series "Rito y Geografía del Cante" illustrates this argument. José María Velázquez interviews Pulpón, a nickname that, appropriately enough, means "octopus." He asks this impresario, who is largely responsible for the Morón Flamenco Festival, why the audience in chattering during the performances. Both Velázquez and Pulpón seem perplexed by enthusiasts who have taken the time and paid the money to attend this marathon session of flamenco performance, but who then ignore the music. Shades of earlier epochs (see Johnson 1995; Levine 1988)?

11. This passion for collecting, far from benign, alienates the Other whose music is collected (Clifford 1988: 193). The

collections create a barrier between the collector from the Others whom he tries to approach, producing an alienation that arises from the simple fact that the collector chooses and selects what is, for Others, most often unchosen, unselected, but rather imposed and received. In just this way Jack Kerouac focused on the ecstasy of jazz music while simultaneously ignoring the poverty of the musicians:

> At lilac evening I walked with every muscle aching amongst the lights of 27th and Welton in the Denver coloured section, wishing I were a Negro, feeling that the best the white world had offered was not enough ecstasy for me, not enough life, joy, kicks, darkness, music not enough night (from the *Dharma Bums*, quoted in Chambers 1976: 157).

Similarly, Jackson Braider describes his flamenco experiences using the imagery of the hallucinogenic ecstasy while ignoring the social aspects of flamenco music: "During the two weeks I attended the tenth Festival Internacional de la Guitarra in Córdoba, I was mainlining rhythms and counter-rhythms night and day. Once you succumb to flamenco, there is little hope of coming back alive" (Braider 1991). Finally, as if to confirm flamenco's potential for raising listeners above all experiences and for conferring superhuman powers, Brook Zern has written, on the jacket of the recent CD *Flamenco: Fire and Grace*, that flamenco will satisfy your desire to find "a place from which you can see the whole world at once."

Chapter 4

Gypsies

Within Spain or beyond, wherever flamenco music is played, listeners expect to hear the Gitano (Gypsy) style with its curt vocals and its polyrhythmic barrages of guitar playing, hand clapping, finger popping, and chatter. In the face of this widespread expectation, critics, scholars, and aficionados have been forced to ask some very tough questions. Is this "flamenco Gitano" the real stuff or is it some sort of Madison Avenue hype? Is this Gitano style the heart and core of the art or is it just flamenco fluff?

In the 1950s Anselmo González Climent and José Carlos de Luna disputed García Lorca's celebrated portrayal of the Gitano style as the trunk of the flamenco tree. *Cante Gitano*, they said, was an important branch, undeniably well-leafed, but still just a branch. In the 1960s, Molina and Mairena reasserted the Gitano thesis, contending that "real" flamenco is nothing if not Gitano, especially as rendered in performances of *soleares, seguiriyas, tangos*, and *bulerías*.[1] In the 1980s and 1990s deep historical research efforts have advanced the debate beyond claim and counterclaim. Some of most remarkable works in this line have portrayed *cante Gitano* as a *tour de force* of musical commercialization or, in straighter talk, a fraud. Many go so far as to suggest that the term "Gitano" refers to nothing of substance, being itself part of the process of commercial invention. For example, García Gómez (1993), Gelardo and Belade (1985), Mercado (1982), Mitchell (1994), and Steingress (1993) all contend that the social category of Gitano is vague, indistinct from the Andalusian lumpen, and trumped up with attractive features and positive values so as to make a killing on the flamenco music circuit. The force of these criticisms is directed to the pro-Gitano literature that swamped discussions of flamenco music in the 1960s and 1970s. The critics claim that the pro-Gitano scholars who generated this literature were benighted by their romanticism and hoodwinked by their nostalgia.

My own view is that such a blanket condemnation is overly
simplistic.

Gitanofilia and Ethnicity

The Gitano debate, with its claims and counterclaims, turns as
much on the concept of ethnicity as it does on the substance of
Andalusian history. Consider, for example, the stridently pro-
Gitano treatise *Misterios del Arte Flamenco* in which Ricardo
Molina (1985) advanced such notions as "the mysterious Gitano
community" and "Gitano racial purity." His vague allusions to
Gitano ethnicity indicate his reliance on the Weberian tradition in
which ethnicity is understood as a function of primordial ties (see
Comaroff and Comaroff 1992: 50). In this same Weberian vein,
Antonio Mairena, in his *Confessions* (1976: 80), spoke of a
mysterious Gitano power, *razón incorpórea*, which has allegedly
shaped the Gitano flamenco style. In other words, Mairena
emphasized distinctive inherited Gitano mental states and
exclusive faculties. Non-Gitano disciples of Mairena, including
José Caballero Bonald, Félix Grande, and Fernando Quiñones,
advanced the pro-Gitano approach to flamenco by describing
Gitanos as a persecuted minority who, in the sixteenth century,
formed a hidden and marginalized social tradition in association
with remnant Moriscos and Jews, and who carried forward a
song style that came to be known as flamenco in the nineteenth
century. In these accounts, one can discern again the Weberian
assumption that ethnicity refers to distinctive mental traits
and dispositions inherited by a group of people. Ethnicity, in
these defenses of flamenco Gitano, consists of an inherited group-
psyche.

Recent opponents of Mairena's concept of ethnicity contend
that Gitanos at the end of the eighteenth century were indistinct
from the landless jobless masses of Andalusians (Mercado 1982:
54; Torrione 1995). If anything, the notion of a Gitano ethnicity
emerged in the wake of French Romanticism (García Gómez
1993: 78). The racy images of hot-blooded Andalusians concocted
by French writers like Gautier encouraged European travel to
southern Spain, which, in turn, kick-started a movement among
the Andalusian poor to style themselves after those narrated

images so as to cash in on tourism. If there is any Gitano ethnicity in this scenario, it is ethnicity wrought rather than inherited. "Gitano" does not name an age-old people who think or feel or play anything authentically. Instead, the term "Gitano" refers to momentarily constructed practices of people who are struggling to enhance their economic situation.

It is both interesting and problematic that these challenges to the pro-Gitano position advance a definition of ethnicity as invented rather than inherited. Ethnicity, in these anti-Gitano arguments, is "a highly situational attribute" (Mitchell 1994: 40). Far from being a survival from the deep past, ethnicity is as a contemporary strategy to deal with the unequal distribution of wealth, power and status. In this way of thinking, the invention of *cante* Gitano is just one facet of the larger tactical and situational process of ethnic invention.

While acknowledging the tactical importance of "invention," many of these scholars contend that invented Gitano ethnicity is fraudulent. The fraud lies in the fact that "the invented" was pawned off as "the inherited," thereby masking the real forces that operated in Andalusian history. Inventions that hide history in this way must be exposed as acts of dissembling nostalgia and must be subjected to a "destructive" sociological–historical analysis (see Handler 1985; Jameson 1991: 19; Rosaldo 1990: 27). Pursuant to this program of exposure and demystification, Steingress argues that the errors of traditional flamencology derive from attributions of significance to the mystical historical abstraction of "Gitano ethnicity" and that those errors should be rectified by adhering to an analysis that accords significance only to synchronic socio-economic and ideological tendencies (1993: 158). His own analysis of those tendencies in the early nineteenth century show that flamencos were people who bootstrapped themselves into existence by imitating the gitanized bohemian style that was then all the rage in Europe. These Gitano "wannabes" profited handsomely from the windfall of European tourism to this Orient that lay within the boundaries of the Occident (Steingress 1993: 332). The force of his argument is directed against a *gitanismo* that portrays invention as inheritance, and that encourages Gitanos to present themselves as something which, he says, they most definitely are not.

To counter Steingress's argument, it should first be emphasized that *all history is inventive*. Those who coopt the past in order to fashion a future are not stepping outside of *real* history. Rather, they are doing history in the only manner possible, that is, by constructing it. Historical fact does not exist in some objective world that is independent of what Rosaldo has described as the inventive "dance of life." Though social class may seem like the infrastructural rock on which a modern society is built, this rock is itself invented (Eagleton 1991: 23). Labor and class are cultural constructs every bit as much as is art, and the historical representation of labor and class is never independent of the creativity of representational discourse (Schrag 1980: 77ff.). In short, history is always invented.

While Steingress and Mitchell may acknowledge the role of invention in history, they seem not to accept its corollary, that *inventions become history*. The invention of "Gitano" in the nineteenth century is not some sort of ethnic epiphenomenon. "Gitano" is not a byproduct of other, more clearly real, historical forces. It is not an inconsequential spinoff of history that can be safely ignored while one gets down to "the real stuff." Rather what was invented yesterday, has become today's reality from which future social practices are launched (see Huyssen 1995: 88; Lipsitz 1990: 136). Though Mitchell lent a sympathetic ear to the Comaroffs' claims about cultural invention (Mitchell 1994: 40), he seems deaf to their equally emphatic claim about the role of invention in the shaping of history: "While ethnicity is the product of specific historical processes, it tends to take on the 'natural' appearance of an autonomous force, a 'principle' capable of determining the course of social life" (Comaroff and Comaroff 1992: 59). At the very least, one can note with Angela McRobbie, that ethnic inventions form and shape ongoing social life through such processes as "reproduction." That is, invented ethnicity, far from being sequestered in the domain of art or entertainment, becomes intertwined "with domestic labor, part of the work of reproduction, the sustaining of the self and others, in preparation for the return to work the following day, work in the world" (McRobbie 1994: 32).

The oversimplification that results when critics dispense with "gitanophilia" as if it were artificial, epiphenomenal, and mere nostalgia, becomes particularly evident when the target of such criticism is examined closely and with attention to detail. Here, I will consider expressions of "gitanophilia" in the documentary film series "Rito y Geografía del Cante," and, in line with the foregoing argument, I will show that Gitano ethnicity in these films is both invented *and* politically effective.

A Critique of "Rito y Geografía del Cante"

The "Rito" documentary film project was hatched in the late 1960s, the decade in which pro-Gitano rhetoric had risen to a fever pitch among flamencologists. It may well be that "invention" goes some distance in explaining its support for the pro-Gitano agenda. As Mitchell says, Gitanos in the 1960s were hard pressed to maintain their differentiation, having fallen on hard times in the 1940s and 1950s. Not only did they suffer through the same "Years of Hunger" as the rest of the population of Spain, but in addition, their traditional economic roles were being eroded by modernizations of all sorts. Cars and trains had replaced mules as primary modes of transportation, hence the traditional Gitano activities of animal trading and mule driving became redundant. Metal working at forges, again a traditional Gitano activity, fell to industrial metallurgy. As a result, the sedentary and erstwhile well-integrated Gitano muleteers and blacksmiths suddenly felt the economic floor drop out from under them. One telling indicator of the power of these external forces to erode the foundation of the Gitano community is the fact that marriages of Gitanos to non-Gitanos rose to some 30% of marriages overall. Thus, the Gitano identity was suffering serious debilitation in the early 1960s,[2] and, according to Mitchell, Mairena came to the rescue by reinventing Gitano ethnicity. Mairena portrayed "cante Gitano" as the root and soul of flamenco, and he developed the concepts of *razón incorpórea* and Gitano hermeticism, and, in these various ways, he operated as a "one-man invention of tradition" (Mitchell 1994: 205), an expression that indicates something of the double-voiced tone of Mitchell's discussion (Mitchell 1994: 205f.). Though he has credited Mairena with ingenuity for reinventing Gitano ethnicity, he has accused Mairena of fabrication. Evidently, though the invention of tradition may be a productive social process, the invention of Gitano tradition in Andalucía has been, for the most part, a sham and a lie. *Mairenismo*, for Mitchell, is just another name for deception.

This cynical view of *mairenismo* bears directly on the inter-

pretation of the "Rito" films insofar as they constitute the most
elaborately formulated and most widely disseminated *mairenista*
effort to date. Though no one has actually undertaken a pointed
criticism of the series – the films have not been available for
study within or beyond Spain until very recently – still "Rito"
seems an apt target for those like Mitchell who consider
mairenismo to be a fraudulent ideology. The focus of such a
criticism could be anticipated from Mitchell's comments on non-
Gitano *mairenistas* who, he says, perpetrated the greater fraud.
Well-meaning, but deluded, non-Gitano scholars cloaked
Mairena's reinvention of Gitano ethnicity in a sanctifying history
of Gitano persecution and passion, and topped it off with a
beatific picture of the Gitano as linchpin of Andalusian cultural
life. In Mitchell's words, "it was not his (Mairena's) fellow
Gitanos but impressionable flamenco aficionados who were
instrumental in realizing the initial success of Mairena's
teachings. The self-appointed savior of Gitano values came along
just when non-Gitano aficionados and intellectuals were in need
of a folk messiah" (Mitchell 1994: 209). The problem, as Mitchell
sees it, was that these aficionados and intellectuals were
benighted by a pervasive and pernicious Andalusian ideology,
and had become, he claims, "tardo-romantics," that is,
anachronous romantics or intellectuals who persisted to
irrational lengths and degrees in their romanticist thinking
(Mitchell 1994: 209). "Not Franco's technocrats hastily pushing
Spain into development," they were "humanists watching the
Spain of their childhood vanish before their eyes." They pined
for ruined places and aged artists, turning their back on the
future in order to reflect lingeringly on the past. Mitchell's
epithet "tardo-romantic" applies, among others, to José Caballero
Bonald, Francisco Moreno Galván, José María Velázquez, and
José Monleón, all gitanophiliac scholars who helped to advance
mairenismo by contributing to the success of the documentary
film series "Rito y Geografía del Cante." The question I now pose
is this. Does the "Rito" series deserve the same criticism that
Mitchell has leveled at the gitanophiliac writers of the period?
Do these films express the "tardo-romanticism," nostalgic
humanism, or irrational passion for ruins that Mitchell sees in so
much pro-Gitano writing. The answer is a good deal more
complex than such a simply framed question suggests.

Franquismo, Gitanismo, Andalucismo and the "Rito" Series

In order to respond to Mitchell's assault on the work of non-Gitano *mairenistas*, we must return our attention to the historical struggles of Andalusians, concentrating above all on their responses to Franco's elevation of Madrid to the status of social hub of the nation in such a way as to marginalize Andalusians, Catalans, and Basques (Collier 1987: 187; Hansen 1977; Harding 1984: 25; Johnston 1991), drowning their pleas for regional independence in a sea of centralist rhetoric.

Andalusian opposition to similar centralist rhetoric had been active since at least 1868, and was most often linked to historical arguments for the distinctiveness of the Andalusian people. These arguments emphasized the age-old diversity of the south, claiming a distinctive Andalusian national identity rooted in the amalgamation of the diverse groups of people who resided in the south prior to 1492. Andalucía was portrayed as a paradisiacal conviviality of Christians, Muslims, Jews, and Gitanos, at least until fifteenth-century Madrid unleashed its iron-fisted program of cultural homogenization (Acosta Sánchez 1978; Moreno Navarro 1977).[3] A common way of emphasizing this quintessentially diverse Andalusian heritage was to tout the contributions of the different populations who constituted the cultural trunk of Andalucía. Always, however – and this point is crucial – this promotion of Muslims, Jews, and Gitanos served both the interests of Andalusian regionalists in their struggle for national recognition and political independence, and the interests of conservative elites to avoid the social changes that would result from land reform and increased industrialization. It was in this complex social climate that Antonio Machado y Alvarez "Demófilo" emphasized Gitanos (Moreno Navarro 1977: 44; see also Acosta Sánchez 1978), and that Blas Infante, *andalucista* extraordinaire, emphasized Muslims, and that Rafael Cansinos Assens emphasized the Jews (see also Sofía Nöel 1977).

Not accidentally, music was a strongly favored vehicle for elucidating and celebrating the Andalusian past. In line with the powerful influence of German Romanticism over Andalusian intellectuals, scholars such as "Demófilo" and Blas Infante fell upon flamenco music as the tell-tale sign of Andalusian heritage, "the characteristic voice of the Andalusian nationality" (Infante Pérez 1980; Acosta Sánchez 1979: 41; see Moreno Navarro 1982: 358; see Barrios 1989: 126), a complex musical style for a uniquely heterogeneous region.

Interestingly, Franco's cultural politics in the 1940s and 1950s succeeded in driving a wedge between these pro-Gitano arguments – as well as the pro-Muslim and pro-Jewish – and the regionalist rhetoric of *andalucistas*. This *franquista* wedge was begun with an active suppression of *andalucismo*: García Lorca, a pro-Gitano *andalucista*, was murdered, and so too Blas Infante, a pro-Muslim *andalucista*. Curiously, however, *gitanismo* itself was tolerated. Resistant Gitano artists were treated as no more than benign irritations to the regime, and more docile Gitanos received positive and favorable treatment in the regime. Such tolerance for Gypsies, who were – and are – widely discriminated against in Europe and the Americas, lent credibility to Franco's claim that Spain's government was neither fascist nor intolerant of cultural diversity. The cost of such tolerance was minimal, since Gitanos were political unorganized, but its purchase was great insofar as the fledgling economic alliance between Spain and the U.S. hung in the balance of such matters as Franco's respect for human rights.

Taking advantage of Franco's permissive attitude with regard to Gitanos, Antonio Mairena, in the 1960s, promoted the Gitano cause with impunity, suggesting *cante Gitano* as a proper sign of Gitano depth and dignity. In his eagerness to promote Gitano interests in the face of the viciousness of the Franco regime, he propounded an account that emphasized Gitano contributions to *cante*, though his handling of other Andalusian contributions was confused and obscure (Steingress 1993: 142). Ironically, when assessing the political consequences of his views, one would have to conclude that Mairena's agenda both abetted and opposed *franquismo*. Like a double-edged sword, Mairena's rhetoric helped to clear the way for Gitanos, but, with an overly hearty backswing, it cut against the interests of *andalucistas*.[4]

This historical sketch, then, presents the background and context for our understanding of the "Rito" series. Specifically, it prepares the way for a response to Mitchell's assault on the non-Gitano *mairenistas* who contributed to the series. To recapitulate, this sketch has emphasized the longstanding opposition between Andalucía and Madrid, the Andalusian use of the concept of "the

Gitano" to symbolize the substantial cultural contrast between Andalucía and Madrid, and the shrewd *franquista* maneuver of suppressing *andalucismo* while winking at *gitanismo* in such as way as to encourage the emergence of a Gitano Power movement (Mairena) pursued independently of the regionalist politics of non-Gitano Andalusians.

Now, to respond to Mitchell, I contend that the *mairenismo* of the non-Gitano scholars who contributed to the "Rito" series should not be understood as a simple reflex of Mairena's reinvention of Gitano ethnicity. Rather, their project should be understood, partly at least, as a shrewd struggle to respond to Franco's redoubtable and smotheringly broad centralist politics. Theirs was an effort to jar the narcotised minds of the popular television audience into consciousness, if not into action. These "Rito" contributors, far from being dreamy-eyed romantics and far from being conservatives who took more delight in weeping over the lost past than in laboring toward a more promising future, were activists who had confronted the cold steel of Franco's bayonets and who had become more familiar than they would have wished with the interiors of Franco's prisons (García Jimenez 1980: 424). They were, in short, shrewd politicians who took advantage of some of Mairena's ideas to advance opposition to Franco and to support the regionalist interests of Andalusians. On this account, the "Rito" documentary film series to which these figures contributed their energies should be understood as a multidimensional discourse that availed itself of Mairena's popularity and political immunity in order to reassert something of the *andalucismo* that had been suppressed in the 1930s and 1940s.

This claim that the "Rito" film series involved subtle resistances riding the coat tails of *mairenismo* was born out in my conversations with the principals of the series. Both Mario Gómez, who directed the series, and Paco Lira, who helped to set up many of the filming sessions, acknowledged a political element in the series though they emphasized that artistic and geographic documentation were their primary objectives. Pedro Turbica, a series co-author, and Romualdo Molina, the series supervisor, stated these same goals. Interestingly, their words made it clear that they were less eager about advancing Mairena's agenda (see, for example, Alvarez Caballero 1988: 11, 72) than about promoting the interests of Andalucía. Of course, all their statements of objective and intent must be taken with a grain salt. Like Carlos Saura – whose statements of intent were discussed briefly in footnote 7 of Chapter 1 – the "Rito" authors, having grown up in the oppressive atmosphere of Franco's Spain, were predictably cautious about expressing their intentions.

Beyond the authors' statements of intent and purpose, we can turn to the films themselves for evidence of the *andalucista* interests that were served by the "Rito" series. We can note, for example, that the programs in this series celebrated Andalusian distinctiveness even as its titular reference to *geografía* intimates. In Franco's Spain, where geography stood for culture (Kovacs 1991), and where banner-waving celebrations of distinctive regional cultures were suspect, "Rito y Geografía del Cante" must have prompted official concern from the outset. All the more so because the cultural characteristics of Andalucía were presented with realistic cinematography (see Nichols 1991; 1994), and without the heavy-handed propagandistic commentary that was characteristic of official "No-Do" productions – *Noticias Documentales*, documentary newsreels produced by the government office established by Franco in 1942. The contrasting images of Gitano and non-Gitano styles were regularly steered, in this series, toward the objective of reminding viewers of the archaic diversity of the region. The authors persistently queried artists about the difference between the Gitano and the non-Gitano styles thereby planting the idea that *cante* is irresolvably diverse, the logical outcome of the heteroglossic conviviality in the south prior to 1492. When a singer such as José Menese, explicitly *antifranquista* and *andalucista* in his political leanings, emphasized the value and importance of the Gitano style, as he did emphatically in program no. 46, one senses that his gitanophilia served the interests of Andalusians more clearly than the interests of Gitanos. Contrastively, the almost mocking treatment of Madrid's stars such as Manolo Caracol (no. 54) and Pepe Marchena (no. 87) was, according to the "Rito" authors, intentionally orchestrated so as to de-emphasize Madrid's contribution to flamenco song.

Nowhere was the role of the Gitano as a remnant of Andalusian heterogeneity emphasized more clearly than in the performance (program no. 95) by the Montoya family with Eduardo El de la Malena, all Gitanos, a performance in which

Lole sings *tangos* in Arabic. The Arabic lyrics reminded viewers of the very Moorish contributions to Andalusian identity that *franquismo* was bent on hiding from view. When presented by Gitanos, the Arabic lyrics clearly and unmistakably directed viewers attentions to pre-1492 Andalucía and to its essential diversity prior to Madrid's domination.

The "Rito" series went to great lengths to emphasize the longstanding coordination of diverse cultural traditions in the south. Andalucía was portrayed as a region of mutual accommodations that encouraged a spirit of universalism (see Acosta Sánchez 1979: 39). In line with this portrayal, Gitanos were presented as distinct but integrated, and never as the exoticized creatures who were so vigorously parodied in Ramon Sender's "Nancy" novels (e.g. Sender 1969). With these characteristics, the "Rito" series aimed, in the words of José Monleón (1967b) to "awaken the critical and political consciousness of viewers." Thus, while the "Rito" series – along with its contributors and authors – may be criticized for advancing the pro-Gitano inventions of Mairena, it should also be credited with political shrewdness. By linking *andalucismo* to a politically immune *mairenismo*, the "Rito" films were able to accomplish the unthinkable, airing a subversive political message on Franco's own television network.

Conclusions

The pro-Gitano leaning of the "Rito" series is less a sign of the documentarian's self-deception and ideological stultification, than an indication of constructive, inventive energies directed to the task of opposing the entrenched oppressions of *franquismo* and of paving the way toward a renewal of Andalusian cultural life. Granted, these inventions are dangerous. As Terry Eagleton would say, "they move under the sign of irony, knowing themselves ineluctably parasitic on their antagonists" (1991: 26). Though they presuppose an essential Andalusian identity, that presupposition should be understood as a "tactical" maneuver whose force and endurance is keyed to the oppression they oppose.[5]

The "Rito" authors and contributors reasserted an *andalucista* view of flamenco music as an alternative to Franco's cultural politics. They clothed that reassertion in Mairena's *gitanismo* so as to both get it past the Spanish censors who might otherwise have silenced the entire project, and to play to the gitanofiliac audiences, both Spanish and American.[6] Clearly the authors were insightful and politically active – hardly tardo-romantic fatalists. Indeed, to persist in this latter criticism is to flirt with the danger of assuming that subjects are unified and that societies are founded on internally consistent ideological systems, a danger that, more than anything else, is a figment of theory (McRobbie 1994: 50). Certainly, the Gitanos and Andalusians of the nineteenth and twentieth centuries were never unified. They never identified themselves wholly as Gitanos or simply as Andalusians. They never had sufficient freedom from centralized political force for such a self-identification. Their expressions in word and in song fed back into their own fragmentary conditions. They invented themselves as "agents" rather than as "subjects," but they did so ironically and in a manner consistent with emancipatory politics that, according to Eagleton, "bring about the material condition that will spell their own demise, and so always have some peculiar self-destruct device built into them" (Eagleton 1991: 26).

The efforts of cultural reinvention are always messy and fragmented, never tidy and whole. As reinventors of *gitanismo* and *andalucismo*, the "Rito" authors and contributors proceeded inventively but were predictably inconsistent and fragmentary in their efforts. That is so because they found themselves caught up in identity negotiations, playing off their *gitanismo* against their *andalucismo* against their *antifranquismo*. Moreover, they were immersed in negotiations through performance, the effect of which was intensification but hardly simplification. As they developed these multidimensional performances of the "Rito" series, they broke the molds of old identities and set new molds into place. Their cultural inventiveness inclined them to support positions that they rarely, if ever, saw or understood in their entirety. The worth of the resulting "Rito" invention can only be assayed in hindsight, by appreciating the larger play of its consequences in history. The value of the *gitanismo* or *andalucismo* in this series is not to be determined within the boundaries of the films themselves, but in the ongoing history of social life to which those films contribute their energies.

Notes

1. The pro-Gitano thesis was developed by Antonio Machado y Alvarez "Demófilo" (see Steingress 1993: 109) and was furthered by Federico García Lorca (1975; see also Grande 1992a,b; Stanton 1978). For a recent version of this thesis see Serrano and Elgorriaga (1991).
2. It should be noted that Torcuato Pérez de Guzmán, from whom Mitchell draws his facts, denies that any of these, developments had any important bearing on Gitano identity, the changes "translated into a growing number of mixed marriages, nearly 30% in the last generation. This is not particularly important. The Gitano core continues as ever it has, a living illustration of adaption without any weakening of identity" (Pérez de Guzmán 1982: 112).
3. Gitano presence in Andalucía is said to predate 1450 or even 1415. There is a widespread assumption among Andalusian Gitanos, at least according to Pedro Peña and many *andalucista* non-Gitanos in the tradition of Blas Infante (Barrios 1989: 27f.), that Gitanos immigrated into Andalucía via North Africa in the centuries before the fifteenth, and that by 1450 they were already well integrated in Andalusian social life.
4. Mairena's treatment of Gitano ethnicity left sympathetic apologists (*mairenistas*) with an ungainly legacy. In spirit and tone, Mairena advanced a free-ranging Gitano ethnocentrism, but, on paper, he operated more cautiously, exploiting the ambiguity of the expression "Gitano–Andaluz" when referring to the ethnic roots of flamenco music. Because of this ambiguity, contemporary debates over *mairenismo* often find flamencologists talking past one another insofar as they refer to the Mairena's spirit or letter, respectively. One recent example of such heated, but unenlightening, debate took place in June of 1995 between Timothy Mitchell and Pedro Peña, guitarist, *cantaor*, scholar, and official representative of the Gitano community in the province of Seville – Peña is the guitarist shown in the cover photo of the Perrate family. Mitchell contended that *mairenismo* was a program built on racist principles. Peña countered this argument, observing that Mairena, far from being chauvinistically Gitano, had always referred to the "Gitano–Andaluz" tradition. The two

proceed to fight to an unproductive standstill with words stretched tight to the point of exploding.

5. The debate about gitanophilia brings to mind four principles that bear on inventions of tradition in popular culture. First, the invention of tradition is rarely an invention ex nihilo, but most often a reconstruction of, or from, extant ideologies: "The hegemonic struggle for power takes place on and across an already constituted field, within which the identities and positions of the contesting groups are already being defined but are never fixed once and for all. Hegemonic politics always involves the ongoing rearticulation of the relations between, and the identity and positions of the ruling bloc and the subordinate factions within the larger social formation" (Grossberg 1992: 245). In the realm of flamenco music, such ideological reconstruction is evident in the early nineteenth-century development of urban bohemian music out of the music of eighteenth-century rural religiosity (Steingress 1993). Given this principle, the *gitanofilia* of the 1960s can be seen as a development out of a combination of *gitanismo*, *antifranquismo*, and *andalucismo*. Second, while ideological reconstructions might be "artificial," they often enter into "historically real" processes, thereby blurring the distinction between the artificial and the real (Comaroff and Comaroff 1992: 59). For example, Eagleton has argued, in opposition to traditional Marxian contrasts of class *realities* with *artifices* such as ideology and identity, that class is itself a cultural construct (1991: 26). Thus, though *andalucista* accounts of flamenco may be artificial (see Steingress 1993: 159), these accounts contributed to a very "real" politics of opposition to Franco. Third, cultural reconstructions regularly spring from a restive social manifold and are, in consequence, multi-dimensional. To treat such reconstructions as cultural singularities is to lapse into essentialist thinking (see Grossberg 1992: 244; McGuigan 1992: 65). Specifically, to suppose that *mairenistas* of the 1960s were simply "tardo-romantics," would be to follow Mitchell into the Gramscian error of homogenizing and essentializing class and ideology (see Golding 1988: 557), treating discourses as if they were one-dimensional (Fiske 1993: 31; Lipsitz 1990: 105). Fourth, cultural reconstructions are advanced less in thought than in bodily practice, that is, in "a range of material practices or

rituals which are always embedded in material institutions" (Eagleton 1991: 148). The meanings and intentions of "Rito" authors, contributors, artists, and viewers as they performed and witnessed their music, form only one part – and not necessarily the most important part – of the resistance exercised by this documentary series. As Eagleton has argued, ideology or ideological resistance is "not primarily a matter of 'ideas.' It is a structure which imposes itself on us without necessarily having to pass through consciousness at all. Viewed psychologically, it is less a system of articulated doctrines than a set of images, symbols and occasionally concepts which we 'live' at an unconscious level" (ibid.).

6. The documentarians' nod to American interests is evident in program no. 85 that features the American Moreen Silver, "María La Marrurra" accompanied by the sterling Gitano guitarist Melchor Marchena, and surrounded by figures such as Antonio Mairena and Rafael Romero. The ironic political purchase of this appeal to American sensibility can be best appreciated against the backdrop of the Franco–Eisenhower accord of the 1950s that paved the way for U.S. military bases in Andalucía (Rota and Morón) which gave Americans such as Donn Pohren an opportunity to sample the "ecstasies" of Spanish culture and to transmit their messages back to eager American tourists.

Chapter 5

The Body

The delights of flamenco song are paradoxical. On the one hand, *cante* is a deeply spiritual practice which appeals to contemplative faculties. On the other hand, the flamenco style is undeniably physical and incontrovertibly corporeal. Its pleasures will be all too familiar to those who enjoy shooting baskets or climbing mountains.

The paradoxical aesthetics of flamenco should not be particularly surprising given the fact that the history of Western music is shot through with struggles between spirit and the body, between the Apollonian and the Dionysian. Interestingly, the vacillation between these two poles in both flamenco art and in flamencology is freighted with political force, the focus of this chapter.

Cante on the Mind

In the European writing about music, bodies have long been relegated to the role of instrument, the medium for the expressive soul (see Barry 1987; Chanan 1994: 33; Small 1977). In the case of flamenco song, this denigration of the body has been emphatic. Flamenco song, it is said, is a spiritual exercise. Félix Grande (1992b) cites F. García Lorca approvingly: "the singer has a profound religious appreciation of the song." Ricardo Molina says that a singer is a "solitary hero" who paves the way for the emergence of "a new being, with a substantial union of body and soul" (1981: 15). Singing, according to most flamencologists, requires of *cantaores* that they establish appropriate moods (Hecht 1994) and set their minds to the task of cutting through superficial layers of experience to reach an inner core of emotion.

A number of flamencologists have argued that flamenco emotions, while deeply personal, nevertheless transcend the individual singer. Hence, the singer's quest is to contact aspects of human "primary processes," universals of the human collective unconscious (cf. Molina 1985; Quiñones 1982; Serrano and Elgorriaga 1991). Arrebola (1991: 15) says that "flamenco is universal, and at the same time Andalusian and Spanish, because of its profound human inspiration and by reason of the elemental force by which it directly expresses radical problems, needs, and experiences common to all human beings." Quiñones tells us that "the primary contents (of *cantes*) are of a simple essence to which all humans can assimilate" (1982).

The key to establishing contact with this transcendental core of emotion is sincerity. When driven by a ferocious sincerity (*duende*), the singer turns radically inward (*ensimismado*):

> With flamenco we endure a transformation. There is introduced into daily life, the site of our identity, an exalted aesthetic atmosphere, the place of liberation. One can summarize it in a succinct word: that word is communion. In flamenco, the shadow, the sorrow, the being, the memory and the mystery of *cante* enter into communion, rescuing identity from the claw of Time and History, and revisiting the transcendental intimacy, the paradise of innocence (Grande 1992a: 85).

Duende functions as "a singer's hidden faculty for introducing us to the ineffable so as to draw us close to the ultimate mystery" (Caballero Bonald 1975: 67). Such an introduction need not avail itself of the paltry powers of words (Grande 1992a; Molina 1981). The power of *cante* is primal, elemental and immediate:

> At the beginning of a song, even when no word is uttered, we feel nevertheless that the flesh of our bodies is detached from us as if thought and expression had been suddenly made into one single sudden movement. In the *ayeo* (the moaned singing that introduces a song), the voice is distinctive and primary. This is its moment of nakedness, of pure expression. Each sound is born of itself but simultaneously erases itself. One finds oneself on the threshold of Creation, just as if language did not exist (Rosales 1987: 35).

Armed with such awesome spiritual powers, singers probe the limits of the human condition, "radical human sentiments" (Molina 1981: 14). They sing of life lived against death (Josephs 1983).

One can discover tell-tale signs of this spiritualization of *cante* in the voice-overs of the documentary series "Rito y Geografía del Cante." Written by José María Velázquez, these brief commentaries everywhere reiterate the themes of sincerity, purity, and authenticity. *Cante* in the "Rito" films is the song of the soul, and not just of the individual soul, but of the universal soul. Velázquez's more recent writings reiterate this same theme and advance its justification:

> In *cante* there exist esthetic, emotional, and intellectual elements, but don't we forget about all these factors in order to focus on and achieve other, more profound levels of communication, that is to say, something which does not even have a name, something which goes well beyond the meaning of the lyric? (Velázquez 1989b).

Velázquez developed this theme of "more profound levels" of flamenco communication by referring back to the notion of *razón incorpórea* introduced by Antonio Mairena (Velázquez 1982; 1989a,b), and by arguing, in his own words, that:

> In the system of communication between people, no one escapes from his isolation except by speaking to another person who is locked into his own isolation, in such a way that understanding always takes place between two distinct and isolated individuals, which is what I consider the helplessness of the human being. In this situation there is born the need for poetry and song, such as the *saeta* or the plaintive song: the call to someone who can hear us. Song is thus enmeshed in the ultimate objectives of human language (Velázquez 1989c).

Here, then, is the basis for Velázquez's commitment to *cante* throughout the "Rito" documentaries. Song, he has argued, is rooted in an inherited competence which was developed in isolation by Andalusians and especially Gitano Andalusians, and which redeems humans from the prison of language and the darkening isolation of social life.

With such accounts, flamencologists marginalize the bodies of singers. They subscribe, implicitly at least, to assumptions about music and mind which leave little or no role for the body, as if "the body is not responding directly to its own sensations of harmony but rather imitating those of the soul, which cannot move of itself" (Franko 1995: 76). Flamencologists pursue conventional Western channels of musical interpretation that, while taken for granted by most people, treat bodies as peripheral and ornamental with respect to significant social action.

However, the *experience* of *cante*, in the "Rito" films for example, contravenes this contemplative esthetic. One need only view a little bit of footage to realize that the body, far from being marginal, is focal and necessary and significant. Indeed, centralization of the body is one the its most powerful, albeit invisible and unnoticed, contributions of flamenco music (for more on marginocentric film see Stam 1989: 163).

Western Song Traditions

Western institutional life has generally handled physical diversity by relegating it to the margins of social experience. In the case of music-making, such processes of marginalization have transformed the heteroglossic manifold of musical practice into products of a pure heart, or a singular mind, or a unified soul, or an authentic spirit. Even in eighteenth-century Paris, where musical sentiment is said to have taken a back seat to sensation, commentators betrayed an urgency to comment on the capability of music to convey ideas (Johnson 1995: 38). Such urgencies, expanded and intensified in the nineteenth century, effectively relegating the muscular chaos of music to the sidelines, though never completely (Middleton 1989).

Heterglossic music has been institutionally overshadowed and discouraged in surprisingly concrete ways, as Goffman illustrates in his discussion of the shaping of conversations between patrons and ticket vendors at the movies (1981b). The ticket vendor's box, with its holes strategically placed for speaking and trading money, stands in for words and effectively channels conversations to a speedy end. The architecture of the ticket booth responds to concrete institutional constraints that encourage patrons to rush forward with a curt word, "Two please!," an indication that institutional repressions can be physical as well as mental.

"Official" institutions from the Middle Ages to the present have constrained song and song interpretation by similarly concrete means. They have exercised their constraining power, especially in the modern era, through the physical device of the stage, a powerful mechanism for encouraging uniformity and for marginalizing diversity. Staged popular music by the mid-nineteenth century usurped all prior aspects of music, redefining them according to its own institutional parameters (Middleton 1989: 13). After 1850, popular performers were distinguished from audiences. Popular stars were highly paid professionals in contradistinction to amateurs. Coaches arose to train those stars to perform their role properly. Claques arose to train audiences to perform *their* role (Attali 1985). And in all these roles, uniformity prevailed over diversity. By the end of the nineteenth century, it was very difficult to maintain an awareness of the diverse range of possibilities for popular song.

The stage constrained musical activity along two paths. On the one hand, the stage played up the concept of song that had been cultivated in the Roman Church, and then transformed it into a model of rationalist–universalist social relations. On the other hand, the stage played up a concept of song that had been cultivated in Protestantism, and transformed it into a model of competitive individualistic social relations. These two narrow channels of musical activity came to dominate musical consciousness by the end of the nineteenth century. They also dominated interpretations of flamenco.

The first channel encouraged social relations in which individuals gave themselves over to communities. Gregorian plain chant exemplifies this form of song in which persons mute aspects of their individuality so as to celebrate communality (Chanan 1994: 32). Plain chant is sung by a group in a monophony. Unlike polyphonic music, which highlights the distinctive contributions of different voices, plain chant eradicates the distinctions between individual voices. Chanters are to blend their voices so completely that a listener hears one voice only, thereby diverting the listeners' ears from the heterogeneity of the singers. Moreover, plain chant is sung in such a way as to deny, in practice, the limitations of the body. In contrast to singing in which sung phrases are matched to the lung capacity of singers, the singing of plain chant proceeds without regard to breath groups. Chanters are advised to take breathes anywhere but at phrase junctures. The resulting song is a single endlessly swelling voice, a heavenly sound unfettered by the normal bodily requirements of breathing. Listeners hear what is, in effect, a disembodied voice that has been liberated from physical limitations.

By the nineteenth century, this mode and model of musical activity was secularized, that is, emptied of its religious significance. Courtly music in Britain, France, and Germany was celebrated as a disembodied music whose the form mirrored the structure of human reason. Romantics writers at the beginning of the nineteenth century embraced such music as a vehicle through which the spirit might express a rationality that individual bodies, in their contingency and concreteness can never know: "Unknown to me," writes Wordsworth, "the workings of my spirit thence are brought" (Barry 1987: 131).

This characterization of music as a vehicle for tapping an invisible and universal wellspring of meaning, has served as a powerful model of and for modern social relations. According to this model, singers, though apparently independent of each other, are capable of being joined by abstract universal ties. Songs operate like the myths described by Joseph Campbell (Campbell 1972). They recover the abstract universal ties that invisibly bind humans together. A singer is a hero who searches out the forces of "Mind-at-Large" thereby joining scattered individuals into a seamless community. Song, understood along these lines, is an utopian project. As a staged spectacle, it seeks to draw performers and audiences together to form a perfect unity. This communal song model has obviously exerted tremendous influence over the interpretation of *cante flamenco*, as one can see from sampling the aforementioned flamencological literature.

Under the impact of the stage, Western song and music was also channeled along a second path that influences contemporary interpretations of *cante*. This second path assumes song to be a competitive expression of individuality. Along this channel, songs spring from individual artists for the purpose of validating their personhood vis-à-vis other individuals. A song is inscribed onto the singer's voice and then sent out into the marketplace for competition and validation. There, through a disembodied voice, the singer vicariously competes with others. The competition of songs results in a community of sorts among singers. However, the communal relations realized through such song are indirect rather than face-to-face, and they are marked by competition rather than by unanimity (see Turner 1984: 174).

This mode of interpreting modern song as both symbol and carrier of unique personhood gained popularity at the same time as body-cosmetics, and for the same reasons, "Cosmetic practices are indicative of a new presentation of self in a society where the self is no longer lodged in formal roles but has to be validated through a competitive public space" (Turner 1984: 174). The actions of singing and of putting on lipstick both serve the individual by enabling him or her to cultivate a self that can compete in the marketplace of public life.

Curiously, but predictably for this musical style that wants to be all things to all people, the "Rito" films encourage both modes of interpretation. They prompt viewers to appreciate *cante* as a communal song in which individuality is submerged, but they also incline viewers toward an understanding of *cante* as an individual song through which the artist breaks free of a stultifying community. But, regardless of the interpretive strategy being promoted, the programs consistently place a heavy emphasis on *cante* as a spiritual exercise, one for which bodies are marginal. On the one hand, the singer who is united to the community through song, hides his idiosyncratic talents behind the spiritual integrity of the community. On the other hand, the singer who breaks free of the community to forge new canons, does so by reason of some inner spiritual genius rather than because of any ordinary aspects of physical or social life. Whether *cante* is interpreted as communal or as competitive, it is always the spirit, never the body, that receives the lion's shared of interpretive attention. Evidently, flamencologists have not yet come to grips with corporeal presence in song.

Though flamencologists have overlooked the flamenco body, a savvy flamenco audience or a sensitive "Rito" viewer will not. In the "Rito" programs, for example, Manuel Agujetas, Manuel Soto "Sordera," Antonio Mairena, la Fernanda de Utrera, La Perrata, María La Sabina, Diego El Perote, Juan Talega are singers that come across as bodies first and foremost. Their songs do not merely *use* their voices, as if their voices were instruments of song. Their songs *are* their voices. Despite the soothingly spiritual tone of the voice-overs in these films, the diverse textures of singers' bodies are persistently unsettling. Some of these flamenco bodies are harsh and daunting, some are languid and fluid, some are old and stiff and barely capable of uttering a sound, some are portly without apology. Some bodies are so young, so bright and smooth and slender as to seem incapable of bearing the frightful weight of the sounds they emit. Their movements and gestures are disturbing. When Manuel Agujetas, La Fernanda, Manuel Soto "Sordera," and Antonio Mairena sing, their fists are clenched and their muscles are raw and straining. These singers are crumpled bodies, doubled over in pain, as if they had just had the wind knocked out of them.

The majority of flamenco scholars persist in asking about the "meaning" of these crumpled postures. Or they compliment the singers for the sincerity of their collapsed condition, as if their pure minds had gotten the upper hand over their weak bodies. However, all such comments miss the mark. They fail to recognize the centrality of the body in song, and serve only to further marginalize the bodies that singers seem bent on centralizing. Contrary to the bulk of flamencological commentary, the songs of these singers are their bodies.

Neither of the two major Western paths for interpretation, i.e. communal song and competitive song, can account for the raw and edgy physicality of these images. The songs that we see are not indications of acts that transcend the physical to search out universal sentiments or to liberate the spirit. The songs that we see are not the songs of solitary heroes. They do not spring from personal insight or creative genius or sincere feeling. These songs are more muscular and neural than conceptual or sentimental. They are examples of "musica practica," "muscular music," songs of the body (Chanan 1994).

Cante and the Body

The remainder of this chapter will argue that flamenco bodies hint at processes other than those described as communal or competitive. Specifically, we need to open up a larger role for both muscle memory and bodily pain in the process of song. Our discussion will focus first on music and memory and then move to the issue of music and pain.

Program no. 40 (see Chapter 9) in the "Rito" series opens with a scene that illustrates something of the connection between body and memory in flamenco song. The scene was shot in a simple and bare tavern in La Cabeza de San Juan, Cádiz, where seven men are gathered, for drinking, smoking, and singing. A man, with a guitar resting upside down on his thighs, taps out a rhythm of *bulerías* that the group turns and twists and elaborates into a symphony of percussive sounds with song and dance. The demeanor of the group throughout the nearly four minutes of performance is relaxed and unconcentrated. . .almost off-handed. Their lack of concentration suggests that their rhythmic competence is managed less by their minds or hearts or spirits than by their nerves and muscles. This rhythmic competence is neither genetically programmed, as suggested by Molina (1985: 63ff.), nor culturally distinctive, as suggested by Mairena (1976: 79). Rather, it is the product of years of repetition. In the simplest terms, the rhythmic competence displayed in program no. 40 is a matter of habit.

As a habit, rhythmic competence might be passed off as peripheral and incidental. It is neither. An increasing amount of evidence suggests that the control of complex musical rhythm is central to human activity (see Calvin 1990: 194; Chanan 1994: 85f.). Moreover, the musical rhythms that are handled by the ear probably involve other senses, the visual, the olfactory, etc. since "the memory of one sense is stored in another: that of tactility in sound, of hearing in taste, of sight in sound" (Serematakis 1994: 216). Rather than being narrow and peripheral, the rhythmic abilities displayed in this program are of broad and central importance.

A significant feature of these abilities is that they are social rather than individual. The habitual control of flamenco rhythms is collaborative; it is a moment of social coordination. Such rhythmic collaboration illustrates another side of what Connerton has called "rites", that is, events of "social memory" through which people establish "continuity with the past" (see Connerton 1989: 44f.).

Connerton's term "rite," like term *rito* in the title of the documentary film series, refers to events that link the present to the past. However, now it should be becoming clear that the links that song establishes are forged by bodies as much as by minds. Habitual control of collaborative rhythms is a transtemporal physical ability that operates more powerfully and effectively than ordinary words. For one thing, such rhythmic abilities are phylogenetically more profound than speech insofar as they are widely shared by non-humans (Donald 1991: 175). For another, these rhythmic abilities are socially profound in the sense that they emanate from what Bakhtin would call "the lower bodily stratum." Like other expressions that arise from this stratum, they pose a distinct challenge to officialdom (Bakhtin 1984: 82ff.). Corporeal song does not "mean" resistance; it rehearses resistance (Franko 1995: 28). Bodily movement – in itself and regardless of what it might express – is a response "to a culture increasingly intolerant of disorder in society, in the individual and in art" (Greenblatt 1990: 69). The performance of bodies in the bar in Cádiz, is both a statement of the physical unity of the group and an effective resistance to the force of intolerance in the society at the time. This oppositional impact comes across in "Rito's" images despite the spiritualizing interpretations that dominate the voice-over commentaries.

In addition to illustrating the link between music and the body's handling of habit, the "Rito" films suggest a link between music and the body's handling of pain. Performances such as those of Manuel Agujetas in program no. 45 reveal a dimension of song that eludes the mentalistic, communal, and competitive channels of mainstream interpretation. Agujetas is a pain specialist. His songs are laced with lamentation, anger, and hatred. They usually begin calmly, with wordless *ayeo* that prefaces his display of grief. But suddenly, as if a jolt of electricity had passed through his body, he is transformed into a man possessed by pain. No longer singing about pain, his singing is itself pained. Not just his voice, but his whole body is taken over by the pain. Every muscle is pained, and every movement communicates pain. To understand his song, one must first understand bodies in pain.

A curious thing about bodies in pain is that they become self-absorbed. They turn their attention inward (Leder 1990; see also Scarry 1985). People in pain truncate their normal outgoing (ecstatic) mode of operation, and begin exploring, feeling, and exclaiming about internal realities that, in the normal course of activity, are overlooked and, for all practical purposes, absent. Pain prompts a curious kind of introspective body-talk.

The curiosity of this introspective talk is that it is rarely useful or productive. Instead, the inwardly directed, self-examining expressions that arise on occasions of pain and death, are communicative dead-ends. They may not even seek out a listener. Consider, for example, the radio commentary presented on the occasion of the crash of the Hindenburg dirigible, May 6, 1937:

> I don't believe. . .I can't even talk to people whose friends are out there. It's a. . .(sobs), I can't talk, ladies and gentlemen, honest. It's a laid-down mass of smoking wreckage, and everybody can hardly breathe. I'm sorry; honest, I can hardly breathe. I'm going to step inside where I cannot see it. Scotty, that's terrible. (sobs) I can't. Listen, folks, I'm going to have to stop for a minute because I've lost my voice (as quoted in Nichols 1991: 220).

Here the Hindenburg commentator has turned radically inward. He has forsaken all hope of describing the events before him. Instead his words bemoan his own failing state. His "I can't talk" is not intended to represent anything or even express anything. The commentator's emotional agitation is so great that he has disengaged himself from the essential features of the communication process, even from the listener. His words are directed to no one in particular and have no identifiable purpose to serve.

In their uselessness, such expressions of bodies-in-pain are exceptional. They deviate from the institutionally established channels that want us to hear all expressions as "conduits of meaning" (Lakoff and Johnson 1980; Lee 1992: 80), mediators of useful information or of sentiment intended by the speaker and sent to the listener. Stepping outside of these institutionally recommended channels, individuals in pain are often oblivious to their listeners. Their complete self-absorption alienates them from the world around. They disregard institutionally approved modes of speaking.

Like the Hindenburg commentator, Manuel Agujetas, singing *seguiriyas*, is focused inward. His whole-body expression is devoted to the task of presenting internal realities that are normally held aside and assumed to be absent from everyday affairs. Not that his self-presentations are supposed to do anything or even mean anything. They are not. Like the Hindenburg commentator, Agujetas is using his voice to introduce his own failed body into the landscape of disasters that is Andalucía.

In his moment of pain, Agujetas resists the rules that govern conventional communicative expressions. Like other singers, his body becomes an engine unto itself. It acts for itself, and often with surprising results. "Things come out of me that I wasn't expecting would come out of me," said José Menese (quoted in Alvarez Caballero 1981: 172).

Flamencologists operating from within the channels of Western expressivity have generally overlooked the importance of the uselessness of *cante quejío* (moaned song). They have continually tried to make *quejíos* mean something or do something. For example, Diaz del Moral complains that "there never appears (in *cante*) any rebellious uprising, any revolutionary impulse, or any urgency for political, social or economic reform" (as summarized by Molina 1985: 49). Herrero (1991: 118) describes *cante* as "hermetic" song. In contrast to jazz, flamenco is closed off, hidden, introverted, and in danger, therefore, of self-suffocation. Gelardo and Belade contend that Andalusian flamenco became, over the past 150 years, toothless. It lost the grit of resistance and the bite of protest during the decadent period of the *cafés cantantes* when, little by little, it was sweetened to please the tastes of the middle classes. Earlier song involved wrenching accounts of life in prison, but the sweetened moan of the *café cantante* substituted the softer themes of love and mother for the gritty theme of life in the prison (1985: 133). In sum, *cante quejío* has been criticized as quietistic and self-indulgent.

Such criticisms take for granted the authority of dominant Western modes of interpreting song. They fail to understand that the "uselessness" of *cante* is its sharpest challenge to an oppressive institutional order that demands of expressions that they serve communicatively useful purposes, and that they mediate communal or competitive social relations. *Cante quejío* floods the floor with the "wonder" of a failed body, leaving witnesses awestruck and bewildered (see Greenblatt 1990: 161ff.), raising awareness levels and producing exhilaration. *Cante quejío* gives pleasure rather than meaning (for more on the pleasures of the voice, see Chanan 1994: 193; Frith 1988: 115; Middleton 1989: 261). It is a voice music, "the materiality of the body speaking its mother tongue" (see Barthes 1977: 188). The words used by Barthes (1977: 181) to describe the sounding body of a Russian church bass apply equally well to the sounding body of a *cantaor*. "Something is there, manifest and stubborn, beyond the meaning of the words, their form, the melisma, and even the style of execution: something which is directly the (*cantaor's*) body, brought to your ears in one and the same movement from deep down in the cavities, the muscles, the membranes."

One can appreciate the "grain of the voice" of a singer like Agujetas by surveying other facets of Andalusian expressive life (see Brandes 1980; Gilmore 1986; 1990) and by appreciating the impact of Spain's economic failure over the past 350 years (Mercado 1982; Mitchell 1990; Weisser 1972) and especially the impact of the repeated failures of liberalizing political movements (Steingress 1993: 201ff.). These stories of past failures explain the appearance of *cante quejío*, but that is not to say that they give it meaning. The "grain of the voice" has no meaning. To persist in the search for meaning of *cante quejío* is to engage in a Procrustean operation of imposing meanings where none exist (for more on such impositions, see Certeau 1988: 250ff.). The "grain of the voice" in *cante quejío* resists conventional modes of musical interpretation. As such, it may also serve as a vehicle of political resistance.[1]

Cante on Television

In the foregoing discussion, *cante quejío* was interpreted without reference to any context of performance. Let us now consider the constraining power of the performance context, the impact of the television broadcast on the reception of *cante*. The fact that the *cantes* of Manuel Agujetas and the *cantes* of the men gathered in the bar in Cádiz are mediated by television encourages viewers to respond to *cante* as conventional song and therefore as a mentalized experience. The video medium reframes *cante* as conventional song, and commentaries throughout the "Rito" documentary series encourage the interpretation of *cante* as either communal or competitive. *Cante* on television comes off as normal song. Semantics is returned to center stage. Corporality is consigned again to the wings. Simon Reynolds would describe this process as a sell-out and not unlike the sell-out of "soul" music:

> Soul was once – a very long time ago – the sound of a psyche breaking up, shattered by desire or loss – a wracked catharsis, an ailing, dejected, broken sound, essentially tragic. Today, soul has become a token of strength of feeling, of strength of being. . . .. Beige

popsters take a vicarious pride in the slow baptism of fire that their chosen genre and its protagonists underwent. Beige vocalists admire and envy the "blacks" for being more in touch with their emotions, their bodies, the unfettered ignorance of their self-expression. . .. Beige vocalists attempt to construct an erstaz black body to signify, what? Health! The vocal dexterity, vigour and power of the soul man amount to. . .passion as workout! In our culture, which sets such a high premium on self-enrichment, the robust, emotive and expressive aspects of soul act as a sort of therapy, helping us to "liberate" ourselves by getting back in touch with ourselves, opening up, unblocking, becoming more functional and therefore (it runs) more free. Under the relentless impact of institutionally mediated forces of interpretation, the broken sound of soul becomes a liberating workout (Reynolds 1990: 82).

The incorporation of examples of *cante* into the "Rito" television series sets flamenco on a path of development not unlike that followed by "soul." The medium of film, being an extension of the stage, encourages viewers to interpret *cante* by way of the interpretive channels of the mainstream. Though the examples of *cante* in these films be resistant expressions, the filmic framing of those examples coopts their powers of resistance, and assimilates them to mainstream communal or competitive songs.

Conclusion

Flamencologists portray flamenco song as heartfelt, sincere, meaningful, even spiritual song, a spiritual journey to the heart of the human condition. Such a view of *cante*, while edifying, fails to accounts for its physicality. When one considers the singers in the films of the "Rito" programs, one discovers a corporality that is conventionally consigned to the margins of musical experience. The intensity and diversity of singers' bodies overshadows the allegedly spiritual mission of *cante*.

In this chapter I have argued that bodies occupy a central rather than a marginal place in *cante*. In moments of music, both rhythmic and painful, the artists' intention become secondary, and their bodies speak for themselves. And wherever bodies speak, it is fruitless to ask what they mean.

Note

1. However, it would be dangerous (Grossberg 1992: 94) to attribute general political significance to *cante* as if it were a consistently applied "anti-structural" force (V. Turner 1969), or a "tactic" (Certeau 1984), or "a countervailing form of positive body awareness" (Leder 1990: 153), or a "hidden transcript" of resistance (Scott 1990) or a "language of resistance" (Doe 1988: 220). Rather, *cante*, like other popular manifestations of the body, is politically ambiguous (see Crowley 1989). Its political valence is negotiated in the concrete events of presentation and uptake.

Chapter 6

Women

In Franco's Spain between 1939–75, flamenco music underwent a radical facelift. Not just flamenco, but all expressions of regional cultural life were swept up in cultural politics that were directed toward the goal of realizing a mystically unified Spain. The diverse traditions, customs, practices and, of course, musics of different regions were represented as elements of the integral body of Spain, analogous to the "Mystical Body" of the Roman Church. It was inevitable that flamenco music, so visible and attractive to people outside of Spain, should have been intensely subjected to this cultural process, and that flamenco should have been transformed into a symbol of Spanish identity.

Dissident artists and scholars expressed their opposition – cautiously at first and then openly after Franco's death – to this thinly veiled co-optation of flamenco music for centralist political purposes. Considering flamenco to be "the characteristic voice of the Andalusian people," they reacted to Franco's *nacionalflamenquismo* as if it were a desecration (see Acosta Sánchez 1979: 40) – *nacionalflamenquismo* was the sneering name they gave to the *franquista* promotion of meretricious spectacles that celebrated the richness of Spanish art while hiding both the poverty and the regional allegiances of the artists. Their resistances to *nacionalflamenquismo* appeared in diverse places and was promoted in a variety ways: José Menese sang songs of protest on university campuses; his lyrics were composed by Francisco Moreno Galván, lyrics that have been described as "passionate battles against irrationality" (Moreno Galván 1993: 7; see also Almazán 1971b); left-leaning magazines such as *Triunfo* published critical commentaries (Almazán 1972; Burgos 1972); and – to zero in on my primary interest – Mario Gómez, Pedro Turbica, and José María Velázquez created the 100-program documentary series "Rito y Geografía del Cante" (1971–3). What makes this last venue of resistance interesting and problematic – if not

Figure 1. José María Velázquez, José Menese and Francisco Moreno Galván in a scene from 'Rito y Geografía del Cante'.

confounding – is the fact that it combined the efforts of many dissident forces and yet it was aired weekly on the heavily censored Spanish National Television network. Predictably, its resistance was hidden beneath its veil of representational imagery, so much so as to challenge viewers to discern the difference between its representations and its resistances. Like so many other efforts of resistance in the history of Spain (Perry 1990; Yovel 1989: 41f.), the "Rito" series is full of irony, a cultural event of extraordinary complexity. Here I will explore some of the subtleties of its resistances to Franco's cultural politics.

"Rito's" resistance was – and had to be – covert and dissembled, but it was effective partly because Franco's cultural politics was simplistic and dichotomous, indeed Manichean, a "politics of original sin" (Steiner 1994), a politics which supposed that "matter, the corporeal, physical bodies in general, obey, or ought to obey, the dictates of the spirit" (Sieburth 1994: 176). Those bent on opposing such a Manichean politics needed only to blur the boundaries of Franco's sharply drawn categories and to obscure the simplistic contrasts that *franquismo* imposed on Spanish social life. In regard to gender, such resistance could consist of nothing more spectacular than disturbing the overly neat *franquista* portrayal of men as public, women as detached, confined, and, except in the absolute privacy of the family, untouchable.

Simplistic contrastive portrayals of gender roles are, of course, far wider and considerably deeper historically than *franquismo*. Franco obviously had no corner on dichotomizing gender theory. Pitt-Rivers, for example, presented the duality of madonna, the private and motherly woman, versus the whore, the public woman, as if it were a central contrast in Mediterranean culture (1977). However, while simplistic dichotomous gender imagery has been conventional in circles that stretch far beyond Franco, nevertheless Franco's use of such imagery was so dramatic, so rigid, and so highly charged with moral value that it deserves the label Manichean.

Here I will revisit discussions of gender and popular culture in the nineteenth century, discussions that prepare the way for understanding the role of gender in Franco's Spain. At that point, I will consider the films of the "Rito" series and the manner in which they quietly but effectively resisted *franquista* gender imagery by diluting and obscuring the moral charge of the

Manichean gender distinctions that were associated with
nacionalflamenquismo.

The Roles of Women in Musical Practice

The contrastive roles of madonna and whore are widely
discussed as cultural fundamentals in Andalusian life (Corbin
and Corbin 1987; Julian Pitt-Rivers 1971: 112–21; Sieburth 1994:
137–87). Women, it is said, are a threat to men. When unconfined,
undisciplined, and unleashed, they become voracious bodies that
threaten to devour men's souls. This imagery may spring from
the earliest roots of Andalusian, if not European, folklore, as
suggested by Pitt-Rivers (1977: 43), or it may harken back to the
early nineteenth century when "women were threatening the
spheres previously occupied only by men," as suggested by
Sieburth (1994: 156). Whatever the source, the imagery is clearly
dichotomous.

Complicating this dichtonomous Andalusian gender imagery
is its association with another cultural dichotomy of reversed
valences, namely highbrow versus lowbrow music. In early
nineteenth-century Spain, though women might be portrayed as
physical threats to masculine spirituality, the musical penchant
attributed to women was credited as rational and progressive.
What we now call highbrow music fell squarely within the
domain of women, and like all the other activities of women, it
was privatized, domesticated, confined. The aesthetic that
dominated such music was Platonist. Musicians sought to
compose and perform a piece that realized a idealized syntactic
plan (see Barry 1987). "Not only opera, but all the large harmonic
forms – symphony, concerto, sonata and tone poem alike – are in
essence psychodramas" (Small 1977: 22). Such rational music
was, like the art of conversation (Burke 1993: 116), increasingly
associated with the interests and styles of aristocratic women,
and accordingly restricted to the household (Leppert 1988: 28ff.).
Indeed, it was considered shameful for distinguished males –
other than dabblers and professionals – to perform music in
public. In England, the Earl of Mornington, father of the Duke
of Wellington, was "the first member of the British aristocracy
who dared to walk through the London streets openly and

unashamedly carrying a violin case" (Leppert 1988: 25). In eighteenth-century France – and therefore in Spain – the trends in highbrow music followed the same course, presenting elite music as the proper domain of women.

Outside the confines of the household, in the streets and plazas of the city, however, that *other* music arose, the male-dominated music of the streets. In the streets, as Hogarth's "The Enraged Musician" suggests, "everything is noise, literal or metaphorical – and added to by the pewterer's shop, hammering on metal, announced by the shop sign at the right (Leppert 1988: 213). This noisy street music of the humble classes, "was ubiquitous, central to their lives in the sense that it seemingly accompanied their every action" (Leppert 1988: 214). Such music inevitably included the component of percussion that had been banished from the reasoned music of the seventeenth century because percussive tones elude rational control – "It was not until late in the seventeenth century that the first percussion instruments were readmitted, the timpani, which could be tuned to a pitch" (Small 1977: 21).

Street music in the cities of eighteenth- and nineteenth-century Europe were, for all intents and purposes, boundary-defining mechanisms. Street music was a noise that made it possible for people to deal with the confusions of urban life. As such, it was integral to public life rather than detached and privatized. And far from being a psychodrama, it was a rambling sound that was used then, as popular music is used now, "as a shield against other people's sounds. . .as a substitute for silence" (Eisenberg 1987: 44).

Some such street music emerged in the public places of late eighteenth-century Andalucía, always in complementary distribution with both the rational music of homelife and the church music of the period (Martin Moreno 1985: 227ff.). It was the music of the brawling popular religiosity of men, the music of boisterous binges carried on in the name of the Virgin, occasions for men to participate in cultural spectacles (Josephs 1983: 124; Steingress 1993: 214). The new atmosphere of cultural conservatism and anti-French *majismo* only encouraged this male-dominated street music. Moreover, in the 1830s and 1840s, this music also served as a symbol for regionalists who, following Herder and the German Romanticists, were eager to locate sources of their distinctive social identity (Burke 1992). From that time to the present, the raw and percussive sounds of flamenco have been celebrated as symbols of Andalusian allegiance. We know about the growing nationalistic popularity of this vulgar lowbrow style in part from Don Preciso's railings, in 1802, against both it and its highbrow counterpart, an Italian operatic style which had at that time become popular (Don Preciso 1982: 21, 199).

Lowbrow popular culture in general, and the noisy percussive street music of flamenco in particular, gained ground in the nineteenth century, it is argued, as the result of some general changes in the roles of women and men, and specifically as a result of the increasing popular fascination with the very dimensions of experience that the aforementioned classical Platonic aesthetic repressed, namely, the physical, the corporeal, the bodily. Urban spaces became increasingly associated with images of "pleasure, excitement, the carnivalesque and disorder" (Featherstone 1991: 25), and with emphases on the repressed lower body that was then associated with women in contrast to the spiritual upper body associated with men:

> In the nineteenth-century bourgeois imagination, the "low" terms of all oppositions blur into an indissociable mass; each is seen as causally linked to others. Thus poverty, illness, dirt, disease, sexuality, animals, the working class, savages, and the prostitute are imagined as inextricably connected. The prostitute become symbolically central to bourgeois fantasy life because she is one channel where everything associated with the "low" can contaminate the "high," bourgeois world. The dread of the low is accompanied by fascination (Sieburth 1994: 143).

Popular culture, then, resulted, from the bourgeois pursuit of this fascination with low womanly physicality (see Huyssen 1986: 44–62).

The bourgeois fascination with "the prostitute" cut two ways. It symbolized the exposure and liberation of what had been repressed, broadly speaking, the liberation of "the female." However, the actual women who participated in this exposure and liberation found themselves confronted by the old antinomies of honor and shame, now even more harshly imposed because of the new economy. Flamenco artists of the late nineteenth and early twentieth centuries lived in a lowbrow underworld dominated by males, a flamenco bar-and-party circuit, a sleazy circumstance excoriated by Salillas (1898) and described in somewhat rosier terms by romanticists such as Hecht (1968), Howson (1965), and Pohren (1980). In its bar-setting, flamenco song rode on waves of alcohol to reach peaks of dubious ecstasy. Mitchell contends that "throughout most of the nineteenth century and a good deal of the twentieth, flamenco music connoted some degree of debauchery or instinctual release" and should therefore be understood less as art than as an "alcohol-assisted catharsis of the ethnic drinking subculture" in Spain (Mitchell 1994: 15, 45). Such ecstatic catharsis mediated by sodden singers may have been acceptable for men, but women were singled out and inevitably relegated to the category of the shameless and the whore. Proper women were said to be out of place in a *juerga* – an all-night binge of song and drink. "A woman's presence in the flamenco bars was not only demeaning for her, it made everyone involved uncomfortable and it interfered with the fluidity of the proceedings. Women were, therefore, fated to be left out of much of the flamenco life of Andalusia" (Pohren 1980: 31).[1] Or if included, they were treated as if they were men, in accordance with general practice in Andalucía: "A woman stripped of her honour becomes a man" (Pitt-Rivers 1977: 45).

The exceptional circumstance that proves the rule with regard to this social norm is the *feria*. Strangely, even paradoxically, seasonal celebrations of the fair and the carnival provide occasions for women to flaunt their culturally defined wildness, their seductive physicality, and their passion, all of which figure so prominently in the popular street life from which they have been all but excluded. In the *feria*, women dress in gaudy and provocative outfits and parade around the fairgrounds situated on the very boundary of the civilized city as it stands against the wild countryside. In this dangerously liminal zone, women, decked out in their racy finery, dance and sing in a way that threatens male self-composure, testing men to the limits of self-discipline, but never beyond (Corbin and Corbin 1987). In contrast to the norm of public street life in which men allow their activities to be infused – unconsciously to be sure – with feminine passion and womanly emotion, the extraordinary postures of fair-going women force men to rethink their quotidian emotionality, inclining them towards a state of passionless and

unflinching self-control, much like the matador who poses with
consummate grace and composure while an enraged bull,
covered with blood and threatening the world with the stench of
death, snaps his horns towards his groin. The role of women in
the *feria* is an exception that explains why women have so often
found no place in the flamenco music of men: a woman's
presence stanches male emotionality, and it does so despite the
historical fact that this male emotionality is derived from an early
nineteenth-century emulation of "the feminine." It is evidently
true that in Andalucía, as elsewhere, men control popular culture
regardless of the significance of women's contributions. Men
were, and are, in the driver's seat, and they typically use their
power to marginalize, exclude, and subordinate women
(Huyssen 1986: 62; Sieburth 1994: 179).

Franco and Women

Franco contributed to this traditional gender imagery with his
Manichean politics, and with his moral reweighing of polarized
gender roles. The effect of such cultural Manicheism on women
was profound. More than merely discriminating against women,
franquista practices virtually annihilated women. In public
affairs, the identity of women was systematically denied
(Hopewell 1986: 113; Yglesias 1977: 95). To be a woman in
Franco's Spain was to be a mother, one who operates within the
realm of the private, and who therefore has *no* standing – not just
less standing – in the public sphere:

> Catholic traditionalism, underwritten by the state, severely limited
> the place of women, relegating them to a sphere defined as narrowly,
> and perhaps more so, than the women's sphere of the nineteenth
> century. Women could aspire to marriage and motherhood but little
> more. The Franco regime literally turned back the clock on the legal
> position of women (Shubert 1990: 214).

With regard to flamenco activities, the Franco years resulted in
the reassertion of the moral imperative of the honor/shame
value complex. On the one hand, *franquista* policies discouraged
the lowbrow cultural circumstances that drew women into
"shamelessness." Flamenco bars in Andalusia, for example, were

nudged out of existence. Simultaneously, the *franquistas* encouraged the development of fraternal associations for the cultivation of interest in flamenco. These fraternities or *peñas* were formed in the 1950s, formalized, licenced, and, one must suppose, subjected to surveillance as were so many similar associations in Spain (Carrillo Alonso 1978: 198; Escribano 1990: 102f.; Hansen 1977: 118). These predominately male clubs focused on the serious – meaning depoliticized – appreciation of the art of flamenco. They provided a forum in which flamenco aesthetes could pursue issues of artistic purity wholly detached from any practical public interests. Such sterile estheticism in flamenco circles was passively complicit with *franquismo* (see Harding 1984: 195ff.). On the other hand, *franquista* policies encouraged the development of flamenco spectacles that presented women as examples of detached femininity and untouchable beauty, and in these respects, women became powerful magnets for tourist dollars.[2]

A remarkably powerful illustration of this traditional gender imagery is visible in the documentary program featuring Gabriel Moreno shown on national television on 31 October 1975, one of a series of programs entitled "Flamenco." The initial credits for this program run across a screen flanked by the profile of a beautiful woman. What is arresting and so deeply disturbing about this imagery is that the woman's profile is not a still photograph that has been made to serve as a screen-framing ornament, but is instead live. Like the living mannequins in a New York City department store, this woman remains fixed and motionless for nearly thirty seconds. Only her occasional eye blinks reveal this beautiful face to be live window-dressing, consciously and intentionally rendered ornamental by the producers of the program. This sort of gender imagery, evident on television, in *tablaos*, and around *peñas*, illustrates the Manichean atmosphere of flamenco life during the Franco regime: men were dominant, and women were detached, sequestered, and unattainable. Lowbrow feminine sexuality was reburied beneath the masculine rationalities of highbrow politics. Feminine regional allegiances – the land and soil of Andalucía are feminine (see Bergamin 1957: 2) – was smothered by a blanket of masculine centralist politics.

Women in the Films of "Rito y Geografia del Cante"

The "Rito y Geografía del Cante" series represented the social scene of flamenco music in the early 1970s while simultaneously resisting it. Its tactics of resistance were covert and rarely explicit. Its subversive intent could always be denied. One arena in which to witness this subtle and deniable form of documentary resistance pertains to the image of women in flamenco music. Specifically, the "Rito" documentarians picked up on some of the tentative and largely unnoticed innovations in both content and style made by female artists in flamenco circles during the Franco years (Molina 1995: 15). By highlighting these innovations throughout the series, the documentarians advanced, against the Manichean gender imagery favored by Franco, a picture of women deeply involved in flamenco while still consummately honorable. The documentarians produced this effect by emphasizing the family as a common and fertile site for musical activity, an emphasis that weakened the longstanding association of flamenco with the complex of "booze-bars-and-babes" while strengthening associations of flamenco with women, wine, and Andalusian family life.

In advance of discussing the reimaging of women in the "Rito" series, it should be noted that not all of its imagery involved a reinvention of women's roles. The series predictably devoted a considerable amount of space to displaying "traditional" flamenco circumstances, that is, to showing the flamenco style associated with *tablaos* (programs nos. 28, 53, 66, 69, 87), and *peñas* (nos 34, 75), and in many of these representations women are decidedly absent or subordinate. For example, it is men alone who are gathered in a tavern in Cádiz for the opening scenes of Fiesta Gitana (no. 14). It is men who huddle around a table in Cádiz, drinking and smoking as if in a private club, while listening to Félix de Utrera and Pericón de Cádiz (no. 79). It is men who are gathered in a somewhat more gentile setting to hear Francisco Palacio Ortega (no. 75). It is just men who are shown listening to Platero de Alcalá (no. 61) and it is just men at the Peña Juan Breva who are shown listening to Diego el Perote (no. 26) and Chato (no. 34). These are scenes of easy fraternity, where men can embrace and even kiss, as Melchor Marchena kisses Francisco Mairena after his *seguiriyas* (no. 21). Women are absent.

Similarly, traditional ideology sometimes peaks through the "Rito" scenes where women are present. In some programs, women are caught somewhere between participant, witness, and decoration, as happens for example in the case of the miniskirted young women who stand alongside Joselero as he sings (no. 68). In other programs, elegant women, clothed in pearls and furs, sit through performances by Beni of Cádiz (no. 56) and through the singing of García Lorca's poems by Beni's older brother Amos (no. 95). These woman seem ill at ease, handling their discomfiture by assuming postures of utter detachment, for example, by picking at a tooth just as the musical intensity has peaked.

While these filmic depictions are conventionally male-centered, nevertheless they never venture into that often parodied domain of masculine activities that includes shameless women. "Rito" programs never mention bordellos or whores despite the fact that such places and such people figured prominently in the history of flamenco. Neither are there scenes of *juergas*, notorious occasions for excessive drinking and shameless womanizing. According to Pedro Turbica, the omission of *juergas* and bordellos from "Rito y Geografía del Cante" is not accidental, but intentional. The series aimed to refurbish the tarnished image of flamenco music, recentering it in the family and household and away from the streets and bordellos. Like García Lorca's writings 50 years earlier, the "Rito" films tried to redeem flamenco, raising it up out of the male-centered debasement into which it had fallen during the Franco years (see García Gómez 1993: 125). The distinctive twist contributed by the "Rito" films to this redemption process was its shift of attention away from flamenco males and toward flamenco females.

Wherever women played central roles in the "Rito" scenes – and that is often – they were presented as pivotal figures, as matriarchs of song. The elderly Fernanda in the program on the Pinini family (no. 19) and the unassuming María La Perrata of the Perrate family (no. 20) were portrayed as central figures who hold their Gitano families together and who make possible the artistry of all their family members (see cover). Tía Anica la Periñaca (no. 80) was portrayed as the pillar of *cante* in Jerez de la Frontera. The *cantaora* María Vargas (no. 42) was essentially – not accidentally or incidentally – a loving mother. Finally, and perhaps most powerfully, Cristobalina Suarez was shown as wife, mother, and *cantaora*. Her performance in program no. 51 ties all three roles together into a single tight knot. In the midst of the furious guitar work of Pedro Bacán, accompanied by hand clapping and table pounding, Cristobalina's powerful voice rings out with tones that – unbelievable though it seems – are soothing to the ears of her son. The child dozes at her breast throughout the performance. The camera zooms in on the sleeping child's face at the conclusion of her song thereby underscoring the significance of the mother–child relationship and securing a significant place for that relationship at the center of flamenco experiences present and past.[3]

Depicted as central figures in flamenco song, "Rito"'s women are active agents, not passive witnesses, and certainly not window dressing for men. For example, in one scene (no. 17) of riotous frivolity in a public place, the bar El Morapio in Sevilla, the focal *bailaora* was portly, elderly and comical. She danced a lascivious *rumba* to the *cante* of Titi of Triana and the guitar of Manolo Brenes in this tavern in Poligono de San Pablo, a Gitano housing project outside of Sevilla. Her antics as a dancer mocked the traditionally conceived "flamenco woman," the beautiful but inactive, unthinking, and untouchable totally self-possessed woman. The footage that presented this mockery of the traditional flamenco female was considered, at the time, to be a flagrant and actionable deviation from *franquista* political imagery – as Pedro Turbica was to discover in a subsequent year when similar footage of Juana la Pipi was pulled by television censors.

Women in the "Rito" films were the linchpins of domestic life, and accordingly, their flamenco song was portrayed as an important component of home life (see no. 10). For example, Lole Montoya (no. 96) was presented in a kitchen, with kids and old folks gathered round a table set with wine. This presentation was particularly riveting because this very beautiful young woman's comportment is completely devoid of the conventional attitudes of either domestic confinement or public alienation – Montoya's performance here virtually launched her long and still very successful career as a *cantaora*. In this humble kitchen surrounded by family, Lole appeared without so much as a hint of lace or frill or spit curl. In contrast to other, more conventional garish and temptingly bare-shouldered presentations of women

– including presentations of las Montoyas themselves in "Rito y Geografía del Baile" – Lole and her kinswomen were shown here as unvarnished, uncultivated, bashfully beautiful women. Her own slightly hesitant style was a refreshing alternative to the conventional feminine air of self-possession that one can discern in the women that appear in Carlos Saura's films (e.g. *Carmen, Amor Brujo, Blood Wedding*).

Among the many factors that facilitated "Rito's" recasting of women in flamenco song, its unusual treatment of alcohol stands out as most interesting. Wine, in these programs, never suggested debauchery, nor did it ever operate as a component of a "drinking subculture." Instead, quite to the contrary, wine symbolized home and family. It was a sacrament of familial unity as illustrated in the photo of the Perrate family gathered in a wine bodega for a session of filming, united around a table set with wine (see cover). Here, wine linked parents and children in moments of song claimed to lie at the very core of flamenco.

That same theme of parent and child mediated by wine was evident in the program (no. 60) on Pedro Lavado, a bar-keep in Puente Genil who easily accommodated his job of dispensing wine to his role as singer and father. Wine, as this program suggests, is itself an art: Pedro Lavado and José María Velázquez visited a local vintner – in one of the few dramatic re-enactments in the "Rito" series – to cultivate both their taste for wine and their taste for song. The transformation of wine into art reaches its culmination in the program devoted to wine (no. 97). Here, somewhat surprisingly, alcoholic intoxication in flamenco circles was explicitly discussed by vintners, aficionados, and *cantaores* who took turns confessing their need for wine. However, consistently throughout this program, wine drinking was handled in the soberest of terms, as a stimulant to song, as a catalyst to artistry, and as a lubricant for performances. Never was there a reference to drunkenness, but always to artistic elevation. The ugliness, the grotesque vulgarity, the lewdness, and the obscenity of the debauched *juergas* of the past were here transformed into moments of alcohol-assisted artistry (see Escribano 1990: 23; Mitchell 1994: 42, 133). Transformed in the "Rito" films, wine became a rite (a *rito*) of Andalusian family life rather than a stain left over from Andalusian bar life. Indeed, in every single one of "Rito's" presentations of families gathered for song, wine was on the table in the foreground. Alcohol was evidently a staple of domestic life, presented here as an emblem of domesticity, always, it seems, leading viewers back to the family relations that were being played up in the "Rito" series.

Conclusion

This film series portrayed women as matriarchs of flamenco, a portrayal which, though undramatic, nevertheless cut against the grain of *nacionalflamenquismo*. The "family-centered" flamenco of this series, with its celebrations of flamenco mothers, children at the breast, and of flamenco fathers encouraging their children to participate in family songfests, was a tacit but effective response to the *nacionalflamenquista* imagery of the Franco years. Paradoxically, the shrewdness of this resistant response lay in its complicity with so many other aspects of Franco's cultural politics. "Family," for example, was a theme of central importance in *franquismo*, so much so that family-centeredness was parodied by the dissident filmmakers of the period (D'Lugo 1994: 96). By using family to cloak their revisionary images of flamenco, the "Rito" filmmakers managed to oppose *franquismo* while seeming to comply. As with all such paradoxical maneuvers, the filmmakers blended selective remembering with tactical forgetting, thereby producing a documentary treatment, which, though a distortion of the history of flamenco, was remarkably productive. Its documentary distortions owe less to carelessness about the past, than to eagerness to build a new future. The emphasis on domestic life rather than on bar life, on sobriety rather than on drunkenness, and on the respectability of females rather than on their sexual attractiveness, constituted a powerful "remembrance" – in Myerhoff's sense of that term – a narrative that reweaves and reintegrates the broken strands of history so as to create a story that might operate effectively, as Dandelion's stories in *Watership Down* operated, to confront contemporary dangers (see Doe 1988: 205; Myerhoff 1982). The fact that the filmmakers made liberal use of selective emphases in presenting these remembrances should not render the series particularly liable to claims that it is unfaithful as a document of history. On the contrary, these "Rito" films embody the principle only lately popularized among social scientists, that documents of memory often make inventive uses of the past for the purpose of "willing backward" the future (Nichols 1994; Nora 1989; Rabinowitz 1994; Terdiman 1993).

Notes

1. Scholarly attempts aimed at rescuing and recuperating the role of women in flamenco have largely consisted of enumerations of the virtues of celebrated *cantaoras* such as Mercedes la Serneta, Pastora Pavón "Niña de los Peines," Anica la Periñaca, and Bernarda and Fernanda de Utrera (Arrebola 1988), though some recent efforts have attempted to discover a vital role played by eighteenth- and nineteenth-century women in preserving and elaborating flamenco song (Auf de Heyde 1995; Catarella 1993: 133).
2. *Tablaos*, for example, were instituted, starting in 1954 with the opening of the "Zambra" in Madrid (Alvarez Caballero 1994: 129). A *tablao* is essentially a bar in which the musical spectacle is emphasized to the point of swamping out all other activity, including conversation. The participants in *tablaos* were primarily foreign tourists predisposed to take in a spectacle.
3. This scene is reminiscent of a similar scene near the end of Edgar Neville's *Duende y Misterio del Flamenco* (1952) in which a young Gitana sings *bulerías* while seated next to her husband, whose clapping hands are wrapped around the waist of their naked child of about 8 months of age. Note that in Neville's film, it is the man who holds the child. This silent smiling young Gitano, and not the woman, is the critical link in family relationships and the symbol of family unity. The woman, decorated in a brightly colored dress, is detached from her husband and child as she concentrates on her song.

Chapter 7

Anglo Perspectives on Flamenco Music

Over the past 100 years, flamenco music has attracted historians, musicians, politicians, poets, and essayists of many stripes. The bulk of these writers have been Spanish. However, Anglo writers, since the time of George Borrow and Richard Ford, in the first half of the nineteenth century, have rarely been reluctant to offer their comments on Spain, Andalucía, and flamenco music. Much of this literature is embarrassingly primitivist and orientalist. For example, Havelock Ellis, writing in 1908, contended that:

> The Spanish character is fundamentally. . .savage. . .His childlike simplicity and intensity of feeling, his hardness and austerity coupled with disdain for the superfluous, his love of idleness tempered by the aptitude for violent action, his indifference to persons and interests outside the circle of his own life – these characteristics and the like, which have always marked the Spaniard, mark also the savage (Ellis 1908: 36f.).

About ten years later, Somerset Maugham pursued a similar theme:

> Daylight was waning as I returned, but when I passed the olive-grove, where many hours before I had heard the malaguena, the same monotonous song still moaned along the air, carrying back my thoughts to the swineherd. I wondered what he thought of while he sang, whether the sad words brought him some dim emotion. How curious was the life he led! I suppose he had never travelled further than his native town; he could neither write nor read. Madrid to him was a city where the streets were paved with silver and the King's palace was of fine gold. He was born and grew to manhood and tended his swine, and some day he would marry and beget children, and at length die and return to the Mother of all things. It seemed to me that nowadays, when civilisation has become the mainstay of our lives, it is only with such things as these that it is possible

to realise the closeness of the tie between mankind and nature. (Maugham 1920: 27).

With his attention fixed on Gypsies and their music, Irving Brown wrote with words that were not much less alienating: "Deep in our hearts we should envy this untamed, passionate race that has never grown up" (1929: 18). And as recently as 1955, V.S. Pritchett argued that "Although Spain often looks like a modern country, it is not. The life of Spanish cities runs much closer to what life was like in England in the seventeenth century" (1955: 180).

Very little, in these anglophone commentaries, stands up to the test of time. Most of them are at once too rich in Anglo ideas about nature and culture and too sparing when it comes to self-reflection and self-criticism. However, two recent works, by Woodall (1992) and by Mitchell (1994), seem more promising than most. Here I will evaluate these works comparing each to the other, and contrasting them both with the Spanish language treatments of the flamenco style.

Spanish Flamencology

Spanish-language treatments of the flamenco style – starting around 1880 – can, as suggested in the preface, be divided into three parts: popularizations, negative criticisms, and genealogical and classificatory appreciations. In the late nineteenth century, the largely negative commentaries of Spanish writers reflected a combination of interests, including an anxious search for a folklore to support nationalistic interests (e.g. Antonio Machado y Alvarez and his sons Manuel and Antonio), and an equally anxious effort to weed out cultural vulgarities from the stock of Spanish culture (e.g. Eugenio Noel 1916), all coupled with a critical interest in cultivating popular music for the twentieth century. As a vehicle of national interest, flamenco's value rose along with the interest in regional folklore and common customs (*costumbrismo*). But, flamenco's status as an art form came in for protracted debate, especially in the popular press, for its vulgarity (see Ríos Ruiz 1993: 37ff.). Intellectuals such as Unamuno and Ortega y Gasset added to the ongoing journalistic vilifications of flamenco by contending that not only is flamenco a moral blemish on Spain, but it is a cultural one as well. Flamenco, they said, was a cheap and culturally debilitating sideshow that was partly responsible for the fecklessness of modern Spanish culture – *la pandereta de España*. In the 1920s, artists like Manuel de Falla and Federico García Lorca fought valiantly – though often rashly (see Grande 1992b) – to parry these criticisms. Their objective was to celebrate a core of flamenco, to cull the riff-raff and to transform the carnivalesque events of flamenco into moments of high art. Arguing from analogous developments in American theater (Levine 1988), one might say that the waxing and waning of flamenco popularity in Spanish writings of this period is a sign of the ongoing struggle over class boundaries within Spain and of the efforts to enhance the international standing of Spain vis-á-vis other countries. It is also the result of the emergence of a consumer society in which works of art were handled as commodities.

During the Franco years between 1939 and 1975, a number of Spanish scholars promoted flamenco as a promising symbol of Spanish national identity (see the *nacionalflamenquismo* that is excoriated by Alvarez Caballero 1992). Other scholars undertook what they assumed was an essentially apolitical activity of charting the history, establishing the genealogy, and refining the categories of *cante*. This latter labor was consistent with the objective of the *Concurso* of 1922 to legitimate flamenco as a high art. Still, other writers took advantage of the silence that was imposed in this historical period to follow out alternative paths of survival and resistance (see Fuentes 1992: 339) to rethink the notions of resistance, marginalization and flamenco music (see for example Caballero Bonald 1975; Molina 1981; Ortiz Nuevo 1985). Throughout all of these phases, the impresarios of commercial flamenco took advantage of tourism to keep flamenco performances afloat. Two recently revised broad accounts of flamenco music through which to sample these Iberian angles on flamenco are Alvarez Caballero (1994) and Ríos Ruiz (1993).

When we juxtapose the books of Alvarez Caballero and Ríos Ruiz with similarly broad anglophone accounts of flamenco by Woodall and Mitchell, some stunning contrasts begin to emerge. Built on the long-lived and somewhat embarrassing tradition of anglophone scholarship, the latter works aim to produce accurate accounts devoid of stereotypical biases, accounts that will contribute to flamenco studies instead of standing quaintly apart. However, what is striking about these works is the degree to which they are driven, without wishing to be driven, by some very familiar anglophone interests. Specifically, Woodall and Mitchell pursue markedly Anglo fascinations with populist and sentimentalist ideas. As a result, readers are bound to be frustrated if they come to these two English books with expectations of finding a recapitulation of Spanish scholarship or, a fortiori, with hopes of reading theoretically impartial accounts of the flamenco style.

The works of Woodall and Mitchell are opposites, like light and dark, like day and night. Woodall's daylit book is a touristic and populist work that presents flamenco as a powerfully attractive haven for homeless souls in a heartless world. Mitchell's dark and brooding book is a demystification that seems bent on stripping away all the attractiveness that writers like Woodall might try to cultivate in flamenco. Mitchell sets himself to the task of exposing and rendering transparent the oppressiveness of the social system in which flamenco developed. In the end, a close reading of Woodall and Mitchell pushes one to reflect on our own Anglo world – both light and dark – as much as it facilitates an appreciation of the world of Andalucía and flamenco music. These books are important more for what they reveal about the social forces in the English-speaking world than for their potential to enlighten one about Spain and flamenco.

In Search of the *Firedance*

Woodall's book is a emotionally charged presentation – as opposed to a detached representation – of flamenco. His is an historical account of the remote forces that influenced flamenco performances of the past and of the proximate forces that have shaped twentieth-century developments of this popular art form. Always, Woodall's writing betrays his love for and commitment to flamenco music and flamenco musicians.

No English-language discussion prior to Woodall's work compares to it in breath of coverage.[1] The chapters on Muslim Spain and on flamenco performance in the first half of the twentieth century are particularly helpful. Woodall, however, is less convincing when he operates as an art critic assessing the relative merits of the early and late Paco de Lucía or the performances of dancers in the *tablaos* of Madrid.

Having acknowledged the fire in *Firedance*, I should note that this book stands betwixt-and-between two major Anglo audiences. The book has evidently soared above the heads of the popular audience of flamenco *aficionados* – at least in America and if one accepts the judgment of Guillermo Salazar (1993) – but it operates beneath and below the level of most Anglo scholars, a conclusion one can draw from the fact that few scholarly journals have reviewed it. Regarding its reception by popular readers, Salazar claims that *In Search of the Firedance* has too many chapters that exceed the popular reader's attention span, e.g. lengthy discussions of historical figures, and balanced and disciplined, rather than doctrinaire, treatments of etiological controversies. In short, Woodall's work is a serious effort to describe and appreciate flamenco music; and, as such, it has evidently been received by popular *aficionados* about as well as a history of punning would be received by an audience at a local comedy club. Most of the people who pick up books like Woodall's are predisposed to contribute minimal intellectual effort for a maximal emotional payoff from reading about flamenco music.

At the same time that Woodall's handling of flamenco history and aesthetics eludes popular readers, his approach to flamenco as a cultural phenomenon "underwhelms" serious scholars, and in the end, alienates the very individuals with whom he might collaborate productively in the study of flamenco. The particular scholars I refer to are those who claim an interest in "popular culture".[2] Their interests are altogether congruent with a major theme in Woodall's treatment of flamenco, namely, that flamenco song is a creative and resistant voice of oppressed and marginalized people. However, beyond sharing an interest in the resilience of the downtrodden with popular culture scholars, Woodall operates with little or nothing of their style and purpose.

For one thing, "popular culture" studies typically devote more space to debating the possibility of, and constraints on, creative resistances by marginalized people than to promoting such resistances, so much so that some have criticized these studies for "giving voice to intellectuals discussing the texts of other intellectuals" rather than giving voice to the downtrodden (Handler 1993: 994). Woodall's book avoids this elitist detachment insofar as it devotes all of its energies to the task of explicating and encouraging flamenco music. But while one could credit Woodall for eschewing elitist discussions, the downside of Woodall's non-elitism is that he is often insensitive to theoretical issues and unable to stand outside of his own assumptions and presuppositions for a fresh take on flamenco.

For example, Woodall leads off his book with the sentence: "modern Spain is a country of noise." Naively, he brushes pass the term "noise" – a term of seismic theoretical significance – so that he can get to the substantive issues he has in mind, namely, the welter of Islamic, Jewish, and Gitano influences that bear on flamenco music. In failing to weigh out the theoretical value of the term "noise," Woodall passes up the opportunity to discuss the most resistant and oppositional features of this style, at least according to scholars Attali (1985), Bailey (1986), Paulson (1988), and Reynolds (1990). Or perhaps he has decided to avoid these matters as too abstract and high flown. But in either case, he has, by his default, alienated students of popular culture. This is just one instance among many wherein Woodall, with hand to plough in the field of flamenco, turns over theoretical diamonds that he ignores in his eagerness to get his crop planted.

Woodall's work is also distinct from studies of popular culture in style. Popular culture studies pursue a rational presentation different from journalistic presentation and different too from the militant rhetoric of the downtrodden. Woodall, however, unlike popular culture scholars, writes a fresh and lively prose that is considerably lighter than the scholarly style of many popular culture studies. But, though his prose is creditably approachable, Woodall's writing incurs its own set of problems. Consider, for example, one of Woodall's highly recognizable manners of presentation, namely, touristic exposition. To put it simply, Woodall often goes about his work as if he were a travel writer.[3] As such and in the long tradition of European travel writing (Mitchell 1988: 26), Woodall's style sets the reader apart from flamenco, thereby rendering flamenco an object of the touristic gaze. Paradoxically, this touristic style also draws the reader into intimacy with flamenco by providing a profusion of unnecessary details that convey a sense of immediate presence to flamenco experiences (see Barthes 1989: 141–8). In Woodall's writing the stylistic vacillation between detachment from, and intimate presence to, flamenco is hidden under the cloak of his own personal fascination with the art – even as Walter Starkie (1935) hid a similar vacillation under his cloth cloak when he traveled through Spain disguised as a Gypsy (see Mitchell 1988: 27). As a result of this hidden vacillation in Woodall's touristic rhetoric, his words operate, not as the transparent windows on the world of flamenco music that they seem to be, but as tools for constructing flamenco as an exotic object. Of such rhetorically constructed objects, Timothy Mitchell – a different Mitchell, one who has written about Egypt rather than about Spain – says "one transfers into the object the principles of one's relation to the object" (Mitchell 1988: 28), thereby creating an exotic "Other."

The most general problem presented by Woodall's book is summarized by McGuigan's (1992) term "uncritical populism." Woodall's treatment of flamenco may be initially attractive for its non-elitist support for the cultural underdog and for celebrating the creative and resistant flamenco voice "singing of the ancient dispossession of a race (and) for salvation from the conditions of poverty and abandonment, from the pain of prejudice and social oblivion" (Woodall 1992: 115). But his book founders for lack of an appreciation of the linkage between that flamenco voice and the economic and political conditions in which that voice is produced (McGuigan 1992: 76). It stumbles because it assumes readers need not concern themselves to confront the unjust and oppressive economic and political system that undergirds that flamenco voice. It assumes that marginalized flamencos will inevitably raise their own resistant voices with inscrutable effectiveness (see Grossberg 1988: 18). In fairness to Woodall, however, his uncritical populism is far from being unique or isolated. Collins (1989: 23), Grossberg (1992: 86), and McGuigan (1992: 76) claim that similar quietistic positions are all too common in popular culture studies because of overemphasis – at least within the Birmingham tradition – on matters of pleasure and consumption in social theory and because of a failure to attend to the conditions in which subaltern voices, so eagerly consumed, are produced (for a comment to the contrary though see Bryan Turner 1992: 203).

Besides encouraging quietism, Woodall's book encourages sentimentalism. Uncritical populists like Woodall encourage "solidarity with ordinary people's capacity to win space from below" (McGuigan 1992: 171), despite the fact that often such a capacity for resistance is stymied or completely absent. Such encouragement verges on sentimentalism because it is necessarily selective. While Woodall encourages flamenco voices, he also ignores the many other instances where oppressed people do not – because they cannot – resist. Second, uncritical populists like Woodall take advantage of the confusions of our postmodern cultural life to encourage what Grossberg calls "sentimental inauthenticity" (see also Featherstone 1991: 72). Woodall operating in a world bereft of epistemological foundations, lacks "the ability to distinguish the relative merit of any site of investment (and, as a result) celebrates the magical possibility of making a difference against impossible odds" (Grossberg 1988: 45). Flamenco is held out as just such a magical object to which readers can attach themselves with all of the emotional intensity that, in other eras, was reserved for commitments to eternal verities: "It is the 'intensity of life' that counts in flamenco" (Woodall 1992: 331), "a search for the most galvanising and most euphoric expression of happiness and despair" (Woodall 1992: 329). That Woodall encourages such emotional attachment is an indication of the sentimentalist agenda behind his writing.[4]

Flamenco Deep Song

Mitchell's book stands a pole apart from Woodall's uncritical populism. In contrast to Woodall's attachment to flamenco, Mitchell is consummately and explicitly detached. He is not an artist or even an *aficionado*, but a "hermit" who stands apart from the flamenco scene hoping to produce an unbiased "revelation of the whole social picture of flamenco" (1994: 26). Far from being an uncritical scholar, Mitchell is super-critical, speaking without any apparent hesitation of "the foul river of flamenco. . .the hot, molten core of depraved folklore. . .sinful flamenco. . .the aesthetic result of the codependency syndrome that prevailed between power-abusing, substance-abusing libertines and their singing, dancing, guitar-strumming menials" (1994: 47, 215). Mitchell's book inhabits a world apart from Woodall's, but whether his world is objective, impartial, and bias-free is another matter.

Mitchell's work offers all that Woodall's does not in the way of structural conditions that undergird the production of flamenco song. Flamenco song, he claims, arose and persists because it is a spectacle through which oppressed people voice their misery in such a way as to evoke expressions of guilt-driven pity from wealthy listeners. *Cante*, on this account, performs a double catharsis, relieving the pain of the poor and the guilt of the wealthy (1994: 107, 137). The upshot is this: both the poor and the wealthy, having been unleashed from their psychological burdens, can walk away content with the world as it is. Hence, flamenco song is fundamentally a homeostatic device that knits together a bipolar society.

Mitchell has given an enormous amount of scholarly energy over to the task of filling in the details of this argument. He has, for example, delved deeply into historical records for evidence of the contributions of blind balladeers, professional moaners, and other disenfranchized non-Gitano Andalusians to the flamenco song style (1994: 78ff.). He has demonstrated the impact of Italian opera singers on lower-class Andalusian proto-flamenco singers who then attracted the interest of the upper classes who were trying to distance themselves from the middle classes in the early nineteenth century – classically structuralist social hydraulics (1994: 120f.). He has offered evidence for the essential role of *señoritos* in the development of flamenco (1994: 178–196). They lavished wealth on impoverished artists, but simultaneously victimized those artists with a deprecatory humor (*gracia*) that is said to be endemic to Andalucía. This whole perverse ensemble was justified in the twentieth century by what Mitchell calls "deliberate regression," that is, an appeal to the purifying zone of the unconscious (1994: 163; see Harbison 1980: xv for the definitive characterization of "deliberate regression").

The role played by Gitanos in the development of this regressive flamenco music comes in for uniform derogation. Mitchell pays lip service to the idea that ethnicity is discursively constructed, but he persists in making an orthographic distinction between "Andalusians" and "gitanos" – some ethnicities are evidently constructed in uppercase and others in lowercase – and in using phrases such as "catchall category of gitano" (1994: 53) and "quasi-ethnic group" (1994: 129). He relies on Manuel Barrios' argument that seventeenth-century Moriscos escaped the very long arm of Spanish Inquisitorial law by passing as Gitanos, thereby confusing the Gitano identity (1994: 55). Additionally, he contends that the alleged Gitano language, *caló*, was neither Gitano nor Romany, but a product of romanticizing writers of the eighteenth and nineteenth centuries (1994: 58).[5]

Ironically, however, the Gitanos who seemed so ill-defined in Mitchell's history of the eighteenth century become well enough defined as the sycophantic professionals exploiting commercial flamenco in the nineteenth. The very group that lacked sufficient identity to contribute to early development of flamenco, suddenly constructed a identity that is clear enough to be fingered for its later degradation. Mitchell does not actually say that Gitanos were primarily responsible for injecting cultural rottenness into the core of the tradition of Andalusian song (1994: 147), but he does not resist the temptation to allow others to say it for him (1994: 213). As Mitchell see it, the *gitanismo* that García Lorca celebrated as the cure for febrile Spain in 1922, was far from being a vaccine, but was instead the virus itself. The Gitano contributions to flamenco music had aggravated, rather than obviated, the tawdry commercialism that symbolized the moral emptiness of Spain at the end of the nineteenth century (see 1994: 175f.).

Finally, Mitchell contends that the significant developments in twentieth-century flamenco were made, not by Manuel Torre and Antonio Mairena with their promotion of an authentic Gitano musical heritage, but by Juan Breva, Antonio Chacón and Pepe Marchena, who, responding to the redistribution of wealth in Spain, brought flamenco to Madrid, raised it out of the murk of "deliberate regression," and tapped into "a free-floating interclass melancholy that effectively transcended the old traumas" (1994: 223). Through these developments, according to Mitchell – the accounts of Ricardo Molina and other "gitanophiliacs" notwithstanding – flamenco escaped from its oppressive Spanish roots and enter into the larger circle of world music.

Mitchell's writing encourages readers to regard flamenco as a theater of guilt and victimization, and not anything like Woodall's spectacle of liberating passion. Nevertheless, a certain sentimentalism also marks the form of Mitchell's work, a Marxist brand of sentimentalism that consists in a search for unity in a social system, the utopist's unity presupposed by Marxist and functionalist social theory (Geoghegan 1987). Associated with

this search for unity are: first, Mitchell's overemphasis on the role
of ideas in the operation of a social system; second, his quest to
explicate ideas and to render them transparent; and third, his
assumption that systemic ideas are inevitably imposed on
subjects rather than constructed by agents.

First, and regarding the overemphasis on ideas, Mitchell
portrays the flamenco world as being held together by a vicious
ideology, that is, a set of victimizing ideas and immobilizing
emotions. While the workings of this vicious ideology are
apparent in the spectacles of flamenco music, they are also
apparent in other cultural venues such as bullfighting (Mitchell
1991), Holy Week religiosity (Mitchell 1990), and popular rites
such as *moros y cristianos* (García Gómez 1993: 184–7; Mitchell
1988). In other words, the vicious ideology of Andalusian social
life is a unified comprehensive and, in Mitchell's words, "pervasive ideology" that orders, however oppressively, the full gamut
of Andalusian cultural activities (Mitchell 1994: 21). This characterization of ideology as a totalizing system of ideas enables
him to portray Andalucía as implicitly and underlyingly unitary.
But, as Eagleton says of the "long tradition of Western Marxism,"
Mitchell's book is one in which "ideas are alloted too high a
status" (Eagleton 1991: 36). As a result of this allotment, the unity
that Mitchell finds in the Andalusian ideology is, however dark,
a sentimentalistic unity. Mitchell's handling of Andalusian social
life would benefit by his spending as much energy discussing
fragmenting practices as he spends discussing unifying ideas,
because ideology, as Eagleton argues, is not "some body of
doctrine, some set of moralizing discourses or ideological
'superstructure,' which keeps the system ticking over. . .[but is]
the routine material logic of everyday life" (Eagleton 1991: 37).

Second, Mitchell seems to pursue the explication of the
Andalusian ideology on the Rousseauean assumption that all
hiddenness is, by nature, vicious and that all transparency is, by
nature, benevolent (see Starobinski 1988 on Rousseauean
transparency). He seems not to countenance the possibility that
"there may be positive kinds of unconscious motivation and
positive forms of functionalism. . . . The fact that a motivation is
concealed, in other words, is not enough in itself to suggest
falsity" (Eagleton 1991: 25). And he seems not to allow for the
possibility that downtrodden Andalusians can and do themselves recognize the injustices in their lives, even as "the majority

of people have a fairly sharp eye to their own rights and interests" (Eagleton 1991: 27).

Finally, Mitchell treats Andalusians as if they were dupes and
patsies of some despicable Andalusian ideology, a treatment that
prompts one to wonder how he understands the agency of
"subjects." In earlier works, he had outlined some criticisms of
sociological automaticity according to which individuals are
pawns of the system (1991: 44), but here that criticism seems to
evaporate. Only dupes and automatons could be on his mind.
What else can one make of his claim that "the reduced role of
nongitanos to that of mere bit players (has been) enthusiastically
seconded by so many nongitano intellectuals. . .because racial
mystification was compatible with their tardo-romantic art
religion" (1994: 216)? Did he never consider the possibility that a
non-Gitano intellectual such as José Caballero Bonald was
capable of making tactical uses of *gitanismo* to mount a resistance
to *franquismo*? Did he never entertain the possibility that the
behaviors of such scholars might be ironic and multidimensional
(see Bauman and Briggs 1993: 66; Collins 1989: 18; Fiske 1993: 21;
Scott 1990: 70ff.)? It does not take a postmodernist to recognize
that ideology is not so much an imposition as a dialog (Eagleton
(1991: 193ff.). "Even an authoritarian discourse is addressed *to*
another and lives only in the other's response, and (therefore)
any ruling power requires a degree of intelligence and initiative
from its subjects" (Eagleton 1991: 46).

Notes

1. The anecdotal books by Donn Pohren (1984; 1988) have served
   as the mainstay of anglophone knowledge about flamenco for
   the past thirty years. However, while Woodall's work is a
   giant step of systematic description beyond Pohren's, it has its
   shortcomings. For one thing, with such broad descriptive
   strokes, Woodall's coverage of issues is sometimes annoyingly
   thin and occasionally erroneous. His treatment (1992: 111f.) of
   the social and historical context of the songs of the Levant

(*las tarantas, los tarantos, murcianas* and *cartageneras*) is weak (compare Cruces Roldán 1993), and his coverage of "Latin-American-based forms" (1992: 109) is sketchy at best (compare Molina and Espín 1992).

Errors are occasionally hidden beneath a camouflage of effusive rhetoric, as, for example: "It would take a labour of Hercules to give a mechanical breakdown of Antonio's triumphs in these years (1950s). He went everywhere and did everything a Spanish dancer could do, using the vast extent of Spain's dance forms – classical, academic, folkloric, flamenco – to create a new ballet each year. He kicked off with his *martinete*, the song-form that until his time existed only for voice and anvil-struck accompaniment; he unleashed it, with Antonio Mairena singing and striking the anvil, in a film called Duende y misterio de flamenco" (p. 237f.). Besides having misspelled Edgar Neville's film title, Woodall has allowed his creativity, here, to get ahead of his perception: Antonio was accompanied, not by Antonio Mairena, but by Pedro Jiménez "El Pili" who sang in a *compás* marked by Antonio's footfalls rather than by anvil-strikes.

2. Generally, these scholars labor in the wake of landmark writings of E.P. Thompson (1963), Raymond Williams (1958), Richard Hoggart (1957), and Stuart Hall (Hall and Whannel 1964), and they consume the writings of Iain Chambers (1986; 1994), John Fiske (1987; 1989; 1993), Lawrence Grossberg (1988; 1992), Dick Hebdige (1979; 1987), Jim McGuigan (1992), and Richard Middleton (1989).

Hebdige's treatment of Jamaican popular music in *Cut'n Mix* (1987) is similar in some respects to Woodall's treatment of flamenco. Like Woodall's book it is historical in content, and emphasizes the social development of an often misunderstood style of popular music.

3. "The Judería is today famous for its small white houses fronted by abundant overspills of flowers. Most famous of all is the callejón de las Flores, a delightful cul-de-sac speckled with pinks, purples, reds and blues in flowerpots handing from the windows, and from where you have a startlingly close view of the Mezquita tower. Thread your way from here on the north side of the Mezquita and you will come to the remains of the tiny synagogue, the only mark left in Córdoba of its once thriving community of Jews" (Woodall 1992: 34).

4. In addition to encouraging an intense emotional attachment to flamenco music, Woodall's work encourages readers to spend time and effort in acquiring a taste for flamenco. Such expenditure of time and effort is, as Featherstone (1991: 18) notes, socially significant because it helps to establish boundaries of social class.

   While Woodall encourages readers to spend time and effort towards cultivating an emotional attachment to flamenco, he does not emphasize the rare, secretive, and exclusive character of that music as do Hecht (1994) or Pohren (1980), for whom flamenco aesthetics is marked by exclusivism as well as by inauthenticity sentimental. The logic of such exclusivism has been explored by Appadurai who notes that "with luxury commodities like oriental rugs, as the distance between consumers and producers is shrunk, the issue of exclusivity gives way to the issue of authenticity" (Appadurai 1986: 44). Hence, the urgency in the writings of Hecht and Pohren to unearth and embrace authentic flamenco performance.

5. Barrios argued that Andalusian Gitanos entered Andalucía by way of North Africa prior to Romanichal migrations into Western Europe, and therefore never spoke either Romany or *caló* (Barrios 1989: 31).

Chapter 8

Music, Resistance, and Popular Culture

Many movements of resistance have unfolded over the past two thousand years of Western history. The clearest and most forceful of these resistances were powered by music. Recall the Albigensian troubadours in the twelfth century, the Franciscan poets in the thirteenth, the Protestant hymnists in the sixteenth, the labor-organizing balladeers of the 1930s, the anti-establishment rockers of the 1960s, and, of course, the *antifranquista* flamencos of the early 1970s. All these musics have been praised as authentic, not so much because they were faithful reflections of some deep dark past, but because they were sincere productions of humans struggling to better their lot in the face of viciousness.

Authentic music puts the starch into popular resistance. For most of us who grew up in the midst of the struggles of the 1960s, such musics are to be cherished, and the musicians, so sincere and courageous, are to be emulated. But where have these authentic musics and these courageous musicians gone? Where are they now when we need them in the 1990s?

Our nostalgia rises to a peak of poignancy when we consider the unusual condition of our post-Soviet/capitalist-China world. The absence of global clashes between diametrically opposed political philosophies has coincided with a decline of the Left, creating a grand confusion amongst those of us who would resist forces of oppression. Today, we are hard put to say who or what should be resisted. No longer do we wage battle against the Draconian statism of the Soviets and, simultaneously, against the American military–industrial–capitalist opposition to that statism. Instead our resistances are fractured into a confusing welter. Some of our movements oppose the domination of the female by the male. Others resist the domination of nature by people. Still others resist the understructure of domination by critiquing the institutions and philosophies that muddy the vision of those trying to identify the sources of domination. We are cursed, it seems, by a plethora of dominations none of which overshadows others in the way that, say, Francoism dominated all other dominations in Spain between 1939 and 1975. As a result of this curse, we are damned if we do and damned if we don't. We can throw all of our energies into resisting sexism, but then we are liable to an accusation of apathy with respect to the ecological crisis. We can devote ourselves to confronting the terrors of human demography but then we will be accused of blindness to the roots of domination.

The study of popular music faces out onto this landscape of confusion. The problem is not that our contemporary popular music is devoid of political motives and social concerns. On the contrary, our songs overflow and threaten to drown us with too much oppositional rhetoric. The problem, some say, is that this overflowing opposition has no center. Contemporary popular music lacks cohesion and integrity. It talks resistance, but it offers no substance. And just below the surface of its feckless rhetoric lies darker realities, not the least of which is that oppositional song-sters are parleying their rhetorics of resistance into mountains of money. Is it any wonder that contemporary scholars find themselves casting a nostalgic glance backwards to times when tactics of resistance were fiercely imagined and boldly deployed? Did not periods of clear and singular oppression sharpen the vision of those who suffered and sang, enabling them to advance unified and cohesive programs with their songs?

This study of the flamenco music, especially the music recorded in Spain in the early 1970s, gives us an occasion for reflecting on just these questions, forcing us to face squarely our own aspirations for popular movements and for the popular music that fuels them. We have seen that Spain during this period was an altogether familiar place. Like North America in the 1960s and 1970s, Spain housed movements of resistance, currents of compliance, and, overarching both, commercialization processes. North Americans had Bob Dylan and Pat Boone, and both raked in money with their astounding record sales. Similarly, Andalucía had Jose Menese and Manolo Escobar and both made bundles of money. However, what distinguished Spain from North America of this same period is the intensity of the oppression. *Franquista* hegemony was so intrusive that it silenced labor unions, muzzled the press, and induced paranoia from Barcelona to Cádiz. In this atmosphere, every aspect of public life was played out with heightened intensity. Compliance and resistance were italicized. The banalities of Spanish popular music were painfully evident. Compliant music was a blandishment for the oppressive regime. But, the music of resistance was as "authentic" as could be found anywhere. At least, so it seems with hindsight.

Appearances, however, are not to be trusted. We have seen, for example, that the oppositional voice of flamenco was frequently hidden beneath a variety of different cloaks, including regional allegiance, ethnic pride, romanticism, and spiritualism. This confusing array of flamenco images puts a huge stumbling block in the path of contemporary commentators who struggle to make sense of flamenco in the 1960s and who often enough end up criticizing musicians and aficionados for failing to motivate opposition or to move people to resist (Gelardo and Belade 1985; Herrero 1991). What, they ask, were the "Rito" authors doing while Spain suffered under the ham-fisted politics of Franco? Were these dreamy-eyed aficionados just frittering away their energies, swooning over the passions of the past?

Such critical commentary is both unrealistic and danger-ous. . .unrealistic because musical resistance under Franco had to be covert. In Catalonia, for example, the "new song movement" or *nova cançó* was largely reliant on the tacit understanding of listeners. Considered in isolation, "the songs were harmless, often innocuous, and at worst, obscure. The meanings attributed to the songs and to the gatherings themselves were beyond the reach of the censor. As a mental exercise, the *nova cançó* was a benign anti-Francoist act" (Johnston 1991: 182). But, when they were sung, these Catalan songs effectively crystallized a resistant politics. A similar resistance emerged in flamenco circles. In the 1960s, though flamenco song was vague and obscure – politically explicit, student-oriented performances by the likes of José Menese and Enrique Morente were exceptional. Flamenco was far from being an obvious engine for resistance. Moreover, resist-ant intellectuals with interests in flamenco, including Caballero Bonald and Moreno Galván, generally heeled to a vague Lorquean aesthetic in their discussions of *cante*, affirming "what was necessary for progress by enlivening the obscure folds of the subconscious and integrating that subconscious into a human project of perfectibility. . .. Its new language integrated it into the world of the cultural progressivist" (García Gómez 1993: 135f.). At the same time that they availed themselves of this Lorquean rhetoric, these intellectuals seemed to sense its danger, the danger of Lorca's characterization of *cante* as "a universal language." Accordingly, they often emphasized regional rather than universal aspects of *cante* (see García Gómez 1993: 119; 128; Mitchell 1994: 160–177). In the end, their intellectual resistance to *franquismo* was strangely twisted and aesthetically confused, but it was nevertheless persistent.

Their confusing intellectualizations together with the ambiguous music that they celebrated are a far cry from the musical movements we dream about when he harken back to utopian and communalistic efforts of Franciscans and Albigensians. This flamenco seems too ambiguous and too compromised. We prefer consistency and monologism, monologism being the idea that legitimate expressions can always be distinguished from the illegitimate, and that every legitimate expression has its rightful place in an underlying order or code or system (Morson and Emerson 1990: 28). In monologistic thinking, a resistant song should be unqualified and uncompromised in its resistance. It should be pure, integral, coherent, and singleminded if it expects to succeed.

This sort of monologistic thinking is dangerous, a wolf in sheep's clothing. Monologism, not money, is the root of all evil, the evil of money consisting of its power to transform all other values into itself so that every value ends up being adjudicated on the desk of a financier (Walzer 1983). In pre-modern Europe, monologistic theology gave rise to repressive Christianity (Schillebeeckx 1969) and to the university as an institution of stifling consensus (MacIntyre 1990: 225). In the seventeenth century, monologistic politics gave rise to a kind of "science" that neutralized the voices of the unruly masses (Shapin and Shaffer 1985). In the nineteenth, monologistic culturological resistance to French intellectual imperialism, energized German romanticism, nationalism, and, later, fascism (Berlin 1991). Finally, contemporary functionalist theory, the sort that undergirds so much scientific flamencology, is a totalizing monolog that hides more than it explicates, tempting one to hope for a social orderliness that no flesh and blood human being could long abide.

Every single-minded, rhetorically coherent, internally consistent monolog, whether that monolog is advanced in the name of governance or in the name of resistance to governance, flirts with oppression and with the homogenizing centripetal forces that Mikhail Bakhtin feared so deeply and resisted so ardently. The lesson he taught us is that monologism from the bottom up is every bit as dangerous as monologism from the top down. Monologistic resistance is like monologistic oppression in that it draws on centripetal forces to homogenize a movement. The content of such resistance may be appealing but, if it is a monolog, then its form is toxic. Fiske errs when he maintains that "when it is in the interests of subordinate formations to contest the power of the dominant in particular circumstances they may need to exercise their agency through the same technologies of power to which the dominant have historically privileged access" (Fiske 1993: 155). Against this view, Bakhtin would suggest that monologistic resistance is never appropriate. Vacillations and inconsistencies such as those that haunted flamenco circles in the 1960s are always preferable to super-ficially satisfying strategies of monological resistance.

Unfortunately, flamenco critics have been upbraiding artists and scholars of the 1960s in the same way Jim McGuigan has criticized "populist" thinkers (McGuigan 1992). In both cases, their accusations dwell on the issue of inconsistency. In McGuigan's view, "populists" are scholars who celebrate the resistant power of the social gallimaufry, the unruly and ill-kempt social manifold. Such populists, it is argued, are misguided insofar as they put their trust in forces that are politically ineffective (see Storey 1993: 182). Though "popular culture" might stimulate edifying conversation, it affords no political leverage. Stated in another way, "populism" lacks a sense of the real wrongs of social life, and of utopian convictions for righting them. Without such moral azimuths, populism lapses into quietism (McGuigan 1992: 81). At the end of his book McGuigan writes with wide-ranging, free-swinging words:

> Various movements for peace, democracy, ecology, for collective and self emancipation, old and new, are mutually implicated in the Utopian project since they all offer vision, "counter-factual models", for a better world. . . .. Until the oppressed of one kind or another are liberated and technology is properly humanised, we cannot speak of *post*modernity. (McGuigan 1992: 246).

McGuigan, like the critics of flamenco, displays a utopist's impatience. "Impatience" is perhaps too frail a word. Utopists are marathoners who wear one shoe that says, "Just do it" and another that says "No excuses." They work hard and they expect results, being driven, at the deepest levels, by the millenarianist–gnostic assumption that humanity has been saved, that the kingdom has been won, and that what remains is to live the redeemed life to its fullest, to its most consistent, and in its most completely monologistic form (see Kumar 1987: 19; Manuel and Manuel 1979: 17; Tinder 1980).

Bakhtin's proposals provide a healthy alternative to such utopianism. In his view, politics is always carried on by heteroglossic bodies, and not by monologic minds. No reasoning faculty – no matter how self-critical – should be allowed to suppress the wanderings and vagaries of human corporality. Humans are destined to play out "a dance that turns neverendingly on itself" (Steiner 1989: 41). There are no essential wrongs, nor can we identify with certainty any fixed set of universal virtues beyond the vague desideratum of "company" (Eagleton 1990: 204) – literally "bread-together-ness". Evil has no essence, and virtue is never absolute. No natural monolog defines and fixes either one. Both are constructed in the practices and narratives of interacting bodies (MacIntyre 1981).

Human beings are essentially uncentered. They develop like my neighbor's front lawn, unprogrammed, and generally unmanageable. They extend wherever and whenever they can, but almost never where the chief administrator intends. The story of human history is at "root" aimless and dull, like the story of grass at growing. However, despite the absence of a per-ceptible plan or appreciable project, still the onward rush of humanity is checked here and advanced there by dint of individual efforts that build on one another and that exert influence beyond the dimensions of any single individual's intention and design – the moral counterpart of the "butterfly effect" (Ermarth 1992: 62ff.; Morson and Emerson 1990: 33).

In this respect, the human moral condition is perfectly consonant with human biology. Moral evolution, like biological evolution, proceeds in meandering paths that are narrowed and stanched or broadened and paved as a result of the failures or successes of individuals to cope with the conditions that confront them. In moral evolution, as in biological, what succeeds is not the grand scheme, but the spotty efforts of casuists and ironists (Ermarth 1992: 99; Rorty 1989; Shweder 1989: 138). No individual can ever rise above the whole process to catch a glimpse of its direction and purpose. The best that one can do is to work eagerly and persistently to see as clearly as one can, always self-critical, always laboring in concert with others, always collaborating to produce the beautiful and to construct the good (Shusterman 1992: 245). In moral evolution, as in biological, the individual's efforts often fail to enhance his or her own life, and regularly such efforts go unwitnessed and unacknowledged. "So it goes," as *Slaughterhouse Five's* Billy Pilgrim would say.

No individual can extricate himself or herself from the fragmentation and the heteroglossia of the human condition. Though one hopes for centeredness and consistency in human experience, art being an expression of such hope, any realization of such a hope should be more cause for worry than for elation. Wherever movements finally achieve consistency and single-mindedness, one should expect that there Draconian forces are operating behind the scenes. With just such a self-critical attitude, Dandelion discerned the meretricious delights of Cow-slip's warren in *Watership Down*.

Flamenco music is no simple thing, artistically or politically. Whether one is referring to a performance of Antonio Mairena or Pepe Marchena and whether one is remembering the songs of Manuel Torre or Juan Breva, always one confronts socio-musical chaos. Multiple voices and manifold interests build upon each other through time, setting an ineffably complex stage for each next performance. The task of critics who face this chaos is less that of winnowing the tradition and sifting out the legitimate from the illegitmate – as if only legitimate flamenco were worth a good listen – but to respond to each performance in such a way as to grow the noise.

Chapter 9

"Rito y Geografía del Cante"

Introduction

The "Rito y Geografía del Cante" documentary series consists of 100 half-hour programs produced by Spanish National Television and aired on Saturday – and later Monday – evenings in Spain between 23 October 1971 and 29 October 1973. The documentaries were shot in 16mm black-and-white film while on location in the different parts of Spain where specific flamenco artists lived and performed and where different "flamenco forms" were popular. Andalucía, southern Spain, is the region in which flamenco music evolved, and, accordingly, the Andalusian cities of Sevilla, Jerez de la Frontera, and Cádiz are frequently featured in this Flamenco documentary film series.

The films in the series were authored by Mario Gómez, Pedro Turbica, and José María Velázquez. The series director was Mario Gómez. Flamencological knowledge was provided by José María Velázquez and Pedro Turbica. The assistant director of photography was Federico G. Larraya. Camera work was done by Manuel Cabanillas, Jesus Lombardia, and Alberto Beato. Juan Matías handled reproduction. Antonio Cardenas, Rafael Viego, and Efrén Gómez were the audio engineers. The film editors were Angelina Barragan Cabecera, Miguel Inlesta, and Manuel Galindo. In addition, Romualdo Molina at Radio Televisión Español (RTVE), was responsible for integrating the "Rito" films into the programming of Channel Two. Paco Lira, an *aficionado* in Sevilla, assisted in setting up sites and occasions for filming many "Rito" programs.

I had access to video copies of 89 programs in the "Rito" series through the Golda Meir Library at the University of Wisconsin-Milwaukee where they have been maintained since 1988. The Library had acquired these materials from Columbia University through the intervention of Professor Dieter Christensen of the Department of Ethnomusicology at Columbia University and with collaboration from Mr Brook Zern. Of the eleven programs that were missing from the UWM collection, I was able to view and study five at the *Centro Andaluz* in Jerez de la Frontera. The remaining programs have been lost or destroyed. The soundtracks of the programs are in excellent condition, and the video images are fair. Because these programs were copied onto videotape from the original 16 mm film, they all lack the subtitles that, at the time of the original airing, were inserted to identify artists. None of tapes illustrate any of the video context – the preceding or subsequent programming in the midst of which these documentaries were aired. Only some of the films in this collection are prefaced and concluded with the original program title and credit sequences.

The chronology of programs that comprise the "Rito y Geografia del Cante" series is somewhat disputed. After comparing RTVE records with program announcements in the popular television guide *Tele-Radio*, and with the program listings offered by the *Centro Andaluz* in Jerez, I constructed the following chronology of "Rito" programs.

Program Titles and Dates of Broadcast

1 "TONÁS" – 23 October 1971[1]
2 "ROMANCES, TANGOS, Y TIENTOS" – 30 October 1971
3 "SEGUIRIYAS" – 6 November 1971
4 "SEGUIRIYAS" – 13 November 1971
5 "CÁDIZ Y LOS PUERTOS" – 20 November 1971
6 "SOLEARES" – 27 November 1971
7 "SOLEARES" – 4 December 1971
8 "EL FANDANGO" – 11 December 1971
9 "DE RONDA A MALAGA" – 18 December 1971
10 "NAVIDAD FLAMENCA" – 15 December 1971
11 "MALAGUEÑAS" – 1 January 1972
12 "DE GRANADA A LA UNION" – 8 January 1972
13 "CANTES PROCEDENTES DEL FOLKLORE" – 15 January 1972
14 "FIESTA GITANA" – 29 January 1972
15 "TONAS" – 5 February 1972 (unavailable)

16 "LA LLAVE DE ORO" – 12 February 1972
17 "TRIANA" – 19 February 1972
18 "BARRIO DE SANTIAGO" – 26 February 1972 (unavailable)
19 "LA FAMILIA DE LOS PININI" – 4 March 1972
20 "LA FAMILIA DE LOS PERRATE" – 11 March 1972
21 "LA CASA DE LOS MAIRENA" – 18 March 1972
22 "MANUEL TORRE Y ANTONIO CHACON" – 25 March 1972
23 "LA SAETA" – 1 April 1972
24 "LA CANTAORA" – 10 April 1972
25 "LA GUITARRA" – 17 April 1972
26 "VIEJOS CANTAORES" – 24 April 1972
27 "CANTE FLAMENCO DE INTERPRETE GITANO" – 1 May 1972
28 "DEL CAFE CANTANTE AL TABLAO" – 8 May 1972
29 "CANTE GITANO CON INTERPRETES NO GITANOS" – 15 May 1972
30 "LA GUITARRA FLAMENCA" – 22 May 1972
31 "FESTIVAL DEL CANTE" – 29 May 1972
32 "EVOLUCION DEL CANTE" – 5 June 1972
33 "FANDANGO DE HUELVA" – 12 June 1972
34 "MALAGA Y LEVANTE" – 19 June 1972
35 "FALLA Y FLAMENCO" – 26 June 1972
36 "SERRANIA" – 3 July 1972
37 "FANDANGOS NATURALES" – 10 July 1972
38 "POR SOLEA" – 17 July 1972
39 "POR SEGUIRIYAS" – 14 July 1972
40 "FIESTA GITANA–BULERIAS" – 31 July 1972
41 "FIESTA GITANA–TANGOS" – 7 August 1972
42 "SABICAS" – 14 August 1972 (unavailable)
43 "MARIA VARGAS" – 21 August 1972[2]
44 "JUAN PEÑA EL LEBRIJANO" – 11 September 1972
45 "AGUJETAS" – 18 September 1972
46 "JOSE MENESE" – 25 September 1972
47 "LA PERLA DE CADIZ" – 2 October 1972
48 "FERNANDO TERREMOTO" – 9 October 1972
49 "LUIS CABALLERO" – 16 October 1972
50 "DIEGO DEL GASTOR" – 25 October 1972
51 "CRISTOBALINA SUAREZ" – 6 November 1972
52 "FOSFORITO" – 13 November 1972
53 "MANOLO CARACOL" (I) – 20 November 1972

54 "MANOLO CARACOL" (II) – 27 November 1972
55 "CHOCOLATE" – 4 December 1972
56 "BENI DE CADIZ" – 11 December 1972
57 "OLIVER DE TRIANA" – 18 December 1972
58 "AMOS RODRIGUEZ" – 25 December 1972
59 "PERRATE DE UTRERA" – 1 January 1973
60 "PEDRO LAVADO" – 9 January 1973
61 "PLATERO DE ALCALA" – 15 January 1973
62 "EL BORRICO" – 22 January 1973
63 "MELCHOR DE MARCHENA" – 29 January 1973
64 "FERNANDA DE UTRERA" – 5 February 1973
65 "BERNARDA DE UTRERA" – 12 February 1973
66 "ANTONIO DE CANILLAS" – 19 February 1973
67 "ENRIQUE MORENTE" – 5 March 1973
68 "JOSELERO DE MORON" – 12 March 1973
69 "MANUEL SOTO SORDERA" – 19 March 1973[3]
70 "RAFAEL ROMERO" – 26 March 1973
71 "DIEGO CLAVEL" – 2 April 1973
72 "ENCARNACION DE SALLAGO" – 9 April 1973
73 "LA SAETA" – 16 April 1973
74 "CAMARON DE LA ISLA" – 23 April 1973
75 "EL PALI" – 30 April 1973
76 "M. RODRIGUEZ-PIES DE PLOMO" – 7 May 1973
    (unavailable)
77 "LA PAQUERA DE JEREZ" – 14 May 1973
78 "PACO DE LUCIA" – 21 May 1973
79 "PERICON DE CADIZ" – 28 May 1973
80 "TIA ANICA LA PERIÑACA" – 4 June 1973
81 "PANSEQUITO" – 11 June 1973
82 "PEPE El DE LA MATRONA" – 18 June 1973
83 "LA PERRATA" – 25 June 1973
84 "ANTONIO MAIRENA" – 2 July 1973 (unavailable)
85 "MARIA LA MARRURRA" – 16 July 1973
86 "PEPE MARTINEZ" – 23 July 1973
87 "PEPE MARCHENA" – 30 July 1973
88 "LOS TORRE" – 6 August 1973
89 "CANTES PRIMITIVOS SIN GUITARRA" – 13 August 1973
90 "DE SAN LUCAR A LA LINEA" – 20 August 1973
91 "CANTES FLAMENCOS IMPORTADOS" – 27 August 1973
92 "EXTREMADURA Y PORTUGAL" – 3 September 1973
93 "LOS CABALES" – 10 September 1973

94 "DE DESPEÑAPERROS HASTA ARRIBA" – 17 September 1973
95 "LORCA Y EL FLAMENCO" – 24 September 1973
96 "DIFUSION DEL FLAMENCO" – 1 October 1973
97 "EL VINO Y EL FLAMENCO" – 8 October 1973
98 "LOS FLAMENCOLOGOS" – 15 October 1973
99 "NINOS CANTAORES" – 22 October 1973
100 "TRAS DOS AÑOS" – 29 October 1973 (unavailable)

3. Official Announcements, Program Summaries and Voice–overs for Programs no. 1–5 of "Rito y Geografía del Cante"

"Tonás" – program no. 1

Official Program Announcement:

> 23 October 1971 (Saturday 9:55) "Intervienen: Juan Talega, Antonio Mairena, Tía Aníca la Piriñaca, El Borrico, Aguetas y José Menese. Se trata del primer programa de la serie, donde se analizan los primitivos cantes gitanos, es decir, los cantes sin guitarra, a través de los más representativos cantaores actuales. Desde su llegada a España en el siglo XV, los gitanos acceptan el folklore andaluz con reminiscencias orientales, y en el XVIII hacen su aparición las primeras formas de cante (*Tele-Radio*, no. 721, p. 50).

Program Summary:
This program treats the deepest roots of *cante*-Gitano. Photo stills and musical vignettes combine with scholarly presentations to convey the idea that during the dark period between the sixteenth and the nineteenth centuries, Gitanos in the south of Spain fused a variety of musical influences, including Islamic and Christian liturgical song. Versions of *tonás, carceleras, romances,* and *martinetes* are sung by Juan Talega, Antonio Mairena, Tío Borrico, Manuel Agujetas, Rafael Romero, Tía Anica la Periñaca, José Menese.

Voice-over comments: "Si la existencia de los Gitanos es, de por sí, oscura, y apenas poseemos datos para establecer una nómina cronológica de su historia, mucho menos podemos fijar con precisión fechas sobre su llegada a España aunque se tiene como dato cierto que una, de su entrada, la hicieron por Barcelona en 1447. El gitano con cierto bagaje musical ya entonces alterado por la continua existencia errante, encontró en Andalucía una expresión folklórica idónea semejante a sus ritmos y jiros de procedencia oriental, quizá localizables en La Persia o La India. . . En las canciones arábigo–andaluzas, los cantos sinagogales, la tradición mozarabe, los romances, hallaron los gitanos un apoyo musical lo suficientemente rico como para que, al cabo de tres siglos de íntima elaboración, del quince al diez y ocho, surjieran los primeras formas de tonás o seguiriyas fraguadas en barrios de Sevilla, Cádiz o Jerez. . .Juan Talega, decano de los cantaores gitanos hasta hace tres meses que murió, nos cantó, en su casa, estos viejos martinetes que representan un anticipo en la búsqueda de lo puro de lo que todavía en la casi inédita labor de unos artistas que no han querido abandonar su procedencia significa la verdadera tradición gitano andaluz. . .Es posible que la ronda de martinetes tenga su explicación en ciertas reminiscencias de cantes romanceados comunitarios. De allí quizá su forma dialogada de cante en la que la temática es clara para todos los componentes de la reunión donde se comunican problemas afínes. El diálogo entre El Borrico y Agujetas surgido espon-taneamente puede servir de muestra. . .Porque, de todos los oficios de los gitanos, desde asentamiento en Andalucía baja, canastero, sillero, latero, paraguero, tratante de ganado, telero, la fragua es lo que más nos interesa por su carácter polémica en relación con el cante."

"Romances, Tangos, y Tientos" – program no. 2

Official Program Announcement:

30 October 1971 "Romances: Familia de los 'Perrates'. Tangos: Antonio Mairena y Fernando 'Terremoto'. Tientos: José Menese. Tangos del Piyayo: Manolillo el Herraor y Angel de Alora. Partiendo de los primeros ritmos gitanos, alboreás y romances, se van mostrando los distintos aspectos de los cantes festeros más primitivos – el tango y su derivación más inmediata, los tientos – para terminar con una ronda de tangos del Piyayo, última y personal derivación de los anteriores" (*Tele-Radio*, no. 722, p. 50).

Program Summary

José María Velázquez sits with Tomás Torre and Antonio Mairena, and asks Mairena about flamenco forms: "Antonio, hemos presentado unas muestras de cantes más prim-itivos, pero sin embargo se habla también de romances o de livianas. ¿Qué cree usted de esto?" In response, Mairena emphasizes the familial foundation of this music, and especially of the form *alboreá* whose purity has been maintained by Gitano families. The sub-sequent footage displays Gitano families in celebration, first, the Pinini family, and then Los Perrates.

Voice-over: "Dentro de las celebraciones Gitanas, el cante festero, tango, romances, alboreás, bulerías, es uno de los elementos que da cohesión a las reuniónes. Solo en esta situación de participación comunitaria se producen cantes con toda la largueza y libertad. En la fiesta de boda la alboreá y los romances se complementan tanto en la melodía como en el ritmo."

Voice-over: "En la reunión de la familia Gitana de los Perrates, artistas de Lebrija y de Utrera, surgieron durante ésta intérpretación de los romances formas entremescla de romance y de alboreá. Este hecho se dá frecuéntemente en las fiestas de boda ya que la alboreá y los romances se complementan tanto en la melodía como en el ritmo."

José María poses the question, ¿"Cómo te explicas tú estas diferencias o este paso del romance primitivo al romances que pudiéramos llamar romance flamenco gitano?"

Voice-over: "En la voz de Menese, los tientos adquieren categoría de un cante que llegado a más, aparecer casi desligados de los tangos y ya en poco no recuerdan su procedencia. Su importancia se puede percibir en que es un cante aun en evolución, un cante con muchas posibilidades de desarrollo."

"Seguiriyas" – program no. 3

Official Program Announcement:

> 6 November 1971 "Cantaores: Tía Anica la Piriñaca, Agujeta y Fernando Terremoto. Presentador: José Manuel Caballero Bonald.

Partiendo de los programas anteriores, se llega a la seguiriya, cante gitano por excelencia, y se recorren todos sus aspectos técnicos, musicales e incluso polémicos sobre su localización origen y desarrollo" (*Tele-Radio*, no. 723, p. 50).

Program Summary:
With a bar-side lecture, José Caballero Bonald steers the attention of viewers to the city of Jerez de la Frontera where *seguiriyas* has been especially well-developed and is currently rendered with great enthusiasm. The venerable Anica la Periñaca (see José Ortiz Nuevo 1987) illustrates *seguiriyas* in her patio. Manuel Agujetas offers a powerful example of *seguiriyas* in a tavern amidst a gathering of flamenco artists that includes El Borrico, El Chosa, Mono, and the guitarists Los Morao. A final example of *seguiriyas* is offered by Fernando Terremoto accompanied by Parilla de Jerez and Manuel Soto Sordera.

The initial voice-over commentary sets the tone: "El Barrio de Santiago de Jerez fue, en la segunda mitad del siglo diez y nueve, uno de los principales núcleos de origen de las seguiriyas. Se tienen noticias de principio que se cantaba sin guitarra ya que de alguna manera conservaban su natural parentesco con el cante de tonás de donde proceden. El señor Manuel Molina, Loco Mateo, Diego El Marrurro, Paco La Luz, Joaquín la Cherna, Tío José la Paula forman parte de la extensa nómina de grandes siguiriyeros jerezanos. Tía Anica la Periñaca recuerda en esta seguiriya al son, todavía sin guitarra, el estilo de maestro Tío José de Paula en companía del Borrico, Tío Paulera, Joselito, Tío de Carra en una reunión de un patio de Santiago."

Manuel Torre is discussed with the following voice-over comments: "Manuel Torre está considerado como el principal creador de seguiriyas de este siglo. Además de introducir cambios y enriquecer las versiones de los maestros anteriores aportó numerosas seguiriyas de inspiración personal que influyen de manera decisiva en los cantaores actuales."

Voice-over: "La interpretación de Fernando Terremoto se caracteriza por su forma libre de expresión donde se entremesclan diversos estilos. Aunque en este caso la segunda letra de la seguiriya pertenesca a Enrique Mellizo y la tercera a Tomás El Nitri, sin embargo su cante hay que clasificarlo como autenticamente jerezano y con elementos de elaboración muy posterior y personal."

"Seguiriyas" – program no. 4

Official Program Announcement:

13 November 1971 "Intervienen: Curro Mairena, Antonio Mairena, "El Chocolate" y Luis Caballero. Presentador: José Manuel Caballero Bonald. En este segundo programa se muestran estilos diferentes de seguiriyas y su posterio adopción por otros sectores flamenco, así como la evolución de este cante" (*Tele-Radio*, no. 724, p. 50.).

Program Summary:
This program begins with street scenes of Triana and a voice-over narrative: "En la Triana del diez y nueve, la familia Gitana de los Canganchos constituyó una de los soportes básicos y más primitivos de seguiriyas y tonás. Del principal miembro de esta familia, Señor Manuel Cagancho, aun pudimos conseguir alguna muestra de este estilo sobrio de seguiriyas conservada por Juan Talega."

Voice-over some scenes of street-life in Triana: "Un fenómeno característica en la formación y evolución del flamenco es el trasiego de los propios artistas de una ciudad a otra en busca de la fuente del cante y en busca también de una atención comercial para su arte, por lo que el cantaor gitano llega incluso a aceptar, ya fuera de su orbita natal, ciertos condicionamientos ciudadanos muchas veces impuestos por el payo."

Voice-over presented as "El Chocolate", accompanied by Eduardo El de la Malena, prepares to sing: "En estas circunstancias puede encontrar al cantaor gitano Antonio Nuñez "El Chocolate" residente de Jerez y afincado en Sevilla, ciudad donde se congregan cantaores de distintos puntos de Andalucía."

Voice-over presented as Luis Caballero, accompanied by Eduardo El de la Malena, prepares to sing: "Así como el cantaor gitano contribuye a la renovación expresiva del cante, el artista no gitano ofrece en la mayoría de los casos elementos musicales nuevos. Desde Silverio Franconetti hasta hoy, este hecho se repite. Silvero, payo de Morón, impulsor de los cafés cantantes se formó el orbe de los maestros gitanos de la época como El Fillo de quien aprendió las cabales dandoles un sello propio y divulgandolas."

The following voice-over introduces Antonio Mairena: "Dentro del confusionismo actual en que parece debatirse la historia del cante, Antonio Mairena representa uno de los pocos puntos con garantías de crédito para un estudio vivo del flamenco. Su dedicación exhaustiva su directa y vinculación al tema, su ortodoxia hacen que su opinión y su experiencia sean imprescindibles para una revisión del presente y del pasado de este arte. A él debemos la resurección de muchos estilos y la conservación de otros como esta seguiriya del cantaor de Arcos, Tomás El Nitri."

"Cádiz y Los Puertos" – program no. 5

Official Program Announcement:

> 20 November 1971 "Intervienen: María la Sabina, Juan Vargas, Perla de Cadiz, Curro la Gamba, Rafael Romero y María la Perrata. Pesentador: Fernando Quiñones. Cádiz posee una serie de cantes que se distinguen de los del resto de la geografía flamenca. El grupo de cantiñas se da solo en la zona gaditana, siendo sus variantes la alegría, romeras, mirabrás, caracoles. También son característicos de esta zona los tangos y las bulerías, de los que se dan una muestra" (*Tele-Radio*, no. 725, p. 50).

Program Summary:
The "Rito" series is a touristic exposition, a panoramic survey of regions and peoples designed for filmic travelers. The initial voice-over of this program on Cádiz and its surrounding port cities exemplifies its touristic character: "Cádiz y los puertos de su bahía, Sanlúcar de Barremeda, Chipiona, El Puerto de Santa María, Chiclana, Puerto Real, y San Fernando, significan en su conjunto uno de los soportes básicos del cante. En esta zona encontramos estilos con personalidades y sellos propios, que la distinguen de los del resto de la provincia como por ejemplo Jerez. En nuestro viaje hemos encontrado dentro de la extensa gama de cantiñas, como romero, mirabrás, rosa, caracoles, que la alegría, es la se conserva una supervivencia más brillante y variada. Tanto La Perla de Cádiz como el gran aficionado Juan Vargas, han preferido para sus interpretaciones esta última modalidad."

The voice-over preface to the presentation of *bulerías* by María la Sabina continues the theme of "Rito" as touristic adventure:

"En nuestra busca de estilos y intérpretes, encontramos a la vieja Gitana María la Sabina que después de veinte años sin cantar hace para este programa unas bulerías de peculiar valía."

A camera mounted on a horse-drawn carriage provides viewers with a tourist's-eye view of the city and bayside streets of Cádiz.

Fernando Quiñones lectures on Cádiz describing it as the site where various musical traditions from northern regions of Spain and from the Americas came together to influence flamenco.

Dialog replaces the more common forms of exposition and interview on rare occasions in the "Rito" films, and more often as as spice than as substance. Here, a brief but spicy debate between four elderly men in a tavern is introduced by a voice-over comment: "En nuestro contacto con los diversos elementos que componen el mundo flamenco damos algunas opiniones de los aficionados quizá los más representativos de Cádiz los hermanos Melu, Paco Neti, El Churi, Peleta, José El Picador."

Cádiz is said to be a region of people who favor the generic flamenco form of *cantiñas*. A voice-over preface to a performance by la Perrata accompanied by Pedro Peña reports on this generic form: "Las cantiñas son los cantes básicos de los estilos gaditanos. Parten de allí las alegrías, mirabrás, caracoles, romeras que no son más que variaciones de las propias cantiñas. Este cante, por su amplitud, tomó formas incluso fuera del área de los cantes gaditanos, como por ejemplo la del Pinini que recuerda la María la Perrata."

Rafael Romero, accompanied by Pedro El del Lunar, sings *mirabrás*, which the accompanying voice-over identifies as a a variety of *cantiñas*: "Una de las variedades de las cantiñas es la mirabrás, cante muy rico musicalmente, que incorpora temas tan populares como los pregones."

The program ends with a *bulería* sung by La Perla de Cádiz. The voice-over suggests that this flamenco form is regularly used as the finale for flamenco gatherings: "A pesar de darse, también en otros puntos en nuestra geografía flamenca, las bulerías, remate de toda reunión y los tangos en este caso difieren de los otros por su tono eminentemente gaditano."

Reflections on the Title Sequence

The title and credit sequence for the "Rito" series presents the themes of the series in a distilled and condensed form. This 45 second sequence that prefaces each program begins with eight seconds of helter-skelter imagery including at least ten shots of different rhythm-making activities, i.e. knuckles pounding on a table, a cane pounding on the floor, the strumming of a guitar, and the clapping of hands. The sound track that backs up these scenes is a *bulería falseta* excerpted from Pedro Peña's performance in program no. 14. The frenzy of attention-grabbing images comes to a halt as the camera focuses on a guitarist – probably Pedro Peña – adjusting his instrument. He says "Un momento, Perico" while he bends a string into tune and then tightens the friction peg of his old-style *cejilla* (capo). He moves somewhat awkwardly, almost as if wrestling with his guitar. In the sound track, that awkwardness is captured in the grinding friction peg. This adjustment lasts eight seconds, a very slow eight seconds in contrast to the dizzying footage that preceded.

These frenzied and jerky segments, both the earlier scenes of percussion and the subsequent scene of guitar adjustment, then give way, in the smoothest of transitions, to thirty seconds of coherent graphics, titles, and credits, all displayed in synchrony with bulería *falsetas* by Diego del Gastor. This segment begins with the network logo emerging from within line drawings of nineteenth-century flamenco figures (Figure 2). Following the presentation of the logo and line drawings, the words: "Presenta Rito y Geografía del Cante . . . según guión de Pedro Turbica, Mario Gómez, José M. Velázquez. . . Dirección: Mario Gómez" move across the screen in steps timed to match the rhythm of the music (see Figures 3–6). The screen is then overlayed with multiple graphic images depicting typical figures of the flamenco past. These figures are moved across the screen in steps matched to the rhythm of the *falseta*.

The 45 seconds of the title and credit footage moves from a phase of noisy and ill-framed action into a phase of coherent and well-organized sound and imagery. In the course of these sequences, viewers confront the juxtapositions of chaos and orderliness, uncenteredness and centeredness, noise and music, confusion and understanding. Each contrast is associated with a temporal phase, the past and the present, respectively. This medley of images and sounds provides viewers with the single strong impression that flamenco is a mysteriously attractive delight, though one not easily penetrated. Its mysteries are best handled by adopting an historical geographical perspective.

This impression is not spoken in so many words, but is instead implied by the visual and audio material of the title sequence. Its message is condensed in images. In the initial fifteen seconds, the noisy but tantalizing confusions of flamenco are conveyed by disjointed and uncentered images. Hands are shown clapping, knocking, tapping, and strumming. These hands are all contemporary hands, photographed in such a way as to capture their rich detail. They are old hands, fast hands, and graceful hands. But they are also hands that are disturbingly disconnected from the mainstream of social life. This sense of disconnection is conveyed in part by the fact that no faces appear with the hands. No heads organize this confusion of flamenco sights and sounds. As a result, the contemporary world of flamenco song comes off as complex and more confusing than any single viewer of any one moment of gaze can appreciate. At the end of this fifteen seconds, viewers are jolted, discomfited, and encouraged to believe that all of their reactions are due to the simple and uncultivated state of affairs of the flamenco music they have encountered. Interestingly, it is the very careful editing of the material that is responsible for this viewer reaction. It is the highly cultivated uncultivatedness of these images that ultimately reaches out and grabs viewers, forcing them to wake up and to give their attention to the program.

The thirty-second sequence that follows resolves some of the tension created in the initial moments. In contrast to the jumpy uncentered images of the first fifteen seconds, the images of the last half of the title sequence are precisely formed and carefully sequenced. The written lines flow from right to left across the screen, and then back again. Then, through a step-like accumulation of images, the screen is gradually filled up. The images that fill the screen are line drawings that, because they display sparse detail, are lucid and easily comprehended. Moreover, these line drawings depict faces, rather than disconnected body parts, and they leave viewers with the impressions that at last they are approaching the center and essence that was lacking early on. Finally, the linear imagery that

Figure 2

Figure 3

Figure 4

Figure 5

Figure 6

fills the screen during this last thirty seconds consists of line drawings of historical figures. This allusion to the past creates an impression that an orderly and well-disciplined appreciation of flamenco will be achieved by reflecting on flamenco roots. Historical continuities will make sense of contemporary confusions. This last thirty seconds of footage suggests that the confusing noise of flamenco will be resolved in a clear understanding provided that viewers contribute respectful and disciplined attention to the linearities and continuities of the flamenco style. The linearity of these images – the fact that the images march across the screen on a line – conveys its own distinctive message. The flamenco tradition, it seems, operates on a single line that moves from deep past to present and future, and that line varies only in intensity as it moves. Flamenco forces here seem to be analogous to geologic forces. The past presses its heritage onto the present.

The two major impressions conveyed by the title sequence as a whole are: that flamenco is a confusing experience, but an appreciation of flamenco music can be achieved by studying the historical continuities of flamenco culture. These two lessons, presented in 46 seconds, summarize the entire series as it stretches across 50 hours of viewing time.

The Historical Context of the "Rito" Series

Some reflection on the historical context of these films will help unpack their complexity (see Nichols 1991: 265; 1994: xiii; Rabinowitz 1994: 21). This reflection will show that these films are not just about music and Andalusian culture. They are also about opposing Franco's centralist politics and advancing a regionalist *andalucismo*.

Considerable contextual evidence supports this claim that the "Rito" film series was, implicitly at least, a political statement rather than as a nostalgic review of flamenco music. Not in the least is the fact that the primary authors – the term "authors" was suggested by Mario Gómez so as to cover the various activities of direction, writing, filming, and editing that were handled by the three principals behind the series – described the project as implicitly *antifranquista* from its inception. Their statements, of course, must be weighed and sifted carefully because, in the final decade of Franco's rule, such political claims became so many rhetorical pirouettes for negotiating the shifting and often paradoxical terrain of *franquismo* (see Miguel 1975: 341ff.). For example, those who favored the economic *tecnocratismo* after 1956, proclaimed themselves liberal vis-á-vis the *franquista* economics of *autarky* (Miguel 1975: 337). After 1965, even falangist rhetoric turned populist with references to socialism, social humanism, the promotion of popular participation in social justice, and the reform of social structure (Miguel 1975: 303f., 348). Ironically, some populist falangists – "blue communists" – went so far as to resurrect the poetry of García Lorca and Rafael Alberti whose works the radical left had been attending to so respectfully (Almazán 1971b; Miguel 1975: 345; Yglesias 1977: 148).

The single most important indicator of the anti-establishment stance taken by the "Rito" series is the fact that it was produced by Channel Two (*Segunda Cadena*) of Spanish National Television (RTVE). This fact may seem insignificant to North Americans who have long been accustomed to multiple and independent channels on commercial television. But it is monumentally significant for Spaniards. During the 1950s and early 1960s, Spaniards had access to one channel of television programming that was strictly controlled by government censors and was consistently responsive to government interests.

Spanish television was conceived and implemented in 1957 to serve the interests of the dictatorial regime of Francisco Franco (Baget Herms 1993; García Jimenez 1980). Programing in the early years was – and was intended to be – a mind-numbing diversion that would distract the populace from politics and sublimate their frustrations (Diaz-Plaja 1974). The Spanish, suspicious of newsprint, took to watching a great deal of television with an uncritical eye (Chislett 1979; Diaz-Plaja 1974: 11; Hooper 1986: 137). According to Hooper, the credulity of the television viewership persisted despite the fact that television was censored more vigorously than other forms of mass communication (Hooper 1986: 138).

It was in this atmosphere that Manuel Fraga Iribarne, the Minister of Tourism and Information, initiated a somewhat liberalizing turn of events. In 1966, Fraga, himself a "quasi-falangist" (Miguel 1975: 76; Payne 1987: 511) encouraged the passage of a more liberal press law – *La Ley de Prensa* is sometimes referred to as the "Fraga Law" (Miguel 1975: 77, 346) – and he initiated *la Segunda Cadena*, a title that means both "second channel" and "second chain", a polysemy that was exploited in satirical criticisms of the day (Diaz-Plaja 1974: 20). Channel Two, a UHF channel, was initially broadcast only in Madrid and Barcelona. By 1970, eleven transmitters were carrying UHF signals to Bilbao, Navacerrada, Alicante, Zaragoza, San Sebastian, Mallorca, and Sevilla. However, it was recognized, in a RTVE report of 1971, that 400 new retransmitters would be required before the entire country could be supplied with a UHF signal. In other words, the service of Channel Two was expanding very slowly, and was unavailable in many parts of the country, especially in isolated provinces and rural areas, at the time of the broadcast of the "Rito" series. The Andalusian populations of Jerez, Cádiz, and Granada, for example, did not receive the series.

Channel Two was slow expand not only because of the delay in implementing the technology, but also because of the complexity of its function in the Franco regime: García Jimenez has characterized that function with powerfully critical rhetoric: "The *Segunda Cadena*, whose evolution has been the slowest, has aired culturally limited, restricted, and elite material that is too refined for the masses and too narrow for the cultivated sectors" (García Jimenez 1980: 380). The assumption in the Franco government and in the Fraga ministry was that the rural areas would not be able to handle serious television content. The urban intellectuals who *could* handle it were too few and too powerless to do much with it. Consequently, amongst television professionals of the day, Channel Two was described with the sneeringly diminutive term *la segunda cadenilla* ("little-channel two") (García Jimenez 1980: 411).

Channel Two may have played a weak role in Spanish television broadcasting, but it was staffed by young, bold, and eager individuals. The Channel Two staff drew heavily from "the generation of '39," that is, people who were born at roughly the time of the Civil War and who grew up studying logical positivism and Marxism, cultivating a critical spirit despite the repressions of the era (García Jimenez 1980: 485). In the late 1960s these young professionals, though meagerly supported, turned out high quality programs (Baget Herms 1993: 174). This surge of creativity was also the result of the fact that Salvador Pons, the director of Channel Two from its inception in 1966, had recruited a number of young Sevillian intellectuals to Channel Two. These young sevillanos, including Carlos Gortari, Claudio Guerín, Romualdo Molina, José Manuel Fernández along with figures like Alfonso Eduardo Pérez Orozco and Josefina Molina, had all worked together in Sevilla on "Radio Vida." On "Radio Vida," according to Eduardo, presentations and discussions were tailored in such a way as to emphasize free and open lines of communication. The overarching agenda was one of secular humanism. According to Romualdo Molina, "Radio Vida," begun in the early 1950s, found cover under the wing of the archbishop, there taking advantage of ecclesiastical protection against *franquista* reprisals for its broadcasts. Thus protected it was able to air broadcasts of flamenco music that were otherwise banned from the airways.

Recruited to the Channel Two, Romualdo Molina and his sevillano associates from "Radio Vida" formed what has been called the Seville school (*la escuela sevillana*). They were said to have carried their pursuit of freedom and openness from radio in Sevilla to the television in Madrid. The incorporation of "the Seville School" into the Channel Two team was consistent with the "liberalization of the press" in the late 1960s (García Jimenez 1980: 418).

This Seville school helped to move Spanish National Television away from propagandistic treatments of flamenco that prevailed in the 1960s (Espín 1994) and toward the serious documentary project of "Rito y Geografía del Cante" that began its weekly broadcasts in October of 1971. The idea for the series was developed by Mario Gómez and Pedro Turbica, both of whom were natives of Madrid and professionals in television production with Channel Two. Pedro Turbica had been cultivating an appreciation of this music as a result of his associations with José María Velázquez who was from Arcos de la Frontera (in the province of Cádiz), and who was familiar from childhood with traditions of Andalusian song. They drew Velázquez into the planning, and the project began to take shape as a serious film documentary series about the concrete circumstances of song and about the unknown singers of *cante* who lived undramatic lives in the towns of Andalucía. The series was to follow the format developed by José Caballero Bonald who, in his then-recent production of an audio anthology of flamenco song, had recorded unknown and largely Gitano singers. "Rito y Geografía del Cante" would operate similarly, but would record on film – rather than on audio record – the humble versions of flamenco song by unknown artists rather than the widely known and highly acclaimed versions of the professional artists who sang in the tablaos and spectacles of Madrid.

The three – Velázquez, Gómez, and Turbica – drew up the plan and submitted it to Romualdo Molina. Molina acted quickly on the project proposal, getting approval back to the three authors within a week. The initial contract called for thirteen programs. Velázquez wrote the commentaries and interview questions, and appeared in the series as the on-screen interviewer. Turbica was the pivotal technician involved the filming process. Gómez administered the project and edited the films. After its initially contracted run of thirteen programs, the series was renewed a number of times, finally tallying up to 100 programs. The first 40 programs concentrated on geographical regions and the flamenco forms that were favored in those regions. The next 50 programs profiled individual artists, and the final ten program developed miscellaneous topics. The series was consistently praised by left-leaning reviewers, but increasingly disdained and ignored in official circles. During the second year of its run, the weekly television guide *Tele–Radio* promoted it with less print and more typographical errors. More significantly, the program budget was cut by almost a third.

The "Rito" authors, in characterizing their project, consistently used the term "liberalization." For these men at this time, the word "liberalization" meant the unleashing of thought and the freeing of expression from constraint and oppression. The "Rito" programs advanced this liberalization by taking advantage of the opportunities opened up by the populist inclinations (*aperturismo*) in the government in the early 1970s (Miguel 1975: 343ff.). Flamenco performances were apt for this use since they were both popular and approved, if not compulsory – it was said in Franco's Spain that "if it isn't prohibited, it is compulsory" (Harding 1984: 178). Most importantly, flamenco performances could be rescripted. By "rescripting," I mean that flamenco events could be reframed, inconspicuously fitted out with a new agenda.

The prevailing agenda behind flamenco performances at the time was *nacionalflamenquismo*. Flamenco music under Franco was carefully cultivated, cosmetically retouched, and strategically orchestrated in such a way as to present an image of flamenco as a component of Spanish national identity (see Almazán 1972; Burgos 1972). In this guise, flamenco grew robust, particularly in Madrid. There *tablaos* and other spectacles became popular, contributing substantially to the tourist boom of the 1960s. "The slogan of the Spanish Office of Tourism, 'Spain Is Different,' was intended to convey the message that all of Spain, had bullfights, endless beaches, and glorious festivals" especially festivals of flamenco song (Kaplan 1992: 193). Crucially, flamenco events were orchestrated in such a way as to give tourists the experience of sampling different facets of Spain's one diamond, different instantiations of the one body of Spain, all united in the same mystical way that the body of Church is united (Maddox 1993: 175; Melloni and Peña Marin 1980: 16; Payne 1980: 23).

Complementing this nationalization of flamenco music was the *franquista* deregionalization of flamenco (see Hansen 1977). The single most significant sign of this de-regionalization was the enactment of a laws in 1959 that required bars in Andalusian cities to close by 12:30 am, an hour when flamenco events would have been just beginning (Pohren 1980: 17). Such laws were thinly veiled attempts to silence musical events that would normally have bred local loyalty and stimulated political debate (Gilmore 1985; Hansen 1977: 118). Signs went up in urban taverns, *Se Prohibe Cante*, ostensibly to control noise but realistically to control local political activity. The *franquista* agenda that underwrote these maneuvers was one of coopting every aspect of regional life that could be used to bolster the centralization of power, while, simultaneously, discouraging every aspect of regional life that seemed to compete with or challenge that power. In consequence, regional life became almost as bland as the portrayal of it in *Crónicas de un Pueblo* (see Chapter 1; Diaz-Plaja 1974: 61–8). Local voices were systematically discouraged from saying anything political, and encouraged instead to attend to personal development (Hansen 1977: 135), or family (Collier 1987: 216), or art (Yglesias 1977: 150), or anything else except politics (Harding 1984: 181). "No one anywhere in the nation dared to articulate what the Left had struggled for. The Falangists not only did away with the revolutionaries; they also reasserted the class relations of the old order, and they won control of people's minds. . .familiar discourses revived and thrived in a seemingly depoliticized guise" (Collier 1987: 216f.). *Nacionalflamenquismo* was a double-edged weapon in Franco's armory for statism, a weapon that encouraged attention to the centers of power while discouraging politics at the margins.

The "Rito" filmmakers set themselves to the task of revising the imagery of *nacionalflamenquismo*. They were able to accomplish this – at least to some degree – by taking advantage of the complexity of flamenco events. "Complexity" here refers to a multilayeredness and a potential for ambiguity that allowed for the simultaneous presentation of countervailing agendas. In one and the same musical performance, messages of resistance could be laminated between messages of complicity. Like a carnival that simultaneously dominates and resists domination (Scott 1990: 178), flamenco performances could be rescripted to seem complicit with *nacionalflamenquismo* while also advancing opposition.

The filmmakers were able to take tactical advantage of the popularity of flamenco to spread their own message of liberalization (*aperturismo*). They often preserved the splendor and popular power of flamenco events, while adding "side-long glances" to revise the impact of those events. Without denying the role of music as a diversion and as an escape from the oppressive politics of Spanish life, the filmmakers exploited this music with coy tactics to encourage popular resistance (for more on tactics, see Certeau 1984: xix). In this regard, Velázquez-Turbica-Gómez took advantage of music in the same way that the novelist Carmen Martín Gaite, writing in roughly the same period, used the romance novel, both as an escape and as a sign of the need for escape (Sieburth 1994: 202). In sum, the "Rito" series rescripted flamenco by exploiting its "multidimensionality" (Lipsitz 1990: 99f.) and its "multiaccentuality" (Fiske 1993: 31; Stewart 1993: 18; Volosinov 1973: 23) and by sedimenting, within its documentary form, a hidden transcript of resistance to the cultural politics of Franco (see Scott 1990).

Realist-Representation in the "Rito" Series

Having introduced the series and outlined its objectives, I will consider here its realistic form. I contend that the realism of the "Rito" films constituted an implicit resistance to Franco's essentialist conception of Spanish culture. Ironically, however, the use of realistic techniques and travel imagery encouraged viewers to embrace a so-called authentic flamenco, thereby opening the back door for another version of the very essentialism that had just been pushed out the front. As a realistic documentary series, "Rito y Geografía del Cante" may have been effective in debunking Franco's cultural politics, but it came dangerously close to creating its own brand of cultural essentialism.

The directors, authors, and supervisors of this documentary film series were generally united in their opposition to Franco's cultural politics, though that objective was clearer in some minds than in others. They were eager to overshadow the *nacional-flamenquismo* that was associated with *franquismo*. Their primary weapon of opposition was filmic realism that made it possible for the truth to shine through the artifices of *franquismo*. This chapter will explore this claim more deeply and will find that the oppositional force of realism is not so simple and direct as it first might seem.[4]

The "Rito" series displays all the definitive characteristics of realist "representational film." The films in this series present long musical sequences uninterrupted by commentary in just the manner recommended by Feld (1976: 298). They display sensitivity and genuine interest on the part of the commentators and interviewers that serve to counter the normal documentary "power relations" of viewers vis-á-vis filmed subjects, as suggested by Baily (1989: 1) and Titon (1992b: 53). They rarely advance one single political line or any one flamencological position, but instead provide broad samples of opinions that enable viewers to reflect on the larger social context of the films – as encouraged by Titon (1992a: 92). Amazingly – given the notoriously staunch regionalism of Andalusians – the films operate impartially, offering a balanced presentation of the art of the different provinces of Andalucía and beyond, as suggested by Zemp (1988: 402). In sum, the "Rito" series is exemplary both as an objective document about, and as a sensitive supporter for, flamenco music.

These realist "representational" techniques in the "Rito" series effectively isolated the Andalusian past from the complicating propagandistic rhetoric associated with Franco's cultural politics, and, as a result, these films contrasted with the documentary style most closely associated with *franquismo*, the style sanctioned by the government's official documentary agency. Paradoxically, however, this realistically represented past in the "Rito" films was itself subtlely put into service for constructing a distinctive and objective Andalusian identity that was then advanced as a significant player in the present. In terms used by Nichols (1994: 5), the "Rito" films "reveal the force of the past on the present. . .implanted within bodies" (1994: 5). My concern is less with the picture of the past as constructed by the films, than with the manner of using that past to deal with the present. As Nichols suggests, "The pressure of the past on the present moment of recounting (a historical latency) can become as much a subject of the story told as the history ostensibly recounted" (1994: 4).

The Andalusian past, isolated from *franquista* propaganda by use of realist documentary methods, is reintroduced to the viewer by way of the trope of travel. "Rito y Geografía del Cante" is a flamenco travelog, undoubtedly a plus in the eyes of the government censors who inspected this project. As a touristic project, the "Rito" films inevitably "colonized the imagination" of viewers–tourists. Like conventional tourists, "Rito" viewers were compelled to gaze at "sights" along their way, as if there were a "collective sense that certain sights must be seen" (MacCannell 1976: 42). The viewers' gaze enframes "the other as spectacle or picture" (Little 1991: 149, 154). Such an "enframing" cannot be a neutral act, no matter how realistically presented the enframed material might be. Rather, the framing gaze objectifies its object, subordinating it to the needs of the one who gazes: "the author's own real homeland serves as an organization center for point of view" (Bakhtin quoted in Stewart 1991: 177; see also Mitchell 1988: 28).

The appeal of gazing and objectifying is the experience of authenticity. "Modern man (sic) has been condemned to look elsewhere, everywhere, for his authenticity, to see if he can catch a glimpse of it reflected in the simplicity, poverty, chastity or purity of others" (MacCannell 1976: 41). This term "authenticity" refers to an essential integrity that is assumed to undergird the fragmentations of quotidian existence and give them meaning. An authentic experience is one that puts individuals "in touch both with a 'real' world and with their 'real' selves" (Handler and Saxton 1988: 243). The "real," like a Platonic essence, is supposed to make sense of all life's "accidents." It is a hierophany of the Wholly Other that is used to refer "on the one hand to the world of everyday life and point, on the other hand, to a world that is experienced as transcending everyday life" (Luckmann 1976: 43).

Presumably, viewers who gaze out onto the landscape of Andalusian flamenco continually bump up against authentic experiences without knowing what they have encountered, and without recognizing the authenticity that stands before them. Perhaps they overlook authenticity because it consists of a wholeness not easily perceived close up or in one glance. Consequently, in order to facilitate the viewers' perception of authenticity, their experience must be prepared and prepackaged in a neat narrative form (Carr 1991: 73ff.; Handler and Saxton 1988: 253), with some manner of storytelling (see Doe 1988: 203ff.) whether in word or image or action. Such tailored narratives often operate by playing off the experience of fracturedness that one *can* perceive against the experience of integrity that one *cannot*. Such storytelling is the power play of "Rito" presentations on Andalusian flamenco, a device for clothing flamenco music in authenticity that establishes its legitimacy (see Nichols 1994: 68). The "Rito" films, like other travel films, narrate authentic flamenco by creating a contrast between a "front region" and a "back region." Like travelers on a tour (see MacCannell 1976), "Rito" viewers are ushered through a variety of artificial spectacles in the flamenco front region and then gradually introduced to the authenticities of the flamenco back region.[5]

No stretch of imagination is needed to recognize the touristic nature of the "Rito" films. The master image of the sojourn is obvious. The first program filmed for the "Rito" series, *Cádiz y Los Puertos* (no. 5), makes it clear that this series is a filmic tour of flamenco country. The voice-over talks specifically about "our journey" and about "our survey of flamenco," a rhetoric intended to cut against the grain of Franco's cultural politics that downplayed Spain's regional contentiousness and celebrated the collaboration of all provinces in corporate Spain. Almost every program in the series contains panoramic cinematography, a commonplace in travelogs. From roof tops, viewers scan Cádiz, Jerez de la Frontera, Lebrija, and Utrera. From trains, viewers see the landscape rushing by as they travel from Despeñaperros to La Unión and from Córdoba to Sevilla. From carriages, viewers discover the narrow streets of Sevilla as they open out onto the grand sights of La Giralda, the Torre del Oro, and the Guadalquivir. From cars, viewers experience the rush of Málaga's central city. From boats, viewers explore the waters around the port cities of Cádiz, Puerto de Santa María, Sanlúcar de Barrameda, and Chiclana. On foot, viewers climb the hills of Morón de la Frontera where they visit the cathedral and glimpse the ruins of the ancient Moslem fortress. All these different panoramic scenes with their distinctive panoramic techniques confirm the centrality of the trope of travel in the "Rito" films.

Occasionally the voice-over commentator explicitly portrays himself as a travel guide: "In this region we find styles with features that distinguish these people from those of other provinces, for example Jerez. On our journey we have found, in the realm of *cantiñas,* such songs as *romeros, mirabras, rosas, caracoles.*" Later in that same program, the voice-over says: "In our survey of styles and interpreters, we found the elderly Gitana María de La Sabina." Here the phrases "our journey" (*nuestro viaje*) and "our search" (*nuestra busca*) indicate the touristic intent of these films. The program on Triana (no. 17) makes reference to "our journey"; the program on "Los Viejos Cantaores" (no. 26) refers to elderly flamencos as "landmarks and relics in the landscape of flamenco geography;" and the program on "Saetas" (no. 23) refers to the "Rito" project as "our sojourn" (*nuestro recorrido*). All these presentations and phrases secure the claim that "Rito" is a travel project.

The first stop on the flamenco tour, of course, is the mandatory site, the flamenco spectacle, the front region of flamenco shows at *tablaos,* festival stages, and recording studios. Such contrived spectacles are not only acknowledged in the "Rito" series, they are self-consciously explored and exploited, as the camera provides viewers with measured glimpses of Rafael Romero, Antonio Canillas, Diego Clavel, and Manolo Caracol on stages in *tablaos* of Madrid. In interviews, Velázquez asks La Paquera, Manuel Soto "Sordera," La Perrata and numerous other artists whether they sing differently for public audiences and for private gatherings, a question predisposes viewers to adopt a cynical frame of mind regarding public performances, even before they hear the artists' responses. Even more direct and provocative is the question addressed to José Pansequito: "It is sometimes said that singing in a *tablao* destroys a singer's quality. . .what do you think?"

Of all the programs that emphasize the superficial attractiveness of flamenco, none advances that message so explicitly as the programs on Pepe Marchena (no. 87) and Manolo Caracol (no. 53, no. 54). Marchena, the consummate showman, is shown wearing his silk ascots, smoking jackets, and jaunty hats. During his club performance, he suffers patiently the adorations of his audience. His fans are occasionally reduced to speechlessness: one woman protests, "what can I say to such a phenomenon?" With respect to Caracol, the camera takes viewers on a cook's tour of his lavish villa complete with ornate swimming pool and gardens. At the end of the tour, viewers are introduced to Caracol as he relaxes in his living room amid a harem of beautiful women.

Additionally, "Rito" samples the international fanfare that has been prompted by flamenco music. The program entitled "Difusión del Flamenco" (no. 96) presents non-Spaniards learning flamenco dance, e.g. an Anglo woman who has come to Spain to study dance, and a singer performing Japanese *cante*. The program on Joselero de Moron (no. 68) shows him coaching the singing of an ardent American aficionado. The program on La Marrurra (no. 85) explores in depth the American fascination with flamenco song. Commenting on this program, one filmmaker said that singers like Mairena could only stand back and smile at the performances of María La Marrurra. On the one hand, she showed such eagerness and such knowledge and passion despite the fact her voice lacked the power of a first-rate *cantaora*, but, on the other hand, she was still a foreigner who had not yet put her finger on the pulse of *real cante*.

The repetition of *tablao* performances, festival performances, the teaching of foreigners, and the performances of foreigners help to define the genre and mark out its limits so that travelers in flamenco-land might figure out where they are. This process of roping the ring of flamenco had been advanced in a significant way by the development of names for flamenco forms. The confusing intermixture of Andalusian sounds in the eighteenth century was, in the nineteenth, carved up and distinguished into distinct regional and rhythmic varieties including *soleá, alegría, fandango,* and *malagueña.* Such form-names acted like so many signposts and fences to define the boundaries of flamenco territory, objectifying the music by setting it apart from the rhythmic noise of everyday life (Attali 1985: 57). The "Rito" program exploited this objectification by making regular use of form names. In one particularly striking example, *pregones,* a vendor's song, was illustrated by showing the rough uses of song in the course of selling wares (no. 72), and then by illustrating the fully mature form *pregones* (no. 79), now sufficiently refined to warrant a distinctive form name. Similar dramatizations illustrate the development of *jabera, jabegote,* and *trillera.* Clearly flamenco songs when named become public objects in their own right and increasingly detached from social relations in which they arose. As Horkheimer and Adorno suggested, "all reification is forgetting" (Jay 1993: 427).

While the "Rito" films present flamenco front region in these ways, they also struggle to move beyond the front so as to confront the back region of flamenco. That is because the back region of flamenco houses authenticity. To this end, "Rito's" cinematographic tour guides deploy a number of tactics. Curiously, all these tactics are consistent with "realist" cinematography. Consider, for example, the authors' frequent exploitation of throwaway details. In a number of programs, Cristobalina de Suarez is shown singing in a humble dining room while seated with family and friends around a table filled with wine and glasses. None of these circumstances is necessary to her song. But a quantum level of unnecessity beyond these matters is the fact that she sings while cradling her young child. This unnecessary detail encourages viewers to credit this scene with a special "reality" and "authenticity," analogous to the authenticity induced by the unnecessary ornamentation on the walls of the chamber of Gerome's painting of *The Snake Charmer and his Audience* (Nochlin 1989).[6]

Sometimes viewers can know perfectly well that unnecessary details are sometimes concocted. For example, in the programs that feature Pericón and La Marrurra, the interviews with the featured artists are interrupted by phone calls. Both phone calls are treated as unanticipated distractions, and were edited into the final footage, according to Pedro Turbica, in order to convey a sense of naturalness and spontaneity. In neither case can one hear the voice of the caller or even catch the drift of the conversation. Viewers must wait until the distracting phone calls are completed before they can rejoin the artists in their interviews. In the course of these distractions, viewers may be aware that the phone calls could have been edited out of the interviews, but were intentionally retained. Yet, despite this awareness, viewers are still inclined to treat these distracting phone calls as signs of candid reality, of the preciousness of the moments they are witnessing.

One of the most common realist techniques used in this series is the technique of opening doors onto moments of intimacy in flamenco artistry. There seemed to be no shortage of such moments. For example, after a particularly hot *bulería*, the Perrate family members (no. 20) take a breather as they sit among the large wine casks of a humble *bodega*. Bernardo searches about for a coolant. He grabs a glass of wine from the table, and pours its contents over his head. No one seems to take much notice, but the camera's gaze is fully focused on him. The inconspicuous playfulness of his act counts powerfully as a sign of the presence of the real and the authentic in this most informal of flamenco gatherings. The viewer, under the mesmerizing influence of this unnecessary throwaway moment, is encouraged to attribute substance to everything else that fills this back region of intimate song. In the same vein, the unrestrained emotion, the candid joy of Manuel Soto "Sordera" at Christmas time (no. 10), in contrast to his very sober demeanor backstage at a Madrid *tablao* (no. 69), offers a particularly powerful witness to the intimate moments of flamenco family life. Ironically and unbeknownst to viewers, this footage was filmed, not in the family homestead in Jerez, but in a rented house in Toledo, about an hour south of Madrid – a dramatic example of constructed authenticity. A similarly powerful construction of the candor and sincerity is evident in the program on Pedro Lavado (no. 60), as a barkeep in Puente Geníl. He is shown as often with an apron serving wine as with a guitarist singing a song. Said to be ignored by those who run in the fast circles of commercial flamenco, he is nevertheless happy to sing, to teach his young boys to sing – as they do on this program – and to enjoy *cante* in obscurity.

Realist documentation, always in search of the flamenco back region, leads the "Rito" authors to favor non-professionals whose behavior exhibits the sincerity of the back region. Oliver de Triana (no. 57), an old potter from Triana, one of a long line of non-Gitanos who have lived cheek by jowl with the celebrated Gitano *cantaores* of Triana, and who maintained their tradition of song in relative obscurity from the time of Ramón El Ollero in the late nineteenth century. María Sabina, a.k.a. María Macías Moreno, and her son, the blacksmith–*cantaor* Santiago Donday (no. 5) are non-professionals on the order of La Perrata, El Borrico, Pedro Lavado, and Oliver de Triana. As with these other non-professionals, their presence in the "Rito" programs helps to constitute the flamenco back region. Sabina, in these films, is a frail old woman who is missing an eye and some teeth – "La Tuerta" (the One-Eyed Woman). She offers nothing in the way of beauty, melody, or even vocal power. On the contrary, her personage conjures up something like a "moldy fig mentality" that insists that *real* flamencos are "old, illiterate, blind, toothless" (Middleton 1989: 143) but deeply committed to the traditions of flamenco song. Her son, Santiago Donday, is a burly hulk of a man with chiseled features and a gravely voice who sings without airs. If there were ever a pair who would qualify as *puro*, that pair would certainly be Sabina and son.

Finally, the simple feminine beauty and grace of Lole Montoya (no. 96) powerfully underscores the value of the authentic back region in contrast to the artificial front region. Viewers, familiar with the bright dresses, dramatic make-up, and contrived poses of *bailaoras* in flamenco spectacles, cannot help but be persuaded by Lole, here the very antithesis of the flashy *bailaora*: The Montoya family is gathered around a table in a humble kitchen. Portly Eduardo El de la Malena – occasionally called Gordito – plays *tangos* while different members of the family, old and young, sing and dance. At one point, Lole steps forward to perform. Any make-up she might be wearing is undetectable. Her clothes – pants and a tie-back blouse – are humble and unremarkable. But her beauty and grace, played up heavily by camera close-ups, is utterly captivating. She is at once angelic, sensuous, and powerful, a "natural" beauty of the flamenco back region.

The "Rito" films make use of still other techniques for convincing viewers that they have come upon the wellspring of authentic flamenco. One such tactic is the revelation of secrets, the disclosure of things normally hidden from view, the unveiling of what is usually veiled. Such disclosure encourages viewers to believe that what had been hidden must be real. This technique of exposé is effective partly because flamenco artistry in general seems to thrive on concealment. Stories abound of flamenco artists who are reluctant to record their music for fear that other artists will copy their style. Manolo de Huelva, who is said to have been afflicted with an advanced form of this sort of paranoia, appeared in no. 30 but would not play. Flamenco maestros are said to occasionally teach errors so as to preserve the uniqueness of their own art. Each performer, it seems, works with a sidelong glance cast on other performers. Everyone searches for highlights in the performances of others while simultaneously shielding their own art from prying eyes. In this atmosphere of concealment and guardedness, the "Rito" series comes along and throws doors wide open to some of the most intimate and hidden features of the flamenco art. Not only can artists be heard by other artists, but they can be seen as well. And *aficionados*, perhaps for the first time, can catch a glimpse of obscure artists whom they have only heard of, but never actually heard, let alone seen. Certainly, the "Rito" programs occasioned the first glimpse by most *aficionados* of the non-professional artists mentioned above.

Diego del Gastor is a case in point. Diego, who died just as the "Rito" series was being broadcast, was a widely acclaimed guitarist (Pohren 1980) but generally reluctant to produce recordings and to teach, though Pohren argues that he simply disliked the dullness and routine of teaching (1988: 298). He was a hidden figure, whom José María Velázquez had to prod and cajole and encourage to perform in the "Rito" series. His *bulería* is heard over and over again on the audio track of the title sequence, as described above. In his own program (no. 50) he performs both as a soloist and as an accompanist, and elsewhere in this series he accompanies such artists as La Fernanda de Utrera, José El Perrate, José Menese, and Joselero de Morón. In other words, with the "Rito" programs, the curtain is raised on Diego del Gastor, the mysterious Diego, the gifted Diego, the impish Diego.

It is not only artists who are exposed in the "Rito" programs. Music too is exposed. For example, *alboreá* is a song that is characteristically performed at private Gitano weddings. As

Manuel Barrios has said: "As a sign of their exclusivity, (Gitanos) presume to deny access to non-Gitanos, to their most secret and intimate ceremonies. Such is the case with the wedding, that no *Payo* ought to see; neither ought any hear their wedding song, la *alboreá*" (quoted in Blas Vega and Ríos Ruiz 1990: 9). Antonio Mairena contends that no "good Gitano sings *la alboreá* outside of its proper place or outside of the sharply marked boundaries of the Gitano family" (Mairena 1976: 81). However, in these "Rito" programs the secret of *la alboreá* is divulged to the general public. Miguél Funi performs a version of it, and, even more strikingly, the subsequent video series "Rito y Geografía del Baile" offers a complete exposé via roving camera. The camera wanders through a Gitano wedding that is being rocked by a choral *alboreá* while the bride and groom are carried around on shoulders, showered with flower petals, and pushed and shoved and nearly bowled over by zealous wedding guests who rip clothes off themselves and others.

The allure of the hidden also prompts the documentarists to emphasize the personalities of artists. "Rito" viewers are provided with abundant opportunities for observing artists in informal settings where the airs of showmanship drop away and where deep-seated interests and private passions shine through. Moreover, viewers are ushered into intimacy with flamenco artists as they chat about personal interests and events of the day. This "Rito" promotion of artists' personalities is consonant with the tendencies of much flamencological writing that seems unable to discuss the art without exploring the artists. For example, Diego del Gastor's art is somehow elucidated by stories about his carelessness with instruments (Pohren 1980), and Antonio Mairena's standing is evidently a function of Manuel Torre's deathbed designation of him as the guardian of *cante* (Mairena 1976: 86). How to justify such dalliance over flamenco personalities? José Caballero Bonald argues this way: flamenco art is nothing more or less than the flamenco artists. "What the singer looks for – we would suppose unconsciously – is to transmit to the few witnesses present at hand his personal history as it has been lived in the caverns of his own instinct or reconstituted from across the expanse of his intimate and moving apprenticeship into humanity" (Caballero Bonald 1975: 54). In short, flamenco song is, by nature, personal song. By this reckoning, a song that has achieved fame is a testimony to the personal worth of the singer. And by contrast, a song that molders in obscurity must be a song of a lesser soul. Of course, no singer wants to be considered lesser, so singers cultivate virtuosity, polish, and professionalism. In all these ways, singers pursue fame as a validation of their own souls.

Obviously, professionalism has contributed a great deal to this personalization of flamenco art. It is an artist's professionalism, self-cultivation, that earns him fame, and etches his personality into the memories of succeeding generations. "Professionalism is essential to break free of anonymity, and the permanent and public exercise of an art is what leads, as often as not, to fame" (Ríos Ruiz 1993: 12). To be remembered as famous is to be remembered through one's art. And, evidently by extension, remembering artists is tantamount to remembering their art.[7] Interestingly, the "Rito" documentarians have traded on this feature of flamenco *afición* and have overlain it with their own purposes and objectives. The "Rito" films enable viewers to eavesdrop on conversations with artists like "El Chocolate", Paco de Lucía, Pepe Marchena, and Rafael Romero, and by doing so they leave viewers convinced that flamenco is an art that is independent of their gazes. Thus, the effect of the personalization of flamenco artistry in the "Rito" series is similar to the effects achieved through its other realist strategies.

In the last quarter of the Franco era, *andalucista* opponents of Franco sought to advance their cause by undercutting Franco's uses of flamenco. They portrayed his *nacionalflamenquismo* as artificial spectacle, a tourist site to be visited while sampling Spain's delights. Real, authentic flamenco, they implied, stands behind and beneath, in the "back region," visible only to those who are willing to set aside the artifice and propaganda of the front. Ironically, the "back region" is no less fictive – literally, constructed – than the "front region." Ironically too, filmic realism, an alleged medium of truth and enemy of fiction, is the style on which this fiction is founded. We have explored these ironies in the course of considering the documentary series "Rito y Geografía del Cante". The intent of the series was to carry viewers beyond the gaudy front regions and on into the authentic back region of flamenco. But we have noted that that back region was itself constructed, specifically, through tactical uses of simplicity and candor, through excessively detailed description, and through dalliance with the personal and private dimensions of flamenco artistry, all consistent with the doctrine of filmic realism.

Authentic flamenco, the prized but normally hidden musical experience explored in the "Rito" films, is a fiction. Though created, with the best of intentions, as an antidote to the tawdry music of the Franco era, its ficticious authenticity presents challenges to subsequent generations, tempting us, for example, to treat the "Rito"version of flamenco as if it were a new-found essence, the Holy Grail, the great white whale. The danger posed here is that we will canonize this version of flamenco, and use it as a fixed standard for assaying contemporary performances, thereby surrendering ourselves to the very ideology that the "Rito" series so vigorously opposed, and, in the end, bailing out of our human responsibility to struggle with our own noise.

Notes

1. This program was favorably reviewed in the radical left *Triunfo* by Almazán (1971a).
2. The program Fiesta Gitana –Tangos is listed on RTVE records as having been presented on 31 August 1972, however, neither this program nor any other program in the "Rito" series was scheduled for appearance (*Tele–Radio* no. 766) in the listings for this week, during which the Olympic games were being played in Munich.
3. The art of Manuel Soto "Sordera" is described in the listings of *Tele–Radio* as having been the primary topic of two programs. However, I found no evidence of a second program, alleged to have been aired on 26 February 1973.
4. Filmic realism often masquerades as objectivity devoid of ideology. But scholars have become increasingly suspicious of such views: "The real world. . .so real that the Real becomes the one basic referent – pure, concrete, fixed, visible, all-too-visible. This is the advent of the whole aesthetic of objectivity" (Minh-ha 1990: 80). Cinematic clear-sightedness is achieved

by the suppression of "the difference that is already there in the so-called origin" (Niranjana 1992: 39). What is represented is made to seem univocal, monologic, internally consistent, or in the parlance of folkoristics pure, authentic, hidden and "primordial" (Comaroff and Comaroff 1992: 50).

Realism in documentary film is achieved through the management of cinematic "gaze." By "gaze" I mean the congeries of world-constructing, history-denying practices that prevail in so-called ocularcentric societies (Jay 1993; Levin 1993). Such practices of gaze do not merely transmit knowledge, they project knowledge – and so they have been understood from Kepler through the Enlightenment (Jay 1993: 62). From the nineteenth century to the present, the practices of gaze were cultivated as powerful creators of knowledge (Crary 1991; Wright 1992: 21) – if not dissemblers of knowledge (Jay 1993: 128ff.) – and have been particularly prominent in the development of cinema.

One problematic effect of ethnographic gaze has been the encouragement of localism in realist portrayals of cultural life, as if cultural life could be summed and described within clear and uncomplicated spatial and temporal boundaries. Ironically, such cultural localism was being promoted by the "Rito" films – against the centralism of *franquismo* – at the same time that elsewhere filmic discourse was experimenting with nonlocalist techniques (Marcus 1995).

5. It is perhaps unnecessary to say that the flamenco song has often been portrayed in scholarly literature as just such a hidden primordial music. García Matos (1987: 34), for example, discusses "the primordial formulas and Spanish folklorics of this song," contending that "in order to find them, when they exist, it is necessary to be aware that any particular version of flamenco might well conceal its most pristine face below the transformations and additions of expressive and stylistic patterns that the particular talent of the singer could have inserted into it."

One can only wonder whether here, as elsewhere, the back region is built out of, and dependent upon, the front region (see Bruner 1993: 326; Culler 1988: 160; Urry 1992: 8). With respect to such a view, however, it should be emphasized that the contrast between front and back is not so simple as it might first seem. Urry (1992), for example, opposed touristic kitsch to what MacCannell calls the touristic back region, but in so doing, he failed to acknowledge the many ways in which the experience of kitsch is entwined with the experience of authenticity. For example, the art of a Balinese dance may be trite, cheap, infantile, deceitful, and lazy. It may be shlock, schmaltz, cursi, poshlust. But often such banality can point the way to authenticity: "Kitsch pretends that each one of its potentially innumerable fakes, and fakes of fakes, contains something of the objective aesthetic value of the styles, conventions, and works that it openly counterfeits" (Calinescu 1987: 252). Kitsch "suggests the way toward the originals" (1987: 262).

6. Realism is the ensemble of techniques that encourages viewers to trust their eyes (Loizos 1993: 9ff.). Not all of the elements in the ensemble of realist techniques are consistently applicable to all situations. For example, realism – as understood by Abercrombie, Lash, and Longhurst (1992) – involves a suppression of authorship. However, if applied to the "Rito" documentaries, this realist strategy of suppressing authorship would suggest that flamenco performers, especially in the nineteenth century, would be anonymous figures. That, however, has not been the case.

Realist film encourages viewers to believe that the visual images before them correspond to the way things are. But, since realism is a doctrine, not a fact, viewers must be educated – indoctrinated – to believe that images correspond to independent realities. Visual images do not inevitably match external objects and events, but rather the process of perception is one in which optical sensations are organized according to the tangible benefits afforded to the viewer (Wright 1992). In other words, the images processed by the gaze of viewers are images that viewers *need* to see. The doctrine of realism hides this need and instead insists on the automatic correspondence of image and reality.

Because realism has been so broadly and repeatedly embraced in modern social life, it is difficult to avoid watching something like a "Rito" program without trusting that the flamenco images flashing on the screen are at least partly reflective of flamenco authenticities. Realist techniques are convincing partly because of their twofold movement: first, realism encourages viewers to trust in what they see;

second, realism rewards that trust by leaving viewers with the feeling that they are privileged witnesses of reality. If viewers see what is "there," then they themselves are, in a sense, "there" by way of the image. If "there" is an exotic or rare place to be, then viewers feel especially privileged. While feeling privileged, viewers are not so likely to critically re-examine their own beliefs. Realist film, in other words, is self-supporting insofar as it encourages viewers to be uncritical. As Nochlin (1989: 38) has suggested, realism encourages viewers to imagine themselves standing in the very center of a most precious scene. As a result of this experience the viewer is elated. . .one might say, validated (Corbett 1990: 99; Guynne 1990: 216ff.; Preziosi 1988: 68).

7. Given that flamenco art seems to be mediated by the flamenco personality, some flamencologists have found it necessary to distinguish different processes of mediation. Climent, for example, argues that personal fame can be achieved in different ways for different song forms. For example, "singers can personalize *fandango* by embroidering it within the limits of the form. In the case of *seguiriyas,* to reach the point of associating an artist's name with an important style is impossible, because just handling the *cante* itself exhausts the bulk of an artist's energy and art" (González Climent 1975: 28). Pepe Marchena, according to Clíment, has crossed the line of acceptable personalization in his "avaricious" pursuit of fame. Presumably though, Tomás Pavón and Juanito Mojama have distinguished themselves properly in their renditions of *soleares* and *seguiriyas.* In their songs, "particularities of technical expression are not displayed but only the vital manner of embodying those styles" (1975: 28).

What Climent calls "styles of *cante*" are derived historically from "particularities of technical expression" that had the good fortune to survive through a number of generations of singers. What was "a technical particularity" a hundred years ago may well qualify as a fundamental matter of "song style" today. And by the same token, the characteristic that he discounts as merely a "particularity of technique" today, e.g. Camarón's technique, may well qualify as a fundamental matter of style 100 years from now. Climent seems unwilling to acknowledge the fact that technique blends into style in the course of history. Having started down the slippery slope of flamenco personalization, Climent tries to turn back when he recognizes the tangled consequences of identifying song and singer.

Bibliography

Abercrombie, Nicholas, S. Lash, and B. Longhurst (1992), "Popular Representation: Recasting Realism," in *Modernity and Identity*, Scott Lash and Jonathan Friedman (eds), Cambridge: Blackwell, pp. 115–40.

Acosta Sánchez, José (1978), *Andalucía: Reconstrucción de una Identidad y la Lucha contra el Centralismo*, Barcelona: Editorial Anagrama.

——, (1979), *Historia y Cultura del Pueblo Andaluz*, Barcelona: Ed. Anagrama.

Aguirre, Angel (1972), "Review," *Cuadernos para el Diálogo*, no. 103, pp. 48–9.

Almazán, Francisco (1971a), "El Mundo de las Tonás en TVE," *Triunfo*, no. 476, pp. 98–9.

——, (1971b), "Jose Menese," *Triunfo*, no. 479, pp. 44–5.

——, (1972), "50 Años del Nacionalflamenquismo," *Triunfo*, no. 50, pp. 32–5.

Alvarez Caballero Angel (1981), *Historia del Cante Flamenco*, Madrid: Alianza Editorial.

——, (1988), *Gitanos, Payos y Flamencos, en los Origines del Flamenco*, Madrid: Editorial Cinterco.

——, (1992), "Del Nacionalflamenquismo al Renacimiento," *Los Intelectuales Ante el Flamenco*, (*Cuadernos Hispanoamericanos*, nos 9/10, pp. 109–20), Madrid: Instituto de Cooperación Iberioamericana.

——, (1993), "Castellanos y Otros Extranjeros," *Candil*, no. 85, pp. 1271–3.

——, (1994), *El Cante Flamenco*, Madrid: Alianza Editorial.

Anderson, Benedict (1983), *Imagined Communities*, New York: Verso.

Appadurai, Arjun (1986), *The Social Life of Things: Commodities in Cultural Perspective*, New York: Cambridge University Press.

Arrebola, Alfredo (1988), "La Mujer en el Cante Flamenco," in *Dos Siglos de Flamenco: Actas de la Conferencia Internacional*, Jerez: Fundación Andaluza de Flamenco, pp. 381–4.

——, (1991), *Introduccion al Folklore Andaluz y Cante Flamenco*, Universidad de Cadiz: Servicio de Publicaciones.

Attali, Jacques (1985), *Noise: The Political Economy of Music*, Minneapolis: University of Minnesota Press.

Auf der Heyde, Mechthild (1995), "Aspectos Genéricos en el Romancero Analuz como Eleméntos de Identidad," paper presented at the Conference, "Arte e Identidad Colectiva," 17 June, Sevilla: Fundación Machado.

Baget Herms, José María (1993), *La Historia de la Televisión Español*, Barcelona: Editorial Diafora

Bailey, Peter (1986), *Music Hall: The Business of Pleasure*, Milton Keynes: Open University Press.

Baily, John (1989), "Filmmaking as Musical Ethnography," *World of Music*, vol. 31, no. 1, pp. 3–20.

Bakhtin, Mikhail (1981), *The Dialogic Imagination*, Austin: University of Texas Press.

——, (1984), *Rabelais and His World*, Bloomington: Indiana University Press.

Barrios, Manuel (1989), *Gitanos, Moriscos, y Cante Flamenco*, Sevilla: Editorial R.C.

——, (1992), "Gitanos y Moriscos," *Candil*, no. 80, pp. 957–62.

Barry, Kevin (1987), *Language, Music and the Sign: A Study in Aesthetics, Poetics and Poetic Practice from Collins to Coleridge*, New York: Cambridge University Press.

Barthes, Roland (1977), *Image–Music–Text*, New York: Hill and Wang.

——, (1989), *The Rustle of Language*, Berkeley: University of California Press.

Bauman, Richard, and Charles Briggs (1993), "Poetics and Performance as Critical Perspectives on Language and Social Life," *Annual Review of Anthropology*, no. 19, pp. 59–88.

Beck, Ulrich, Anthony Giddens, and Scott Lash (1994), *Reflexive Modernization: Politics, Tradition and Aesthetics in the Modern Social Order*, Stanford: Stanford University Press.

Bergamin, José (1957), *Cante Hondo*, Paris: Seuil.

Berlin, Isaiah (1991), *The Crooked Timber of Humanity*, New York: Knopf.

Berman, Marshall (1982), *All That Is Solid Melts Into Air*, New York: Penguin.

Bernal Rodríguez, M. (1982), "La Andalucía Conocida por los Españoles," in *Historia de Andalucía VII: La Andalucía Contemporánea (1868–1983)*, Madrid: Cupsa Editorial, pp. 297–313.

Bernstein, Richard (1992), *The New Constellation: The Ethical–Political Horizons of Modernity/Postmodernity*, Cambridge: MIT Press.

Besas, Peter (1985), *Behind the Spanish Lens: Spanish Cinema under Fascism and Democracy*, Denver: Arden Press.

Blas Vega, José (1978), *Conversaciones Flamencas con Aurelio de Cádiz*, Madrid: Librería Valle.

——, (1987), *Los Cafés Cantantes de Sevilla*, Madrid: Editoral Cinterco.

——, (1990), *Vida y Cante de Antonio Chacón: La Edad de Oro del Flamenco*, Madrid: Editorial Cinterco.

——, and Manuel Ríos Ruiz (eds), (1990), *Diccionario Enciclopédico Ilustrado del Flamenco*, Madrid: Editorial Cinterco.

Braider, Jackson (1991), "Cante flamenco" *Acoustic Guitar*, vol. 2, no. 2, pp. 30–6.

Brandes, Stanley (1980), *Metaphors of Masculinity: Sex and Status in Andalusian Folklore*, Philadelphia: University of Pennsylvania Press.

——, (1990), "Sardana: Catalan Dance and Catalan National Identity," *Journal of American Folklore*, vol. 103, no. 407, pp. 24–41.

Brown, Irving (1929), *Deep Song: Adventures with Gypsy Songs and Singers in Andalusia and Other Lands*, New York: Harper.

Bruner, Edward (1993), "Epilogue," in *Creativity/Anthropology*, Smadar Lavie, Kirin Narayan, and Renato Rosaldo (eds), Ithaca: Cornell University Press, pp. 321–34.

Bryant, Shasta (1973), *The Spanish Ballad in English*, Lexington: University of Kentucky Press.

Burgos, Antonio (1971), *Andalucía, Tercer Mundo?*, Barcelona: Ediciones 29.

——, (1972), "Los Jornaleros del Flamenco," *Triunfo*, no. 506, pp. 23–5.

——, (1980), *Libelo contra Madrid*, Barcelona: Ediciones Planeta.

Burke, Peter (1992), "We, The people: Popular Culture and Popular Identity in Modern Europe," in *Modernity and Identity*, Scott Lash and Jonathan Friedman (eds), Cambridge: Blackwell, pp. 293–308.

——, (1993), *The Art of Conversation*, Ithaca: Cornell University Press.

Caballero Bonald, José (1975), *Luces y Sombras del Flamenco*, Madrid: Editorial Lumen.

Calhoun, Craig (1992), "Introduction: Habermas and the Public Sphere," in *Habermas and the Public Sphere*, Craig Calhoun (ed.), Cambridge: MIT Press.

Calinescu, Matei (1987), *Five Faces of Modernity*, Durham: Duke University Press.

Calvin, William (1990), *The Cerebral Symphony: Seashore Reflections on the Structure of Consciousness*, New York: Bantam.

Campbell, Joseph (1972), *Myths to Live By*, New York: Viking.

Cansinos Assens, Rafael (1985, originally 1933), *La Copla Andaluza*, Granada: Editoriales Andaluzas Unidas.

Carr, David (1991), *Time, Narrative, and History*, Bloomington: Indiana University Press.

Carrillo Alonso, Antonio (1978), *El Cante Flamenco como Expresión y Liberación*, Almería: Editorial Cajal.

Catarella, Teresa (1993), *El Romancero Gitano–Andaluz de Juan José Niño*, Sevilla: Fundación Machado.

Certeau, Michel de (1984), *The Practice of Everyday Life*. Berkeley: University of California Press.

——, (1986), *Heterologies*, Minneapolis: University of Minnesota Press.

——, (1988), *The Writing of History*, New York: Columbia University Press.

Chambers, Iain (1976), "A Strategy for Living," in *Resistance Through Rituals*, Stuart Hall and T. Jefferson (eds), London: Hutchinson, pp. 157–66.

——, (1986), *Popular Culture: The Metropolitan Experience*, New York: Metheun.

——, (1994), *Migrancy Culture Identity*, New York: Routledge.

Chanan, Michael (1994), *Musica Practica: The Social Practice of Western Music from Gregorian Chant to Postmodernism*, New York: Verso.

Chislett, William (1979), *The Spanish Media Since Franco*, London: Writers and Scholars Education Trust.

Clifford, James (1988), *The Predicament of Culture: Twentieth-Century Ethnography, Literature and Art*, Cambridge: Harvard University Press.

Cobo, Eugenio (1994), "Review," *La Caña*, no. 7, p. 77.

Collier, George (1987), *Socialists of Rural Andalusia: Unacknowledged Revolutionaries of the Second Republic*, Stanford: Stanford University Press.

Collin, Rodney (1931), *Palms and Patios: Andalusian Essays*, London: Heath, Cranton, Ltd.

Collins, Jim (1989), *Uncommon Cultures: Popular Culture and Postmodernism*, New York: Routledge.

Comaroff, John and Jean Comaroff (1992), *Ethnography and the Historical Imagination*, Boulder: Westview Press.

Connerton, Paul (1989), *How Societies Remember*, New York: Cambridge University Press.

Corbett, John (1990), "Free, Single, and Disengaged: Listening Pleasure and the Popular Music Object," *October*, no. 54, pp. 79–101.

Corbin, J.R. and M.P. Corbin (1987), *Urbane Thought: Culture and Class in an Andalusian City*, Brookfield: Gower Publishing Company.

Crary, Jonathan (1990), *Techniques of the Observer*, Cambridge: MIT Press.

Crowley, Tony (1989), "Bakhtin and the History of Language," in *Bakhtin and Cultural Theory*, Ken Hirschkop and David Shepherd (eds), New York: Manchester University Press, pp. 68–90.

Cruces Roldán, Cristina (1993), "*Clamaba un Minero Asi. . .": Identidades Sociales y Trabajo en los Cantes Mineros*, Murcia: Universidad de Murcia.

Culler, Jonathan (1988), *Framing the Sign*, Norman: University of Oklahoma Press.

D'Lugo, Marvin (1991), *The Films of Carlos Saura: The Practice of Seeing*, Princeton: Princeton University Press.

——, (1994), "Authorship and the Concept of National Cinema in Spain," in *The Construction of Authorship: Textual Appropriation in Law and Literature*, Martha Woodmansee and Peter Jaszi (eds), Durham: Duke University Press, pp. 327–42.

Dennett, Daniel (1991), *Consciousness Explained*, Boston: Little Brown.

Diaz–Plaja, Fernando (1974), *La Pantalla Chica*, Barcelona: Plaza y Janes.

Doe, John (1988), *Speak into the Mirror: A Story of Linguistic Anthropology*, Lanham: University Press of America.

Don Preciso (1982, originally 1802), *Colección de Los Majores Coplas de Seguidillas, Tiranas, y Polos que se han Compuesto para Cantar a La Guitarra*, Córdoba: Andalucía.

Donald, Merlin (1991), *Origins of the Modern Mind: Three Stages in the Evolution of Culture and Cognition*, Cambridge: Harvard University Press.

Dos Passos, John (1926), *Rosinante To the Road Again*, New York: George H. Doran.

Drillon, Lilyane, José Monleón, José Ortiz Nuevo, and Salvador Távora (eds), (1975), *Quejío: Informe*, Madrid: Ediciones Demófilo.

Duranti, Alessandro (1993), "Intentions, Self, and Responsibility: an Essay in Samoan Ethnopragmatics," in *Responsibility and Evidence in Oral Discourse*, Jane Hill and Judith Irvine (eds), New York: Cambridge University Press, pp. 24–47.

Eagleton, Terry (1990), *The Ideology of the Aesthetic*, Cambridge: Blackwell.

——, (1991), *Ideology: An Introduction*, New York: Verso.

Eco, Umberto (1976), *A Theory of Semiotics*, Bloomington: Indiana University Press.

Edelman, Gerald (1992), *Bright Air, Brilliant Fire: On the Matter of Mind*, New York: Basic Books.

Eisenberg, Evan (1987), *The Recording Angel*, New York: Penguin.

Ellis, Havelock (1908), *The Soul of Spain*, New York: Houghton Mifflin.

Ermarth, Elizabeth (1992), *Sequel to History: Postmodernism and the Crisis of Representational Time*, Princeton: Princeton University Press.

Escribano, Antonio (1990), *Y Madrid Se Hizo Flamenco*, Madrid: Editorial Avapiés.

Espín, Miguel (1994), "El Flamenco y La Televisión: Crónica de Infidelidades," *La Caña*, no. 7, pp. 19–23.

Falla, Manuel de (1947), *Escritos*, Madrid: Publicaciones de la Comisaria General de la Música.

Faur, José (1986), *Golden Doves with Silver Dots: Semiotics and Textuality in Rabbinic Traditions*, Bloomington: Indiana University Press.

Featherstone, Mike (1991), *Consumer Culture and Postmodernism*, London: Sage.

——, (1992), "The Heroic Life and the Everyday Life," in *Culture Theory and Culture Change*, Mike Featherstone (ed.), Beverly Hills: Sage, pp. 159–82.

Feld, Steven (1976), "Ethnomusicology and Visual Communication," *Ethnomusicology*, vol. 20, no. 2, pp. 293–325.

——, (1990), "Wept Thoughts," *Oral Tradition*, vol. 5, nos 2/3, pp. 241–66.

Fernandez Bañuls, Juan Alberto and José María Pérez Orozco (eds), (1983), *La Poesia Flamenca Lírica en Andaluz*, Sevilla: Ayuntamiento de Sevilla.

Ferraro, Thomas (1989), "Blood in the Marketplace: The Business of Family in the Godfather Narratives," in *The Invention of Ethnicity*, Werner Sollors (ed.), New York: Oxford University Press, pp. 176–208.

Fiske, John (1987), *Television Culture*, London: Metheun.

——, (1989), *Understanding Popular Culture*, Boston: Unwin Hyman.

——, (1993), *Power Plays, Power Works*, New York: Verso.

Frank, Waldo (1926), *Virgin Spain*, New York: Boni & Liveright.

Franko, Mark (1995), *Dancing Modernism/Performing Politics*, Bloomington: Indiana University Press.

Frith, Simon (1987), "Why do Songs have Words?," in *Lost In Music: Culture Style and the Musical Event*, Avron Levine White (ed.) (Sociological Review Monograph), pp. 77–106.

——, (1988), *Music for Pleasure: Essays in the Sociology of Pop*, New York: Routledge.

Fuentes, Carlos (1992), *The Buried Mirror*, New York: Houghton Mifflin.

García, Angel, Vicente Morales, and Leovigildo Aguilar (1991), "Mayte Martín," *Candil*, no. 76, pp. 755–8.

García Chicón, Agustín (1987), *Valores Antropológicos del Cante Jondo*, Màlaga: Diputación Provincial de Málaga.

García Gómez, Génesis (1993), *Cante Flamenco, Cante Minero: Una Interpretación Sociocultural*, Barcelona: Editorial Anthropos.

García Jimenez, Jesús (1980), *Radiotelevisión y Política Cultural en el Franquismo*, Madrid: Consejo Superior de Investigaciones Científicas.

García Lorca, Federico (1975), *Deep Song and Other Prose*, New York: New Directions.

García Matos, Manuel (1987), *Sobre El Flamenco: Estudios y Notas*, Madrid: Editorial Cinterco.

Gardiner, Michael (1992), *The Dialogics of Critique: M.M. Bakhtin and the Theory of Ideology*, New York: Routledge.

Geertz, Clifford (1995), *After the Fact*, Cambridge: Harvard University Press.

Gelardo, José and Francine Belade (1985), *Sociedad y Cante Flamenco*, Murcia: Editorial Regional.

Geoghegan, Vincent (1987), *Utopianism and Marxism*, New York: Metheun.

Gilmore, David (1980), *The People of the Plain: Class and Community in Lower Andalusia*, New York: Columbia University Press.

——, (1985), "The Role of the Bar in Andalusian Rural Society: Observations on the Political Culture under Franco," *Journal of Anthropological Research*, vol. 41, no. 3, pp. 263–78.

——, (1986), "Mother–Son Intimacy and the Dual View of Woman in Andalusia," *Ethos*, vol. 14, pp. 227–51.

——, (1990), "Men and Women in Southern Spain: 'Domestic Power' Revisited," *American Anthropologist*, vol. 92, no. 4, pp.953–70.

Goffman, Erving (1974), *Frame Analysis*, New York: Harper & Row.

——, (1981a), *Forms of Talk*, Philadelphia: University of Pennsylvania Press.

——, (1981b), "Felicity's Condition," *American Journal of Sociology*, vol. 89, no. 1, pp. 1–53.

Golding, Sue (1988), "The Concept of the Philosophy of Praxis in the Quaderni of Antonio Gramsci," in *Marxism and the Interpretation of Culture*, Cary Nelson and Lawrence Grossberg (eds), Urbana, IL: University of Illinois, pp. 543–64.

Goldman, Robert (1992), *Reading Ads Socially*, New York: Routledge.

Gómez Pérez, Agustín (1978), *El Neoclasicismo Flamenco: El Mairenismo, El Caracolismo*, Córdoba: Ediciones Demófilo.

González Climent, Anselmo (1964/1953), *Flamencología*, Madrid: Escelicer.

——, (1975), *Pepe Marchena y La Opera Flamenca*, Córdoba: Ediciones Demófilo.

Goodwin, Charles and Alessandro Duranti (eds), (1994), *Rethinking Context*, New York: Cambridge University Press.

Grande, Félix (1979), *Memoria del Flamenco*, two volumes, Madrid: Espasa Calpé.

——, (1985), *Agenda Flamenca*, Sevilla: Editoriales Andaluzas Unidas.

——, (1986), "No Queremos Morir," *Diario 16*, 1 December.

——, (1992a), "Teoría del Duende," *Los Intelectuales ante el Flamenco* (*Cuadernos Hispanoamericanos*, vols 9/10), Madrid: Gráficas.

——, (1992b), *García Lorca y El Flamenco*, Madrid: Mondadori.

Greenblatt, Stephen (1990), *Learning to Curse: Essays in Early Modern Culture*, New York: Routledge.

Greenfeld, Liah (1992), *Nationalism: Five Roads to Modernity*, Cambridge: Harvard University Press.

Grossberg, Lawrence (1988), *It's A Sin: Essays on Postmodernism, Politics and Culture*, Sydney: Power Publications.

——, (1992), *We Gotta Get Out of This Place*, New York: Routledge.

Guynne, William (1990), *A Cinema of Nonfiction*, North Carolina: Fairleigh Dickinson University Press.

Hall, Stuart and P. Whannell: (1964), *The Popular Arts*, London: Hutchinson.

Handelman, Susan (1982), *The Slayers of Moses: The Emergence of Rabbinic Interpretation in Modern Literary Theory*, Albany: SUNY Press.

Handler, Richard (1985), "On Dialog and Destructive Analysis: Problems in Narrating Nationalism and Ethnicity," *Journal of Anthropological Research*, vol. 41, no. 2, pp. 171–82.

——, (1993), "Anthropology is Dead! Long Live Anthropology!" *American Anthropology*, vol. 94, no. 4, pp. 991–5.

——, and William Saxton (1988), "Dyssimulation: Reflexivity, Narrative, and the Quest for Authenticity in 'Living History'", *Cultural Anthropology*, vol. 3, no. 3, pp. 242–60.

Hansen, Edward C. (1977), *Rural Catalonia under the Franco Regime: The Fate of Regional Culture since the Spanish Civil War*, New York: Cambridge University Press.

Harbison, Robert (1980), *Deliberate Regression*, New York: Knopf.

Harding, Susan Friend (1984), *Remaking Ibieca: Rural Life in Aragon under Franco*, Chapel Hill: University of North Carolina Press.

Hebdige, Dick (1979), *Subculture – The Meaning of Style*, London: Metheun.

——, (1987), *Cut'n Mix*, London: Comedia.

Hecht, Paul (1994, originally 1968), *The Wind Cried*, Westport, CT: The Bold Strummer.

Herbert, Christopher (1991), *Culture and Anomie: Ethnographic Imagination in the Nineteenth Century*, Chicago: University of Chicago Press.

Herrero, Germán (1991), *De Jerez a Nueva Orleans: Análisis Comparativo del Flamenco y del Jazz*, Granada: Editorial Don Quijote.

Hobsbawm, Eric and Terence Ranger (eds) (1983), *The Invention of Tradition*, New York: Cambridge University Press.

Hoggart, Richard (1957), *The Uses of Literacy*, London: Chatto and Windus.

Holquist, Michael (1990), *Dialogism: Bakhtin and his World*, New York: Routledge.

Honneth, Axel (1991), *The Critique of Power: Reflective Stages in a Critical Social Theory*, Cambridge: MIT Press.

Hooper, John (1986), *The Spaniards: A Portrait of the New Spain*, New York: Viking.

Hopewell, John (1987), *Out of the Past: Spanish Cinema After Franco*, London: British Film Institute.

Howson, Gerald (1965), *The Flamencos of Cádiz Bay*. London: Hutchinson.

Hutcheon, Linda (1995), *Irony's Edge: The Theory and Politics of Irony*, New York: Routledge.

Huyssen, Andreas (1986), *After the Great Divide: Modernism, Mass Culture, Postmodernism*, Bloomington: Indiana University Press.

——, (1995), *Twilight Memories: Marking Time in a Culture of Amnesia*, New York: Routledge.

Illich, Ivan and Barry Sanders (1989), *ABC: The Alphabetization of the Popular Mind*, New York: Vintage.

Infante Pérez, Blas (1980, originally 1930), *Orígenes de lo Flamenco y Secreto del Cante Jondo*, Manuel Barrios (ed.), Sevilla: Consejería de Cultura de la Junta de Andalucía.

Jacobs, Michael (1990), *A Guide to Andalusia*, New York: Viking.

Jameson, Frederic (1983), "Postmodernism and Consumer Society," in *The Anti-Aesthetic: Essays on Postmodern Culture*, Hal Foster (ed.), Port Townsend: Washington Bay Press, pp. 111–25.

——, (1991), *Postmodernism or, The Cultural Logic of Late Capitalism*, Durham: Duke University Press.

Jay, Martin (1993), *Downcast Eyes: The Denigration of Vision in Twentieth-Century French Thought*, Berkeley: University of California Press.

Johnson, James H. (1995), *Listening in Paris: A Cultural History*, Berkeley: University of California Press.

Johnston, Hank (1991), *Tales of Nationalism: Catalonia, 1939–1979*, New Brunswick: Rutgers University Press.

Josephs, Allen (1983), *The White Wall of Spain*, Ames: University of Iowa Press.

Kaplan, Temma (1992), *Red City, Blue Period: Social Movements in Picasso's Barcelona*, Berkeley: University of California Press.

Keil, Charles and Steven Feld (1994), *Music Grooves*, Chicago: University of Chicago Press.

Kendon, Adam (ed.) (1981), *Nonverbal Communication, Interaction, and Gesture*, The Hague: Mouton.

Kinder, Marsha (1983), "The Children of Franco in the New Spanish Cinema," *Quarterly Review of Film Studies*, vol. 8, no. 2, pp. 57–76.

Kirshenblatt-Gimblett, Barbara (1991), "Objects of Ethnography," in *Exhibiting Cultures: The Poetics and Poltics of Museum Display*, Ivan Karp and Steven D. Lavine (eds), Washington, DC: Smithsonian Institution Press, pp. 386–443.

Kittler, Frederich (1990), *Discourse Networks, 1800/1900*, Stanford: Stanford University Press.

Kovacs, Katherine (1991), "The Plain in Spain: Geography and National Identity in Spanish Cinema," *Quarterly Reviews of Film and Video*, vol. 13, no. 4, pp. 17–46.

Kumar, Krishan (1987), *Utopia and Anti-Utopia in Modern Times*, Cambridge: Blackwell.

Lafuente, Rafael (1955), *Los Gitanos, El Flamenco, y Los Flamencos*, Barcelona: Barna.

Lakoff, George and Mark Johnson (1980), *Metaphors We Live By*, Chicago: University of Chicago Press.

Larrea, Arcadio (1974), *El Flamenco en su Raíz*, Madrid: Editorial Nacional.

Lavaur, Luis (1976), *Teoría Romantica del Cante Flamenco*, Madrid: Editoral Nacional.

Leder, Drew (1990), *The Absent Body*, Chicago: Chicago University Press.

Lee, David (1992), *Competing Discourses: Perspective and Ideology in Language*, New York: Longman.

Leppert, Richard (1988), *Music and Image: Domesticity, Ideology, and Socio-Cultural Formation in Eighteenth Century England*, New York: Cambridge University Press.

Lévi-Strauss, Claude (1969), *The Raw and the Cooked: Introduction to the Science of Mythology*, New York: Harper Torchbooks.

Levin, David Michael (ed.), (1993), *Modernity and the Hegemony of Vision*. Berkeley: University of California Press.

Levine, Lawrence (1988), *High Brow/Low Brow: The Emergence of Cultural Hierarchy in America*, Cambridge: Harvard University Press.

Lipsitz, George (1990), *Time Passages: Collective Memory and American Popular Culture*, Minneapolis: University of Minneapolis Press.

Little, Kenneth (1991), "On Safari: The Visual Politics of a Tourist Representation," in *The Varieties of Sensory Experience: A Sourcebook in the Anthropology of the Senses*, David Howes (ed.), Toronto: University of Toronto Press. pp. 148–66.

Loizos, Peter (1993), *Innovation in Ethnographic Film: From Innocence to Self-Consciousness, 1955–95*, Manchester: Manchester University Press.

Lomax, Alan (1968), *Folksong Style and Culture*, Washington, DC: American Association for the Advancement of Science.

Luckmann, Thomas (1976), *The Invisible Religion*, New York: Macmillan.

Luna, José Carlos de (1942, originally 1926), *De Cante Grande y Cante Chico*, Madrid: Editorial Escelicer.

——, (1951), *Gitanos de la Bética*, Madrid: Espesa.

MacCannell, Dean (1976), *The Tourist*, New York: Schocken.

MacDougall, David (1994), "Films of Memory," in *Visualizing Theory: Selected Essays from V.A.R. 1990–1994*, Lucien Taylor (ed.), New York: Routledge, pp. 260–70.

McGuigan, Jim (1992), *Cultural Populism*, New York: Routledge.

MacIntyre, Alasdair (1981), *After Virtue: A Study in Moral Theory*, South Bend: Notre Dame University.

——, (1990), *Three Rival Versions of Moral Inquiry*, Southbend: Notre Dame University Press.

McRobbie, Angela (1994), *Postmodernism and Popular Culture*, New York: Routledge.

Machado y Alvarez, Antonio (1975, originally 1881), *Colección de cantes Flamenco*, Madrid: Ediciones Demófilo.

Maddox, Richard (1993), *El Castillo: The Politics of Tradition in an Andalusian Town*, Urbana: University of Illinois Press.

Mairena, Antonio (1976), *Las Confessiones de Antonio Mairena*, Alberto García Ulecia (ed.), Sevilla: Universidad de Sevilla.

Manfredi Cano, Domingo (1955), *Geografía del Cante Jondo*, Madrid: Grifón.

——, (1973), *Cante y Baile Flamenco*, Leon: Editorial Everest-Leon.

Manuel, Peter (1988), "Evolution and Structure in Flamenco Harmony," *Current Musicology*, no. 42, pp. 46–57.

——, (1989), "Andalusian, Gypsy, and Class Identity in the Contemporary Flamenco Complex," *Ethnomusicology*, vol. 33, no. 1, pp. 47–55.

——, (1993), *Cassette Culture: Popular Music and Technology in North India*, Chicago: University of Chicago Press.

Manuel, Frank and Fritzie Manuel (1979), *Utopian Thought in the Western World*, Cambridge: Harvard University Press.

Maravall, José Antonio (1978), *Dictatorship and Political Dissent: Workers and Students in Franco's Spain*, London: Tavistock.

——, (1986), *The Culture of the Baroque: Analysis of a Historical Structure*, Minneapolis: University of Minnesota Press.

Marcus, George (1992), "Past, Present, and Emergent Identities," in *Modernity and Identity*, Scott Lash and Jonathan Friedman (eds), Cambridge: Blackwell, pp. 309–30.

——, (1995), "The Modernist Sensibility in Recent Ethnographic Writing and the Cinematic Metaphor of Montage," *Fields of Vision: Essays in Film Studies, Visual Anthropology, and Photography*, Leslie Devereaux and Roger Hillman (eds), Berkeley: University of California Press, pp. 35–55.

Martin Moreno, Antonio (1985), *Historia de la Música Andaluza*, Sevilla: Editoriales Andaluzas Unidas.

Mattelart, Herbert (1992), "Life as Style: Putting the 'World' in the Music," *Baffler* vol. 5, pp. 103–9.

Maugham, William Somerset (1920), *Andalusia: Sketches and Impressions*, New York: Knopf.

Melloni, Alessandra y Cristina Peña Marin (1980), *El Discurso Político en La Prensa Madrileña del Franquismo*, Roma: Bulzoni.

Mercado, José (1982), *Seguidilla Gitana*, Madrid: Taurus.

Middleton, Richard (1989), *Studying Popular Music*, Philadelphia: Open University Press.

Miguel, Armando de (1975), *Sociología del Franquismo: Análisis Ideológico de los Ministros del Régimen*, Barcelona: Editorial Euros.

Minh-ha, Trinh T. (1990), "Documentary Is/Not a Name," *October*, no. 52, pp. 76–98.

Mitchell, Timothy (1988), *Colonizing Egypt*, New York: Cambridge University Press.

Mitchell, Timothy (1988), *Violence and Piety in Spanish Folklore*, Philadelphia: University of Pennsylvania Press.

——, (1990), *Passional Culture: Emotion, Religion, and Society in Southern Spain*, Philadelphia: University of Pennsylvania Press.

——, (1991), *Blood Sport: A Social History of Spanish Bullfighting*, Philadelphia: University of Pennsylvania Press.

——, (1994), *Flamenco Deep Song*, New Haven: Yale University Press.

Molina, Ricardo (1981, originally 1965), *Cante Flamenco*, Madrid: Taurus.

——, (1985, originally 1967), *Misterios del Arte Flamenco*, Sevilla: Editoriales Andaluzas Unidas.

——, and Antonio Mairena (1979, originally 1963), *Mundo y Formas del Cante Flamenco*, Sevilla: Librería Al-Andalús.

Molina, Romualdo and Miguel Espín (1992), *Flamenco de Ida y Vuelta*, Sevilla: Editorial Guadalquivir.

——, (1994), "Tunel del Tiempo: Emiliano Piedra y Carlos Saura," *La Caña*, no. 7, pp. 48–53.

——, (1995), "La Década del Fandango (1929–1939)," unpublished manuscript.

Monleón, José (1967a), *Lo Que Sabemos del Flamenco*, Madrid: Gregorio del Toro.

——, (1967b), "Las Películas de La Crisis," *Triunfo*, no. 276, pp. 19–25.

——, (1974), *García Lorca: Vida y Obra de un Poeta*, Barcelona: Aymá.

Moreno Galván, Francisco (1993), *Letras Flamencas de Francisco Moreno Galván*, Madrid: Universidad Autónoma de Madrid.

Moreno Navarro, Isidoro (1977), *Andalucía: Subdesarrollo, Clases Sociales y Regionalismo*, Madrid: Manifesto Editorial.

——, (1982), "Hacia la Generalización de la Conciencia de Identidad," in *Historia de Andalucía*, vol. VII, Antonio Miguel Bernal (ed.), Madrid: Cupsa Editorial, pp. 355–80.

——, (1993), *Andalucia: Identidad y Cultura*, Málaga: Librería Agora.

Morson, Gary and Caryl Emerson (1990), *Mikhail Bakhtin: The Creation of a Prosaics*, Stanford: Stanford University Press.

Myerhoff, Barbara (1982), "Life History Among the Elderly: Performance, Visibility, and Remembering," in *A Crack in the Mirror*, Jay Ruby (ed.), Philadelphia: University of Pennsylvania Press, pp. 99–120.

Noakes, Greg (1994), "Exploring Flamenco's Arab Roots," *Aramco World*, November/December, pp. 33–7.

Nichols, Bill (1991), *Representing Reality: Issues and Concepts in Documentary*, Bloomington: Indiana University Press.

——, (1994), *Blurred Boundaries: Questions of Meaning in Contemporary Culture*, Bloomington: Indiana University Press.

Niranjana, Tejaswini (1992), *Siting Translation: History, Post-structuralism, and the Colonial Context*, Berkeley: University of California Press.

Nochlin, Linda (1989), *The Politics of Vision*, New York: Harper & Row.

Noel, Eugenio (1916), *Señoritos, Chulos, Fenómenos, Gitanos y Flamencos*, Madrid: Renacimiento.

Nöel, Sofía (1977), "Relaciones con los Diversos Grupos Etnicos con el Cante Jondo", *Cuadernos Hispanoamericanos*, no. 324, pp. 485–96.

Nora, Pierre (1989), "Between Memory and History: Les Lieux de Memoire," *Representations*, no. 26, pp. 7–25.

Nuñez del Prado, Guillermo (1986, originally 1904), *Cantaores Andaluces*, Sevilla: Editoriales Andaluzas Unidas.

Ortiz Nuevo, José L., and Juan Martinez Vilchez (1975), *Las Mil y Una Historias de Pericón de Cádiz*, Madrid: Ediciones Demófilo.

——, (1985), *Pensamiento Político en el Cante Flamenco*, Sevilla: Editoriales Andaluzas Unidas.

——, (1987), *Anica La Periñaca: Yo Tenía muy Güena Estrella*, Madrid: Libros Hiperion.

——, and Pepe El de la Matrona (1975), *Recuerdos de un Cantaor Sevillano*, Madrid: Ediciones Demófilo.

——, (1990), *Se Sabe Algo? Viaje al Conocimiento al Arte Flamenco en La Prensa Sevillana del XIX*, Sevilla: Editorial El Carro de la Nieve.

Orvell, Miles (1989), *The Real Thing: Imitation and Authenticity in American Culture 1880–1940*, Durham: University of North Carolina Press.

Ossman, Susan (1994), *Picturing Casablanca*, Berkeley: University of California Press.

Paulson, William (1988), *The Noise of Culture: Literary Texts in a World of Information*, Ithaca: Cornell University Press.

Payne, Stanley (1980), *Fascism*, Madison: University of Wisconsin Press.

——, (1987), *The Franco Regime: 1936–1975*, Madison: University of Wisconsin Press.

Pérez de Guzmán, Torcuato (1982), *Los Gitano Herreros de Sevillas*, Sevilla: Ayuntamiento de Sevilla.

Perry, Mary Elizabeth (1990), *Gender and Disorder in Early Modern Seville*, Princeton: Princeton University Press.

Phillips, Miriam (1987), "The Trained and the Natural Gypsy Flamenco Dancer," *Proceedings of the Gypsy Lore Society*.

Pinnell, Richard (1993), *The Rio Platense Guitar*, Westport: The Bold Strummer.

Pitt-Rivers, Julian (1971), *People of the Sierra*, Chicago: University of Chicago Press.

——, (1977), *The Fate of Shechem or the Politics of Sex: Essays in the Anthropology of the Mediterranean*, New York: Cambridge University Press.

Pohren, Donn (1980), *A Way of Life*, Madrid: Society for Spanish Studies.

——, (1984, originally 1962), *The Art of Flamenco*, Madrid: Society for Spanish Studies.

——, (1988, originally 1964), *Lives and Legends of Flamenco*, Madrid: Society for Spanish Studies.

——, (1994), "La Epoca Dorada," *Candil*, no. 94, pp. 1711–21.

Poster, Mark (1990), *The Mode of Information: Poststructuralism and Social Context*, Chicago: University of Chicago Press.

Pratt, Mary Louise (1992), *Imperial Eyes*, New York: Routledge.

Pratt, Ray (1990), *Rhythm and Resistance: The Political Uses of American Popular Music*, Washington, DC: Smithsonian Press.

Preziosi, Donald (1988), *Rethinking Art History: Meditations on a Coy Science*, New Haven: Yale University Press.

Pritchett, V.S. (1955), *The Spanish Temper*, New York: Knopf.

Quiñones, Fernando (1964), *De Cádiz y Sus Cantes*, Cádiz: Ateo.

——, (1982, originally 1971), *El Flamenco, Vida y Muerte*, Barcelona: Editorial Laia.

——, (1989), *Antonio Mairena, Su Obra, y Su Significado*, Madrid: Editorial Cinterco.

——, (1994), *What is Flamenco?* Madrid: Editorial Cinterco.

Rabinowitz, Paula (1994), *They Must Be Represented: The Politics of Documentary*, New York: Verso.

Reynolds, Simon (1990), *Blissed Out: The Raptures of Rock*, London: Serpent's Tail.

Ríos Ruiz, Manuel (1972), *Introducción al Cante Flamenco: Aproximaciones a la Historia y a las Formas de un Arte Gitano–Andaluz*, Madrid: Editorial Istmo.

——, (1988), "Una Literature Fundacional 1937–1987," in *Dos Siglos de Flamenco, Actas de la Conferencia Internacional*, 15–21 June, Jerez de la Frontera: Fundación Andaluza de Flamenco, pp. 241–50.

——, (1993), *Historias y Teorías del Cante Jondo*, Madrid: Taller El Búcaro.

Root, Deborah (1988), "Speaking Christian: Orthodoxy and Difference in 16th Century Spain," *Representations*, no. 23, pp. 118–34.

Rorty, Richard (1989), *Contingency, Irony, and Solidarity*, New York: Cambridge University Press.

Rosaldo, Renato (1990), "Others of Invention," *VLS*, February, pp. 27–9.

Rosales, Luis (1987), *Esa Angustia Llamada Andalucía*, Madrid: Editorial Cinterco.

Rosen, Charles (1995), "Beethoven's Triumph," *New York Review of Books*, vol. 42, no. 14, pp. 52–6.

Rossy, Hipólito (1966), *Teoría del Cante Jondo*, Barcelona: Credsa.

Said, Edward W. (1979), *Orientalism*, New York: Random House.

Salazar, Guilllermo (1993), "Review of *In Search of the Firedance*," *The Journal of Flamenco Artistry*, vol. 2, no. 2, p. 15.

Salillas, Rafael (1898), *Hampa: Antropología Picaresca*, Madrid: Librería de Victoriano Suarez.

Samuel, Geoffrey (1990), *Mind, Body and Culture: Anthropology and the Biological Interface*, New York: Cambridge University Press.

Scarry, Elaine (1985), *The Body in Pain: The Making and Unmaking of the World*, New York: Oxford University Press.

Schievelbusch, Wolfgang (1992), *Tastes of Paradise*, New York: Pantheon.

Schillebeeckx, Edward (1969), "Silence and Speaking about God in a Secularized World," *The Spirit and Power of Christian Secularity*, Albert Schlitzer (ed.), Southbend: University of Notre Dame Press, pp. 156–80.

Schrag, Calvin (1980), *Radical Reflection and the Origin of the Human Sciences*, Lafayette: Purdue University Press.

——, (1986), *Communicative Praxis and the Space of Subjectivity*, Lafayette: Purdue University Press.

Schuchardt, Hugo (1990, originally 1881), *Los Cantes Flamenco*, Gerhard Steingress, Eva Feenstra and Michael Wolf (trans.), Sevilla: Fundación Machado.

Scott, James (1990), *Domination and the Arts of Resistance: Hidden Transcripts*, New Haven: Yale University.

Seltzer, Mark (1992), *Bodies and Machines*, New York: Routledge.

Sender, Ramon (1969), *La Tésis de Nancy*, Madrid: Magisterio.

Serematakis, C. Nadia (1994), "The Memory of the Senses," in *Visualizing Theory: Selected Essays from V.A.R. 1990–1994*, Lucien Taylor (ed.), New York: Routledge, pp. 214–29.

Serrano, Juan and José Elgorriaga (1991), *Flamenco, Body and Soul: An Aficionado's Introduction*, Fresno: California State University Press.

Shapin, Steven and Simon Shaffer (1985), *Leviathan and the Air-Pump: Hobbes, Boyle and the Experimental Life*, Princeton: Princeton University Press.

Shell, Marc (1991), "Marranos (Pigs), or from Coexistence to Toleration," *Critical Inquiry*, no. 17, pp. 306–35.

Shubert, Adrian (1990), *A Social History of Modern Spain*, London: Unwin Hyman.

Shusterman, Richard (1992), *Pragmatist Aesthetics*, Cambridge: Blackwell.

Sieburth, Stephanie (1994), *Inventing High and Low: Literature, Mass Culture, and Uneven Modernity in Spain*, Durham: Duke University Press.

Silverman, David and Brian Torode (1980), *The Material Word*, New York: Routledge.

Shweder, Richard (1989) "Post-Nietszchean Anthropology," *Relativism: Interpretation and Confrontation*, M. Krausz (ed.), South Bend: University of Notre Dame Press, pp. 100–39.

Small, Christopher (1977), *Music. Society. Education: A Radical Examination of the Prophetic Function of Music in Western, Eastern, and African Culture With its Impact on Society and Its Use in Education*, London: John Calder.

Smith, Olivia (1985), *The Politics of Language 1791–1819*, New York: Oxford University Press.

Stallybrass, Peter and Allon White (1986), *The Politics and Poetics of Transgression*, Ithaca: Cornell University Press.

Stam, Robert (1989), *Subversive Pleasures*, Baltimore, MD: Johns Hopkins University Press.

Stanton, Edward (1978), *The Tragic Myth: Lorca and Cante Jondo*, Lexington: University of Kentucky Press.

Starkie, Walter (1935), *Spanish Raggle-taggle: Adventures with a Fiddle in North Spain*, New York: Dutton.

Starobinski, Jean (1988), *Jean-Jacques Rousseau: Transparency and Obstruction*, Chicago: University of Chicago Press.

Steiner, George (1989), *Real Presences*, Chicago: University of Chicago Press.

——, (1994), "Franco's Games," *The New Yorker*, vol. 70, no. 33, pp. 116–20.

Steingress, Gerhard (1988), "La Aparición del Cante Flamenco en el Teatro Jerezano del Siglo XIX," in *Dos Siglos de Flamenco: Actas de la Conferencia Internacional*, Jerez: Fundación Andaluza de Flamenco, pp. 343–78.

——, (1993), *Sociología del Cante Flamenco*, Jerez: Centro Andaluz.

——, (1994), "De Ciegos, Saeteros, y Flamencos: Una Reflexión sobre el Origen y Evolución del Jondo en Cante Flamenco," *Demófilo: Revista de Cultura Tradicional*, no. 12, pp. 93–107.

——, (1995), "Ambiente Flamenco y Bohemia Andaluza," unpublished manuscript.

Stewart, Susan (1991), *Crimes of Writing: Problems in the Containment of Representation*, New York: Oxford University Press.

——, (1993), *On Longing*, Durham: Duke University Press.

Storey, John (1993), *An Introductory Guide to Cultural Theory and Popular Culture*, Athens: University of Georgia Press.

Stratton, John (1989), "Postmodernism and Popular Music," *Theory, Culture and Society*, vol. 6, no. 1, pp. 31–57.

Taruskin, Richard (1993), "Of Kings and Divas" *New Republic*, no. 1417, pp. 31–44.

Terdiman, Richard (1985), *Discourse/Counter-Discourse: The Theory and Practice of Symbolic Resistance in Nineteenth-Century France*, Ithaca: Cornell University Press.

——, (1993), *Present Past: Modernity and the Memory Crisis*, Ithaca: Cornell University.

Thomas, Nickolas (1991), *Entangled Objects: Exchange Material Culture and Colonialism in the Pacific*, Cambridge: Harvard University Press.

Thompson, E.P. (1963), *The Making of the English Working Class*, London: Gollancz.

Tilley, Christopher (1990), *Reading Material Culture*, Cambridge: Blackwell.

Tinder, Glenn (1980), *The Tragic Ideal of Community*, Baton Rouge: Louisiana University Press.

Titon, Jeff Todd (1992a), "Representation and Authority in Ethnographic Film/Video: Production," *Ethnomusicology*, vol. 36, no. 1, pp. 89–94.

——, (1992b), "Style and Meaning in Contemporary Documentary Film," *Appalachian Journal*, no. 20, pp. 44–55.

Torrione, Margarita (1995), "El Traje Antiguo de los Gitanos: Alteridad y Castigo," *Cuadernos Hispanoamericanos*, no. 536, pp. 19–42.

Turner, Bryan (1984), *The Body and Society: Explorations in Social Theory*, Cambridge: Blackwell.

——, (1992), "Ideology and Utopia in the Formation of an Intelligentsia," in *Culture Theory and Cultural Change*, Mike Featherstone (ed.), London: Sage, pp. 183–210.

Turner, Victor (1969), *The Ritual Process: Structure and Anti-structure*, Chicago: Aldine.

Urban, Greg (1991), *A Discourse-centered Approach to Culture: Native South American Myths and Rituals*, Austin: University of Texas.

Urry, John (1992), *The Tourist Gaze*, London: Sage.

Varela, Francisco, Evan Thompson, and Eleanor Rosch (1993), *The Embodied Mind: Cognitive Science and Human Experience*, Cambridge: MIT Press.

Velázquez, José María (1979), "Antonio Mairena: Cincuenta Años de Cante," *La Calle*, 23 April, pp. 61–5.

——, (1980), "Juan El Lebrijano, en la Frontera," *La Calle*, 8 March.

——, (1982), "Datos Perdidos," *Pianissimo*, pp. 53–55.

——, (1989a), "Los Sordera: Saga del Cante," *El Europeo*, 3 October, pp. 77–81.

——, (1989b), "Fosforito: El 'Cantaor' de Fondo," *El País*, 23 July, pp. 20–8.

——, (1989c), "Transparencia del Flamenco o el Cante Detenido," *Cuadernos Hispanoamericanos*, no. 464, pp. 145–52.

Vélez, Julio (1976), *Flamenco: Una Aproximación Crítica*, Madrid: Editorial Akal.

Vittucci, Mateo (1990), *The Language of Spanish Dance*, Norman: University of Oklahoma Press.

Volland, Anita (1985), "Bulerías: Form and Context of a Gitano Music Dance Genre," *Papers from the Fourth and Fifth Annual Meetings of Gypsy Lore Society, North American Chapter*, Joanne Grumet (ed.), New York: Gypsy Lore Society, North American Chapter, pp. 151–63.

Volosinov, V.N. (1973), *Marxism and the Philosophy of Language*, Cambridge: Harvard University Press.

Walzer, Michael (1983), *Spheres of Justice: A Defense of Pluralism and Equality*, New York: Basic.

Weisser, Michael (1972), *The Peasants of the Montes: The Roots of Rural Rebellion in Spain*, Chicago: University of Chicago Press.

White, Hayden (1987), *The Content of the Form: Narrative, Discourse, and Historical Representation*, Baltimore: Johns Hopkins University Press.

Whitney, Carol (1974), *Flamenco, Foreigners, and Academia*, Unpublished Ph.D. thesis, Middletown: Wesleyan University.

Williams, Raymond (1958), *Culture and Society*, London: Chatto and Windus.

Woodall, James (1992), *In Search of the Firedance*, London: Sinclair-Stevenson.

Wouters, Cas (1986), "Formalization and Informalization: Changing Tension Balances in Civilizing Processes," *Theory, Culture & Society*, vo. 3, no. 2, pp. 1–18.

Wright, Terence (1992), "Photography: Theories of Realism and Convention," *Anthropology and Photography*, Elizabeth Edwards (ed.), New Haven: Yale University Press.

Yerga Lancharro, Manuel (1991), "Bendito Seas, Título de Opera Flamenca," *Candil*, no. 78, pp. 882–4.

Yglesias, José (1977), *The Franco Years*, New York: Bobbs-Merrill.

Yovel, Yirmiyahu (1989), *Spinoza and Other Heretics: The Marrano of Reason*, vol. 2, Princeton: Princeton University Press.

Zavala, Iris and José María Diez Borque (1974), *Historia de la Literatura Espanola*, Madrid: Guadiana.

Zemp, Hugo (1988), "Filming Music and Looking at Music Films," *Ethnomusicology*, vol. 32, no. 3, pp. 393–427.

——, (1989), "Filming Voice Technique: The Making of 'The Song of Harmonics'", *World of Music*, no. 31, pp. 56–83.

Zern, Brook (1973), "Paralelismo y Coincidencia entre el Cante Negro y el Cante Gitano," *Revista Flamenca*, no. 3, pp. 12–13.

——, (1975), "Duende," *Revista Flamenca*, no. 7, pp. 26–9.

——, (1987), "Flamencología," *Guitar Review*, no. 71, pp. 23–4.

Ziolkowski, Theodore (1990), *German Romanticism and Its Institutions*, Princeton: Princeton University Press.

Index